IMAGES
of America

AROUND BUTLER

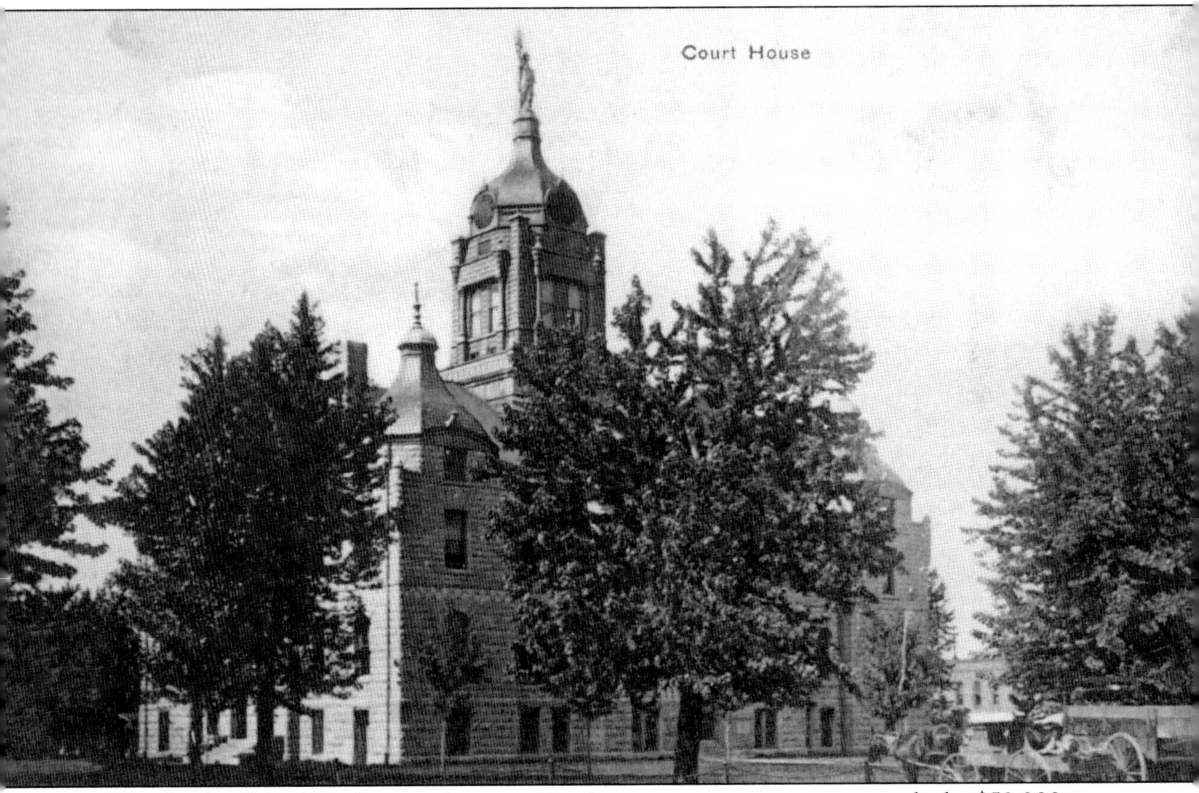

The third and final Butler courthouse, a Carthage-stone structure, was worth the $50,000 it cost the community. An early newspaper article called the edifice "a monument to the enterprise and progress of the county." Nothing says up-and-coming like a bit of grand architecture, and the courthouse was sure to attract its share of trade and tourism to the city. (Courtesy of the Bates County Historical Society.)

On the Cover: Fire chief Frank Mabbott (center) and company sit for a portrait outside the Butler Fire Department in May 1900. A local cigar manufacturer so admired these men and their work that he created a special brand—Pride of Butler—in their honor and had this image printed on the inside of the box's lid. (Courtesy of the Bates County Historical Society and the Eddie Herrman Collection.)

IMAGES
of America

AROUND BUTLER

Vance Woods and Brian Phillips

ARCADIA
PUBLISHING

ISBN 978-0-7385-9866-6

Published by Arcadia Publishing
Charleston, South Carolina

Printed in the United States of America

Library of Congress Control Number: 2012947094

For all general information, please contact Arcadia Publishing:
Telephone 843-853-2070
Fax 843-853-0044
E-mail sales@arcadiapublishing.com
For customer service and orders:
Toll-Free 1-888-313-2665

Visit us on the Internet at www.arcadiapublishing.com

To Fern and Aubrey Durst, for giving me a place to call home
—Vance

Contents

ACKNOWLEDGMENTS

The authors would like to thank the Bates County Historical Society for their generosity in granting us access to their archives, and especially Peggy Buhr, director of the Bates County Museum, for her patience, kindness, and assistance once the work of sifting through the piles of material and information began. Without them, this project would not have been possible. We would also like to express our appreciation for the tireless work and endless patience of our publisher, Liz Gurley, whose advice and encouragement kept us on our feet as the work progressed.

This book would also have been impossible without the influence of two other very important people. First, thanks to the late Eddie Herrman, whose tireless research into all things Butler over the years ensured that we would find not only photographs to work with, but also delightful stories to accompany them. Also, many thanks to Cameron Herrell, master of genealogical data, whose work behind the scenes has been invaluable in the completion of this book.

Thanks to Lowell Logan, Mildred and Walter Wright, Lucille Lindsay, Vickie and Jim Wackerman, Randy Weiss, Barbara Herrell, Missie Good, Len Bartz of Bartz Photography, Wendell Teagarden, Eileen Vannatta, Pam Woods, Dean Durst, Alan J. Mundey, and Will Tollerton for allowing us to sift through and enjoy their treasures with them. Thank you all for sharing your memories with us.

Finally, I (Vance) would like to personally thank Bruce Evans for his patience with my chronic absences over the last several months, Terry VanSandt for taking the time to show me one of the most interesting places I have ever seen, Jana Chaney for teaching me to believe I could write, Chuck McDaniel for teaching me how to do it, and finally, my wonderful wife, Tammy, who has pulled me off my knees and tossed me back on the horse more times than any man could hope or expect: May the next 10 years be as amazing as the first.

INTRODUCTION

On July 19, 2010, the good people of Butler, Missouri, gathered around the town square and formed into ranks, aiming flashlights into the sky to spell out the following message: "Butler—Shine On!" While many called this a Mayberry-esque gesture, the sound and fury typical of small-town life, it underlines a developing irony that ought to give pause to the most jaded of observers. It asks increasingly important questions: how long will places like this small Missouri town be able to shine, and how long will it be before no one living remembers that they were ever there? How long before Butler (and other places like it) disappears beneath the onslaught of interstate upgrades and interchange-oriented marketing that tend inevitably to drain the life from traditional mom-and-pop culture? More importantly, who will miss it when it is gone?

There is a name for those who give in to this sort of historical and cultural melodrama; they are primitivists, people who cannot deal with development and so hide behind the myth of the Golden Years. But to assume that all praise of the past amounts to naive primitivist idealism is also to risk a skewed picture of history. Not all progress is truly progressive, and not all backwards-looking is a sign of backward thinking. Most, if not all, existing societies are nearly enough removed from an agrarian origin that memories of that state are still easily accessed by the general public. Make no mistake, though; that moment of recall is fleeting, and when those memories disappear, so much dies with them. The characters, voices, stories, and moments found in Main Street diners say more about Americans as a people—as they were and as they are—than any comprehensive survey ever could.

In Butler's case, the future may be closer than anyone would like to imagine. US Highway 71 (US 71), which connects the town with Kansas City to the north, is currently being upgraded to form a transport corridor running south to Shreveport. Regulations governing this sort of development spell potential disaster for small, traditional communities constructed on the town-square model. Controlled access is required, which means the loss of intersections not involving over- or underpasses; speed limits are legally higher, allowing for quicker passage and less time to observe passing scenery (creating the proverbial "blink-and-miss-it" phenomenon); legal minimums call for shallower grades and wider lanes, leading to blasting and the exercise of eminent domain. The interplay of these factors can create a domino effect, which leads, ultimately, to a decline in the quality of life in surrounding communities.

Meanwhile, behind the barrier of highway business exists the surprisingly delightful story of a folk, the truest expression of public history. Towns like Butler have it all, from the decidedly ridiculous to the disastrously tragic. While these details may be viewed by some historians as mere footnotes—the larger page being devoted to historic events of a more earth-shattering, paradigm-shifting nature—to the people who lived them, they are everything. Their stories illuminate the human psyche in a manner unmatched by the broad and sweeping narratives so familiar to the high school history student. The protagonists may not be Napoleons or Washingtons, but they are captivating in their own right, and well worth scholarly attention. However, as the transportation arteries of the nation become more and more clogged, the opportunities for such study fade into the blur of passing countryside.

In the face of this danger, how to respond? It is not exactly feasible to suggest returning to the old pioneers' practice of trail blazing; multilane highways are here to stay. But it is absurd to suggest that they are the solution to everything society needs. So, what is the answer? How are these little histories to be kept from drowning in a sea of asphalt and gasoline fumes?

First, it is important to slow down, look around, and take a breather now and then. Not all must happen in such a hurry. Where is the fire? The back roads beckon. They may not provide as direct a route, but they do reveal some things that interstates simply cannot. Perhaps such a route will enable the traveler to commune with the spirit of a place and not just blink as it passes by.

More importantly, it is advisable for historians (professional and otherwise) to set aside for a moment the oft-examined French Revolution and Gettysburg Address. Instead, the gaze of history must shift to the man on the street, to the comparatively tiny world of daily existence, because these things are why the larger history matters. If these stories are lost, it will not matter who said what or what battle happened where and on what day. It is not that the bigger picture is not worth research and discussion, but that, all too often, the things that are thought of as the bigger picture are really those that should serve as the picture frame. In reality, the "bigger picture" is comprised of the lives, deaths, hopes, cares, dreams, and failures of individuals like the men and women of Butler.

If Butler is to "shine on," then it is the historian's responsibility to flip the switch, to focus on the ways in which history is built on a daily basis, not after it is lived but as it is lived. Somewhere, underneath the hardened shell of an asphalt world, lurks a living core of memories and moments in time that, if unearthed with care, may provide a key to who we are, where we have been, and where we are headed—in short, the key to all the history books we think we already understand.

One

In the Beginning(s)

The history of Bates County is one of many beginnings. Originally, it was Osage territory. In 1821, days before Missouri's admission as the 24th state in the union, the first European settlement was established at Harmony Mission. The mission lasted only 15 years, but by that time, the county had been officially organized (for the first time). In 1833, two counties, Van Buren (later Cass) and Bates, were created; for the moment, though, they were still attached administratively to Jackson County to the north. Not until January 29, 1841, when it was reorganized as an independent unit, did the story of Bates County truly begin. Then, in 1851, there was an unexpected twist: for two years, Bates County became Vernon County. Papinville, county seat since 1847, failed to make the cut by three quarters of a mile and was left stranded outside its own county lines. The people of Papinville protested, taking the situation to court. The vote was overturned, boundaries reverted, and things went back to the way they had been.

For its troubles, Papinville was shortly stripped of its rank, and in 1856, the title of county seat went permanently to Butler, a newly organized town at the county's heart. However, the situation still was not fully in hand. Five years later, the Civil War broke out, and Missouri's border counties exploded in rage and savagery. In 1863, three counties—Jackson, Cass, and Bates—and part of a fourth, Vernon, were evacuated, with large portions being put to the torch in accordance with Brig. Gen. Thomas Ewing's infamous Order No. 11. For three years, Bates County was a virtual wasteland; houses were burned, livestock was confiscated, and its inhabitants vanished.

In 1866, people began trickling back, and Butler came into its own as county seat. It alone of the prewar settlements regained and surpassed its former status. It is there, then, that the story of the life, death, and rebirth of Bates County must find its focus.

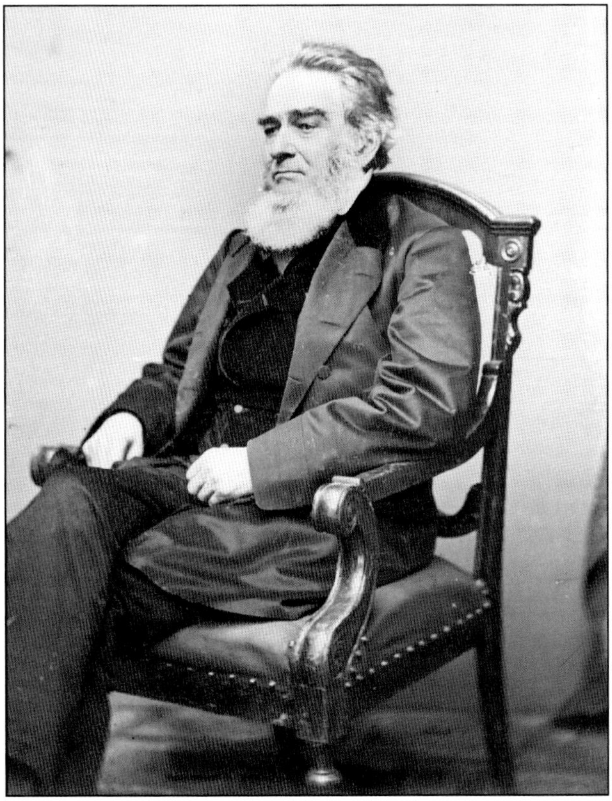

Bates County was named after Edward Bates (pictured at left)—according to the Old Settlers' Society, at least. The constitutive act of 1833 explicitly attributes that honor to Bates's brother Frederick, governor of Missouri from 1824 to 1825. Some suggest that Edward, Lincoln's attorney general during the Civil War, was a more politically correct candidate than his slaveholding brother, thus accounting for the later "confusion." (Courtesy of the Library of Congress.)

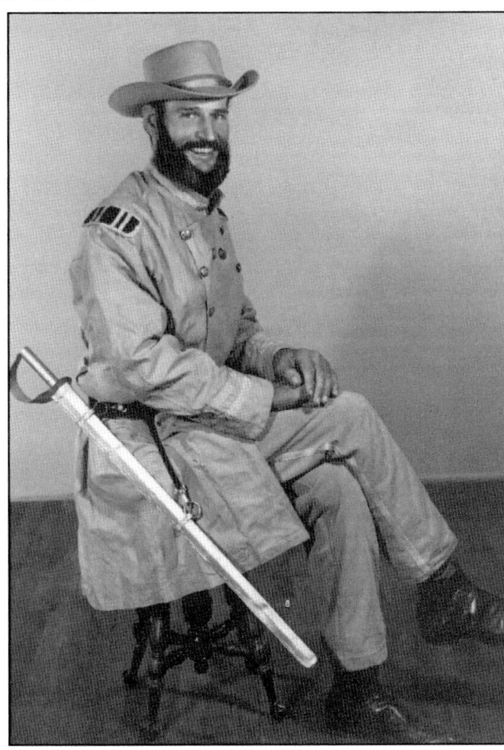

Clifford Bruner, posing as Gen. William Orlando Butler, sits for a portrait during the 1956 centennial celebration. Butler, the Kentucky-born Democratic vice presidential candidate in 1848, was extremely popular with the organizers of the town that would become his namesake. Many of them hailed from his home state, and many of them shared Southern Democratic sympathies, a combination that gave birth to a community. (Courtesy of the Bates County Historical Society.)

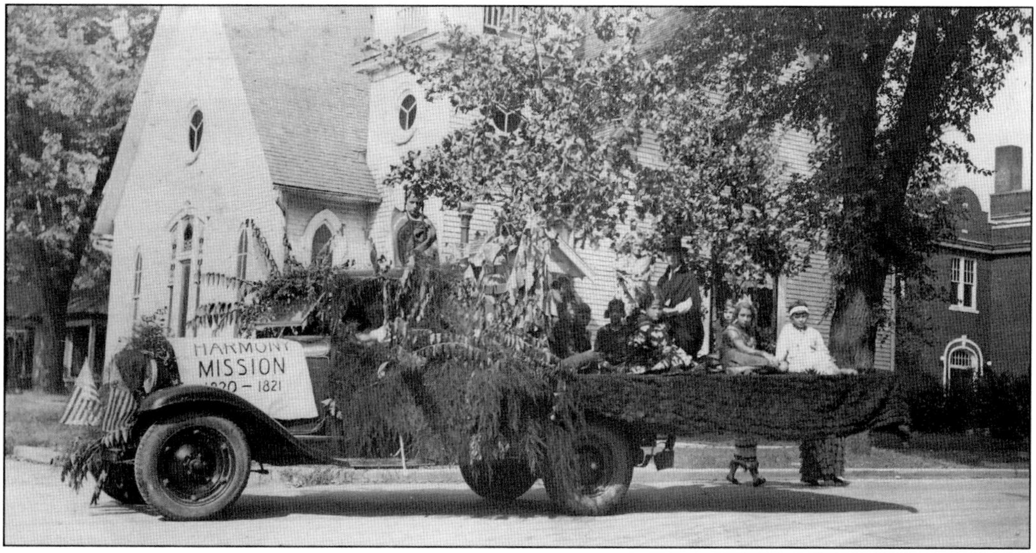

This 1931 parade float depicts the encounter between Osage Indians and Harmony Mission settlers in 1821. Emissaries of the United Foreign Missionary Society, these first white settlers traveled by invitation of Osage chief Payouska, but their school-building efforts met with limited success. Harmony Mission lasted little more than a decade, but the settlement of Bates County had begun. (Courtesy of the Bates County Historical Society and the Eddie Herrman Collection.)

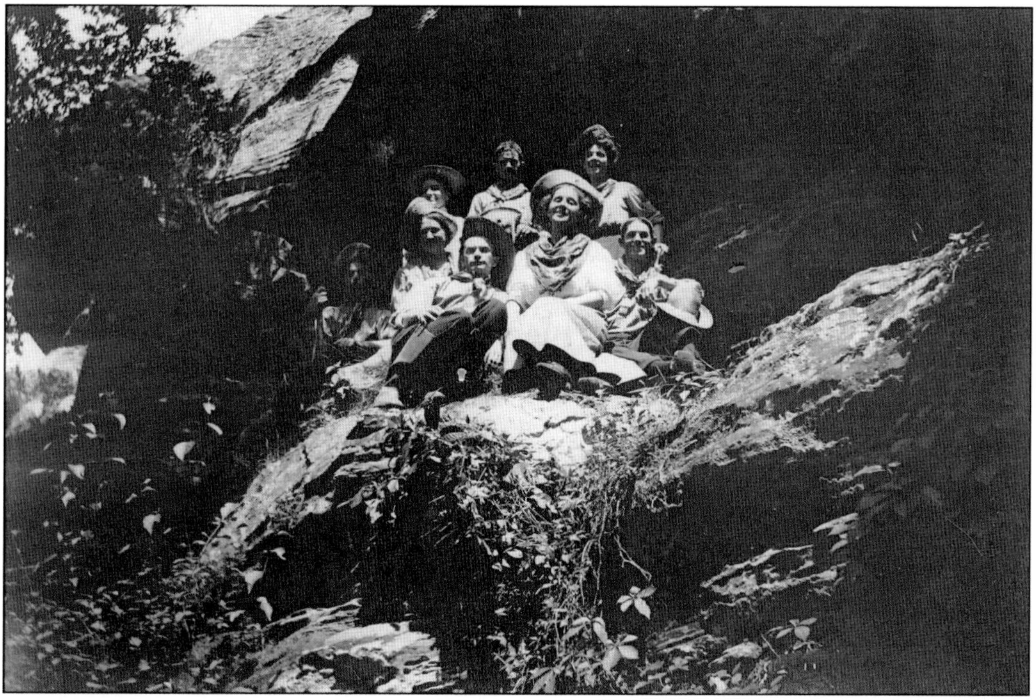

Halley's Bluffs, a natural formation southeast of town, was a favorite destination of Butler youth. It was also the setting of the county's earliest love story. In 1822, a noble Frenchman named Auguste Letier, in search of his father, met an Osage girl named Denignon at the Bluffs. They married and returned to France, marquis and marchioness, Bates County's original "royal family." (Courtesy of the Bates County Historical Society.)

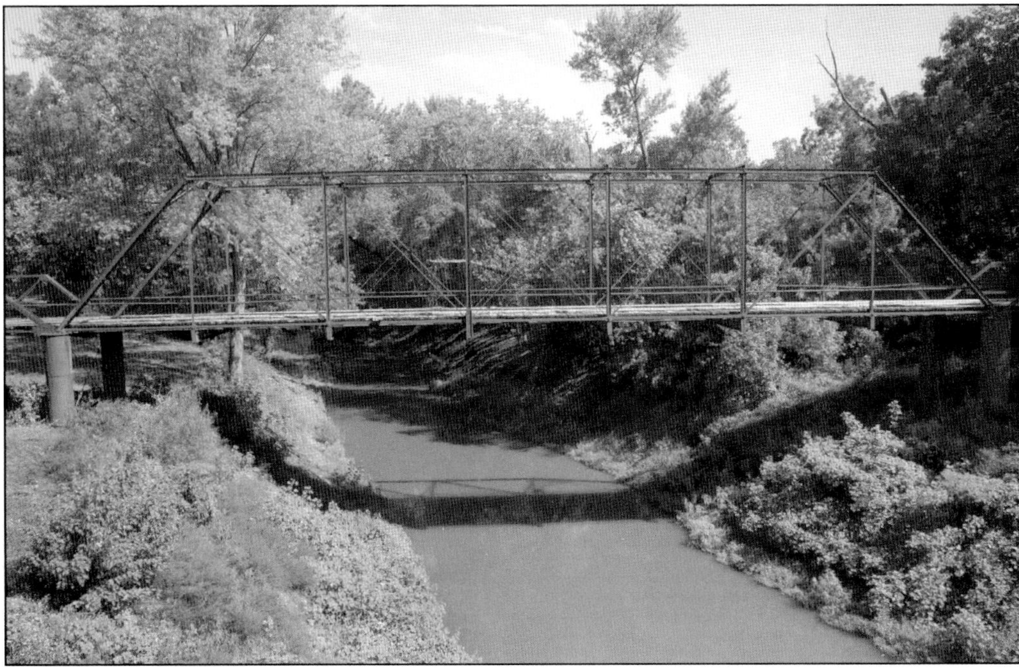

The Marais des Cygnes Bridge in Papinville was built in 1873 and entered in the National Register of Historic Places on October 22, 2002. Papinville, built on 70 acres donated by early settler and merchant Melicourt Papin, was platted in 1847 and served as county seat until 1856. Before the Civil War, it was a heavy trade center, even receiving the occasional steamboat at its docks. (Photograph by Vance Woods.)

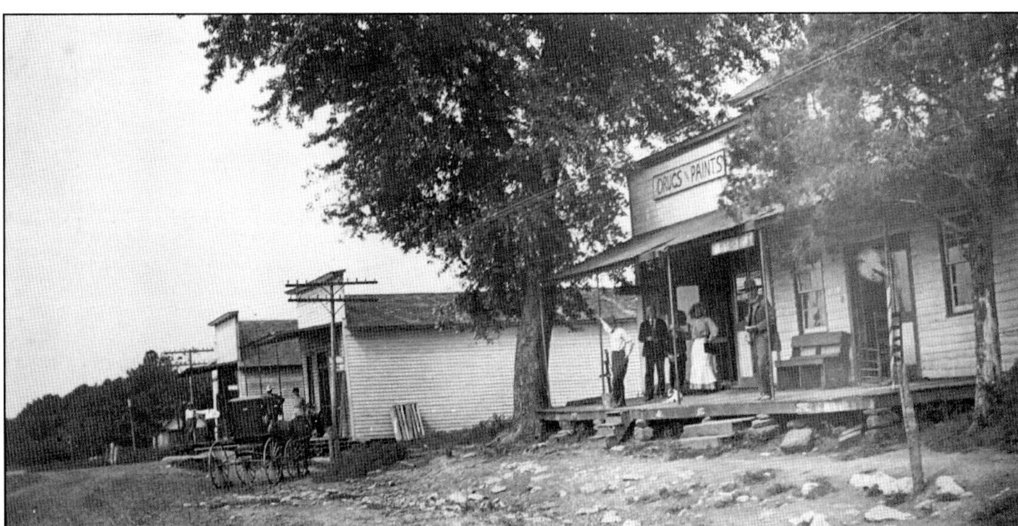

Johnstown, a major player in Bates County affairs during the 1840s and 1850s, is a concrete example of the effect war and economic change can have upon a community. Evacuated in 1862 in accordance with Order No. 11 and circumvented after the war by increasingly important rail routes, Johnstown never recovered its former status. Today, it has all but disappeared from the map. (Courtesy of the Bates County Historical Society.)

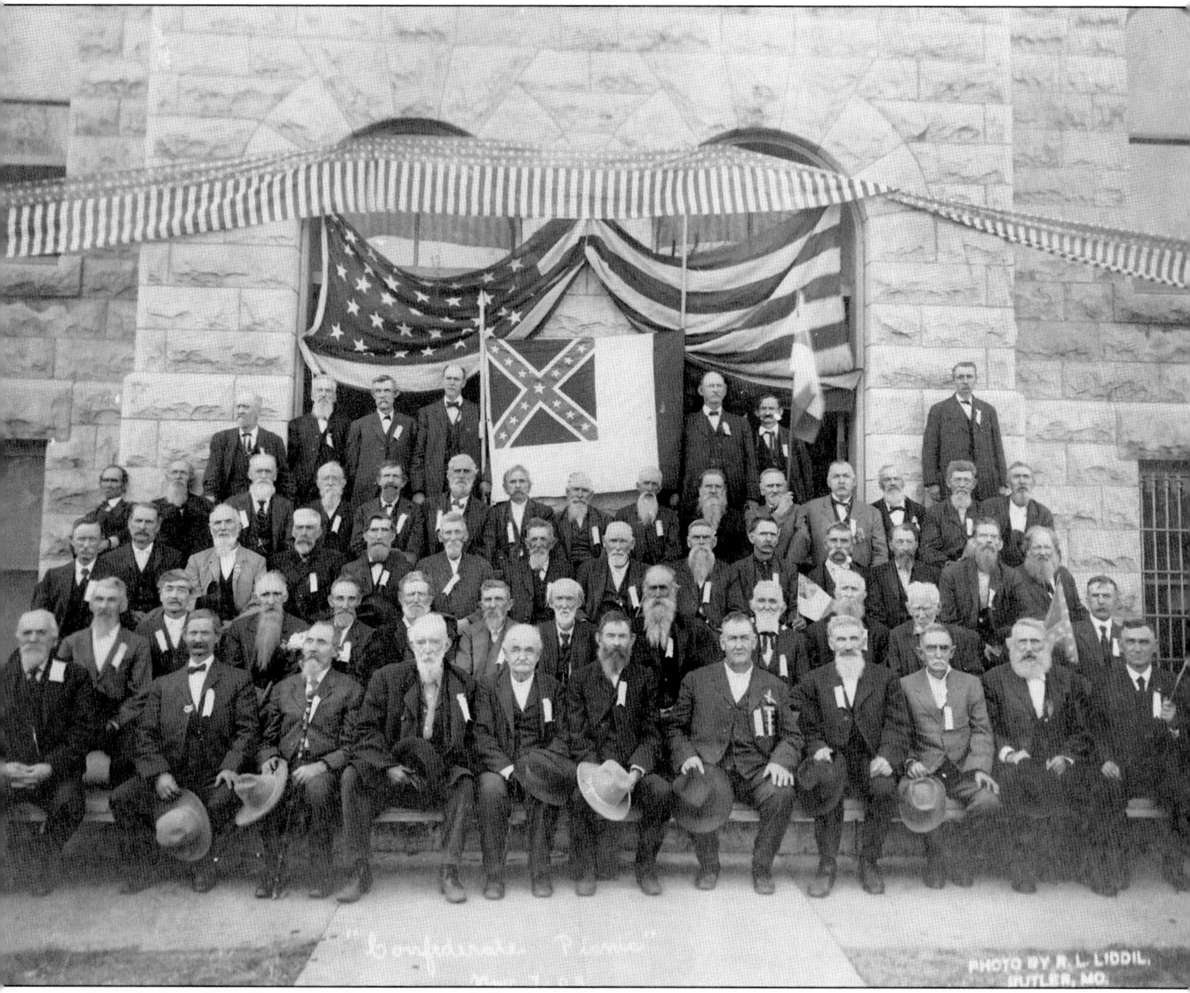

Taken by Butler photographer R.L. Liddil, this photograph captures a November 1908 reunion of Bates County's Confederate veterans at the county courthouse. At the outset of the Civil War, Southern sympathies ran so high in Bates County that historian William Atkeson subscribed the entire population, for all practical purposes, to the cause of the Confederacy. (Courtesy of the Bates County Historical Society and the Eddie Herrman Collection.)

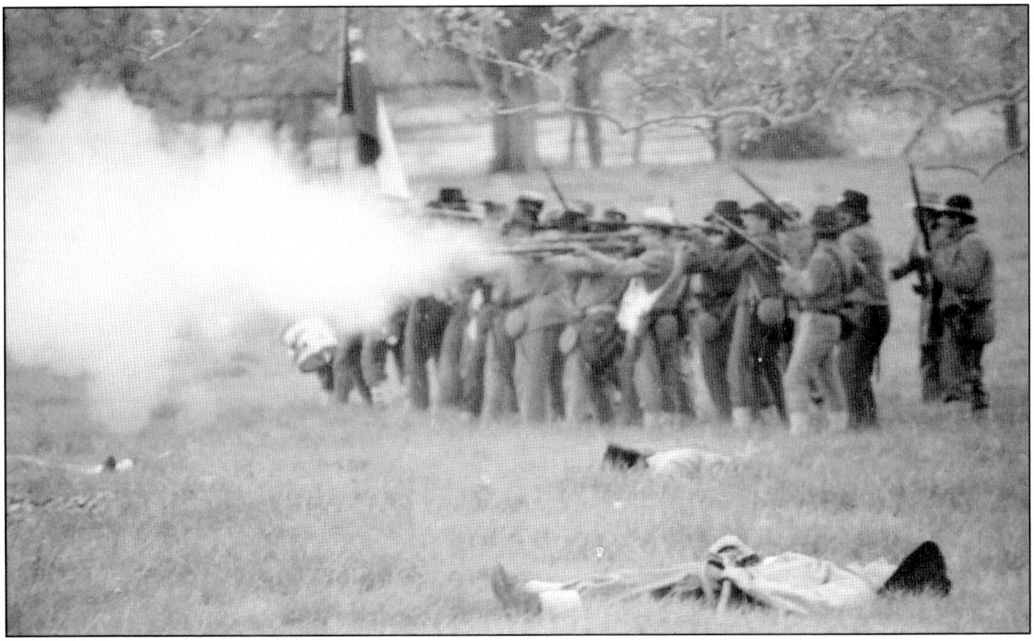

April 19 and 20, 1986, was Civil War Weekend in Butler, celebrating the 25th anniversary of the Bates County Historical Society. Reenactments transported spectators to May 1862, portraying a Confederate attack on Union supply lines. It was a festive occasion, complete with parasol-toting wives watching from the sidelines—but the real war in Bates County was neither festive nor formal; it was a bloody, destructive business. Butler's courthouse was burned in 1860 to prevent sympathizers from harboring rebels, and the confused violence along the Missouri-Kansas line, perpetrated by secessionists, Unionists, abolitionists, and ruffians embracing no cause but their own, left many innocent people dead and sent many others running for their lives. Peripheral though it was, western Missouri is acknowledged by historians as one of the most brutal theaters of the Civil War. (Both, courtesy of the Bates County Historical Society.)

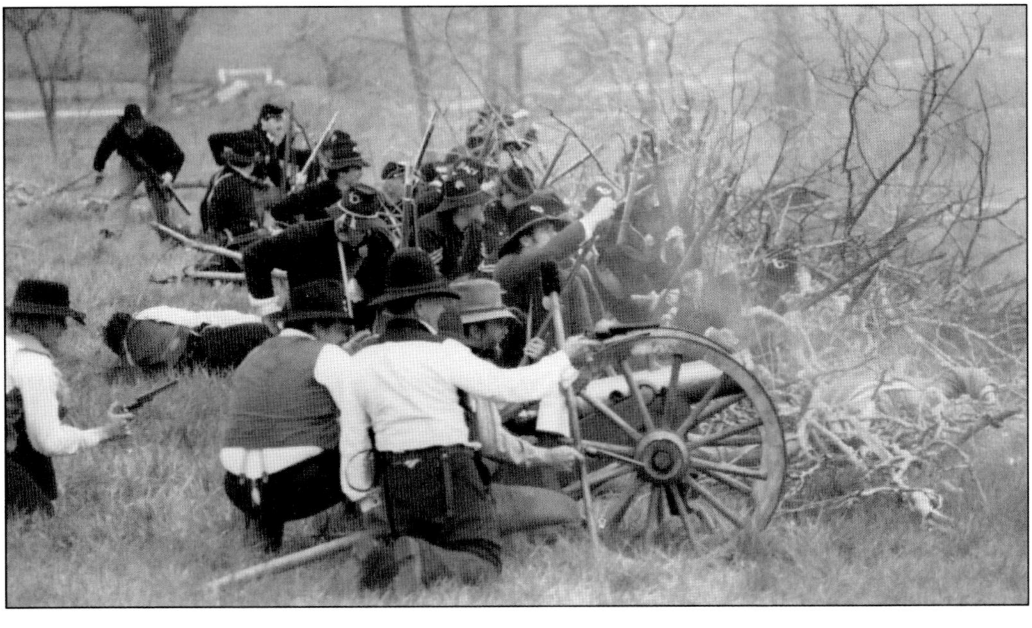

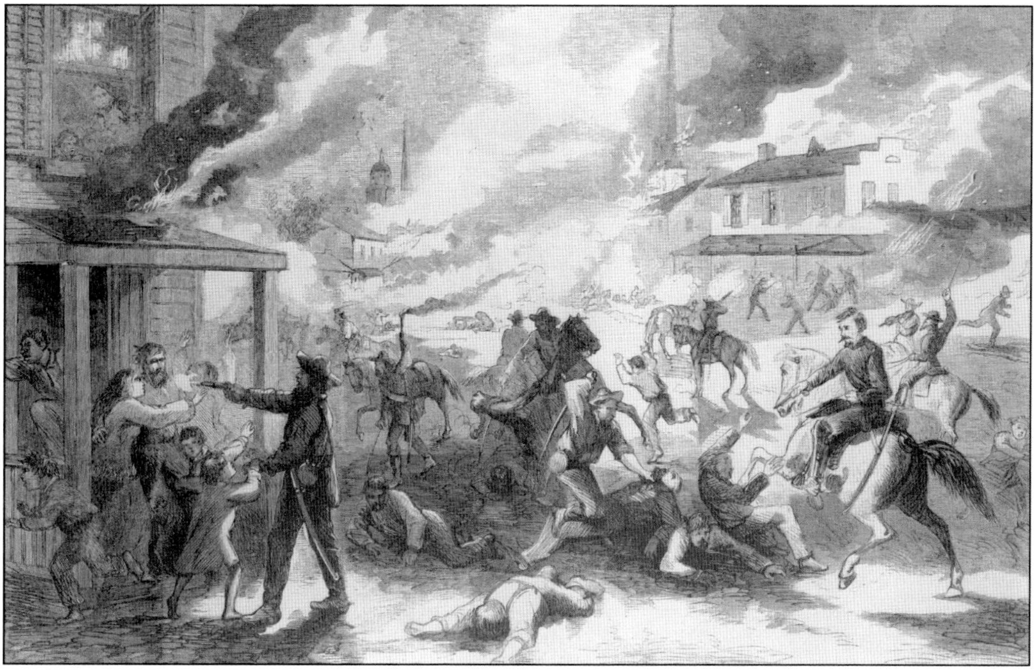

At 5:00 a.m. on August 21, 1863, William Clarke Quantrill and his bushwhackers—including 50 men from Bates and Cass Counties—fell upon a sleeping Lawrence, Kansas, unleashing, in William Connelley's words, "a carnival of death and a gorge of innocent blood." By 9:00 a.m., the marauders had gone, leaving a city in ashes and over 100 men dead in the streets. (Courtesy of the Library of Congress.)

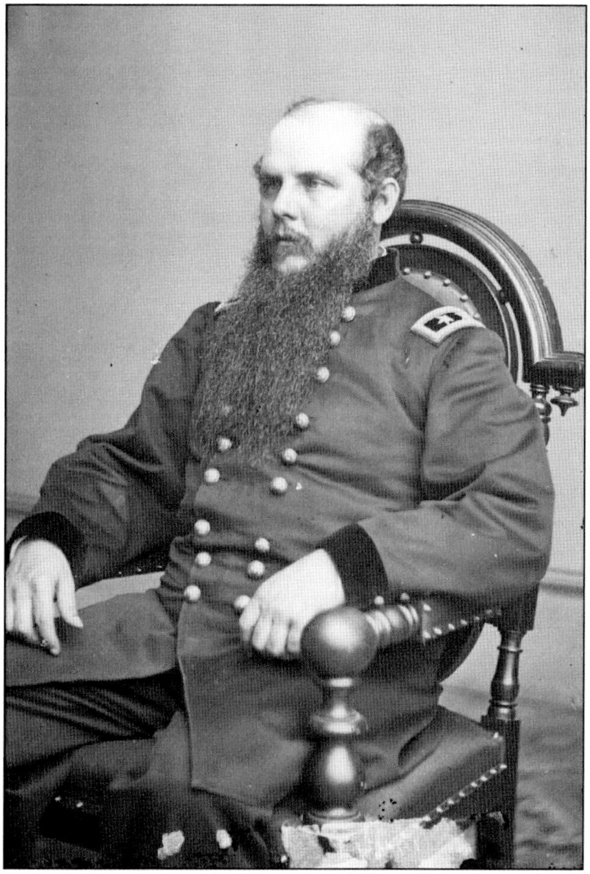

Four days after the Lawrence massacre, a communiqué went out from Maj. Gen. John M. Schofield's headquarters in St. Louis. In the message, the commander of the Department of Missouri feared the only effective deterrent along the border would be "total devastation," giving his subordinate in the west, Thomas Ewing, carte blanche to respond as he saw fit. (Courtesy of the Library of Congress.)

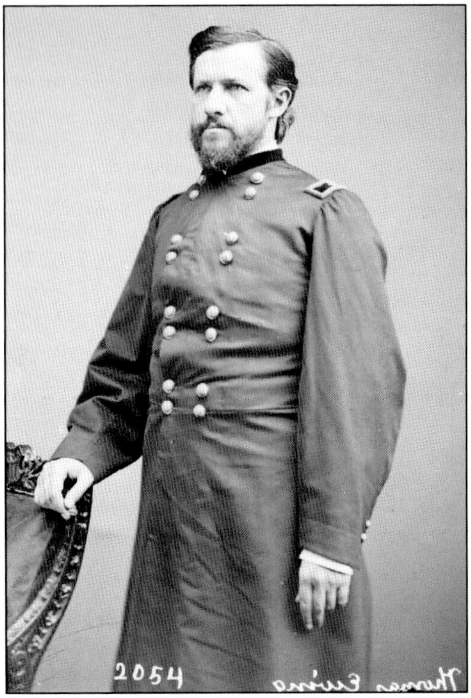

On August 25, 1863, Brig. Gen. Thomas Ewing issued General Order No. 11. The people had 15 days to either get to a military post and prove their loyalty to the Union or admit their disloyalty and get out of the state. Fiery destruction ensued. By the time the smoke cleared, Bates County stood desolate and empty; many of its citizens never returned. (Courtesy of the Library of Congress.)

When people began filtering back into Bates County in 1866, they had no courthouse and no money to build one. For three years, they had to make do with a "court-shack," a 24-by-40-foot frame structure in the northeast corner of the Butler square. It was not until 1869 that they were able to begin work on this, their new county headquarters. (Courtesy of the Bates County Historical Society.)

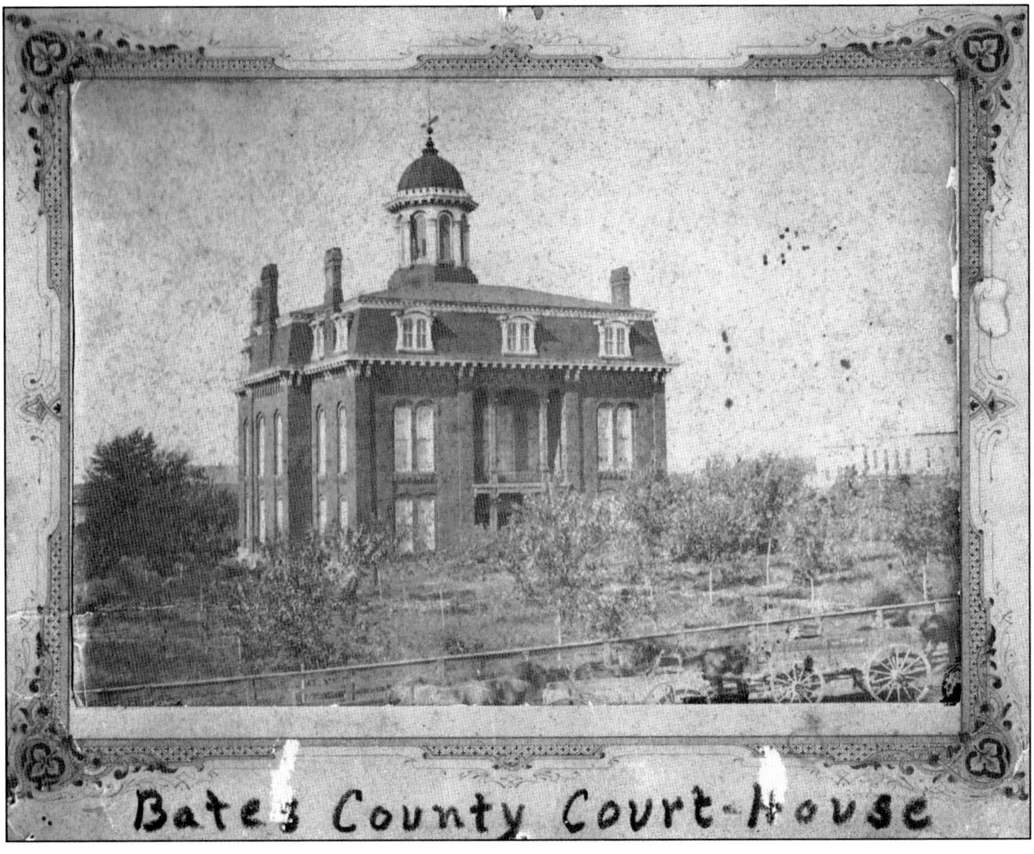

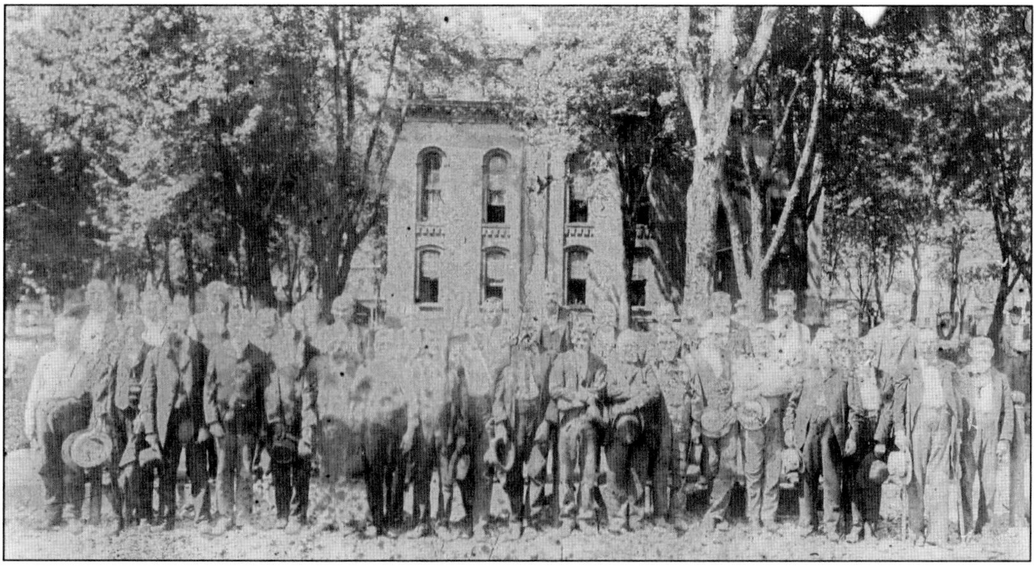

A group of pioneers pose in front of the county courthouse around 1895 in perhaps one of the earliest photographs of the Old Settlers. This society organized officially on May 22, 1897. Open to men and women, providing the applicant have resided in Bates County for at least 25 years, the Old Settlers set themselves the goal of preserving the history of their county. (Courtesy of the Bates County Historical Society.)

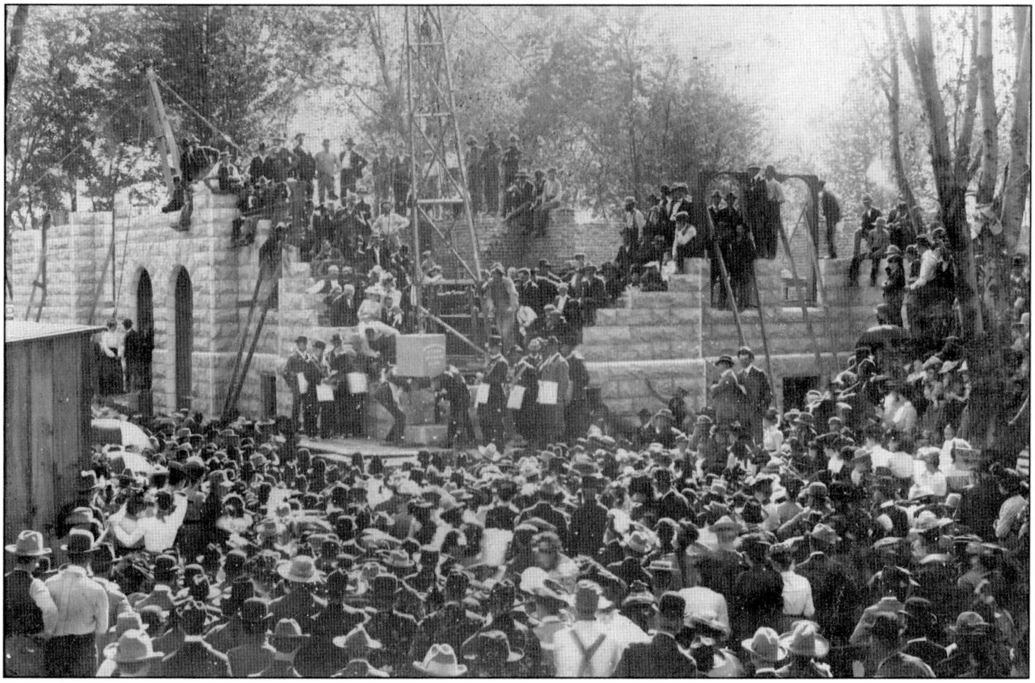

The cornerstone of the county's present courthouse was laid in Butler on October 10, 1901, by members of the local Masonic lodge, and the entire community turned out to mark the occasion. In 1900, the 19th-century structure had been declared unsafe, and plans for a replacement were prepared. The new building was completed in July 1902. (Courtesy of the Bates County Historical Society.)

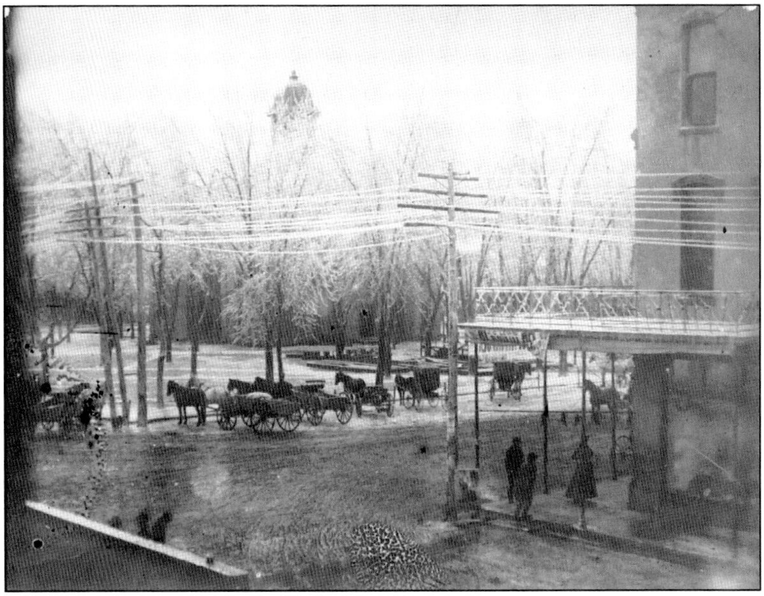

Ice storms, like this one in the winter of 1900, are not uncommon in Bates County. Beautiful to behold, with every surface sparkling, they can also create difficulties for those with work to be done. This one likely put a damper on the demolition of the courthouse, underway in the background. (Courtesy of the Bates County Historical Society and the Eddie Herrman Collection.)

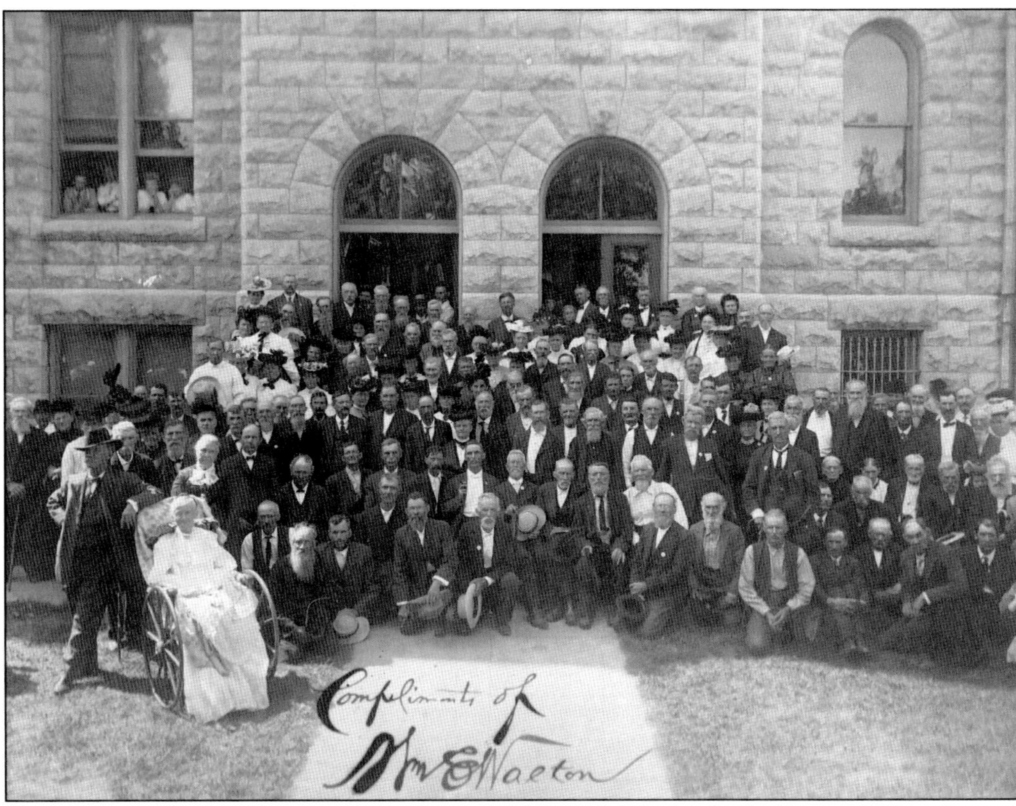

In what is possibly the most famous photograph ever taken in Bates County, the oldest Old Settlers gather at the courthouse in 1903 to celebrate the sixth anniversary of the Old Settlers' Society. Featured are the members in attendance who lived in the county prior to the Civil War. (Courtesy of the Bates County Historical Society and the Eddie Herrman Collection.)

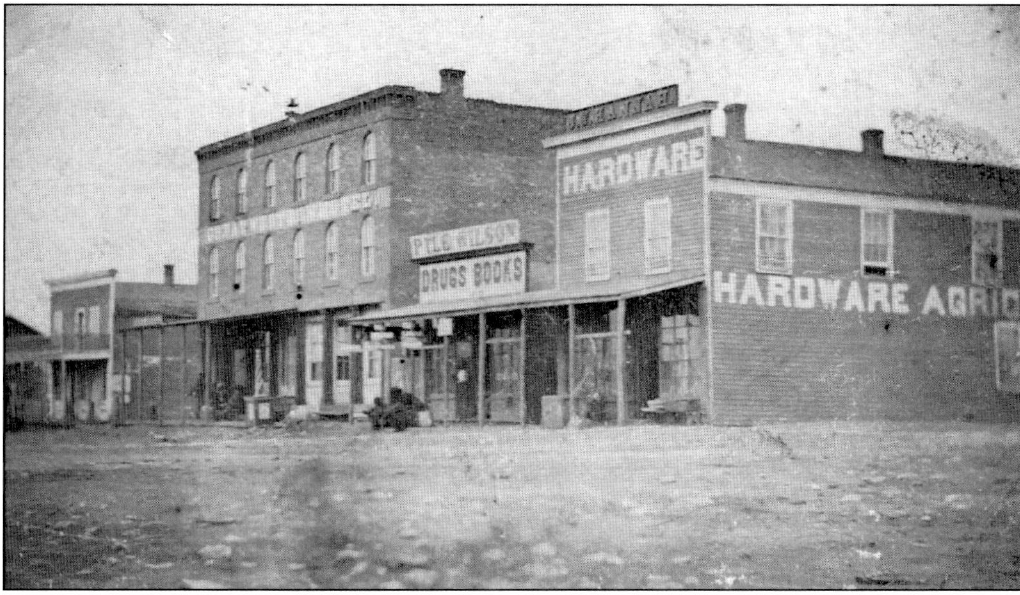

This photograph of the east side of the Butler square, at the intersection of Main and Dakota Streets, dates from 1868 and is reputed to be the oldest extant photograph of the community. It features the Great Western Hotel (second from left), Pyle and Wilson's Drug, and, on the corner, J.W. Hannah's hardware store. (Courtesy of the Bates County Historical Society and the Eddie Herrman Collection.)

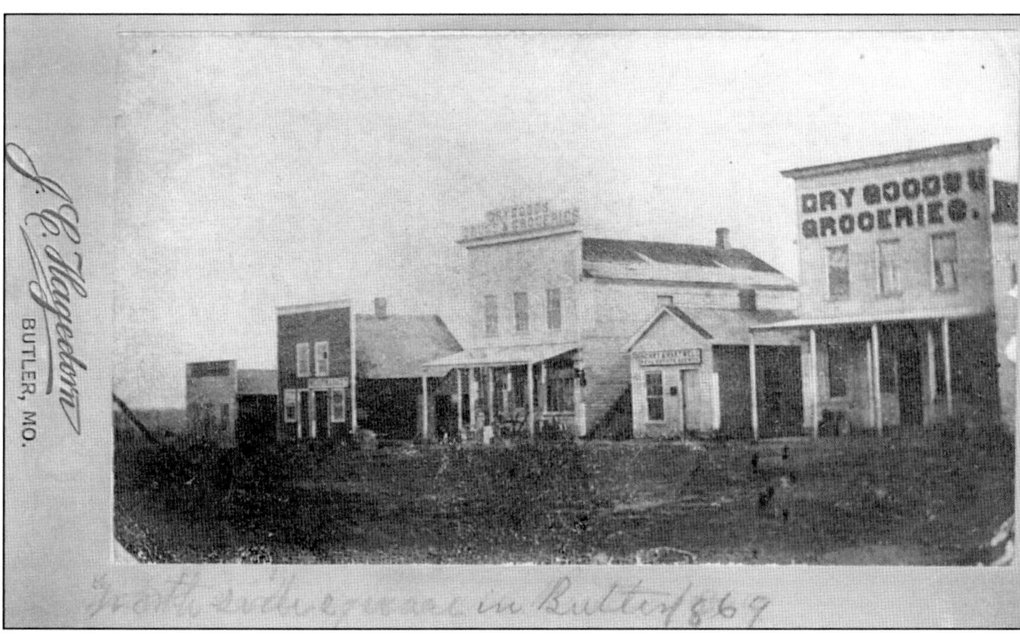

Said to date from 1869, this photograph offers an early view of the north side of the Butler square. Sandwiched between the two dry-goods stores on the right was the one-story office of realtors Henry and Hartwell. This space was later rented out to the US Postal Service for use as the Butler Post Office. (Courtesy of the Bates County Historical Society and the Eddie Herrman Collection.)

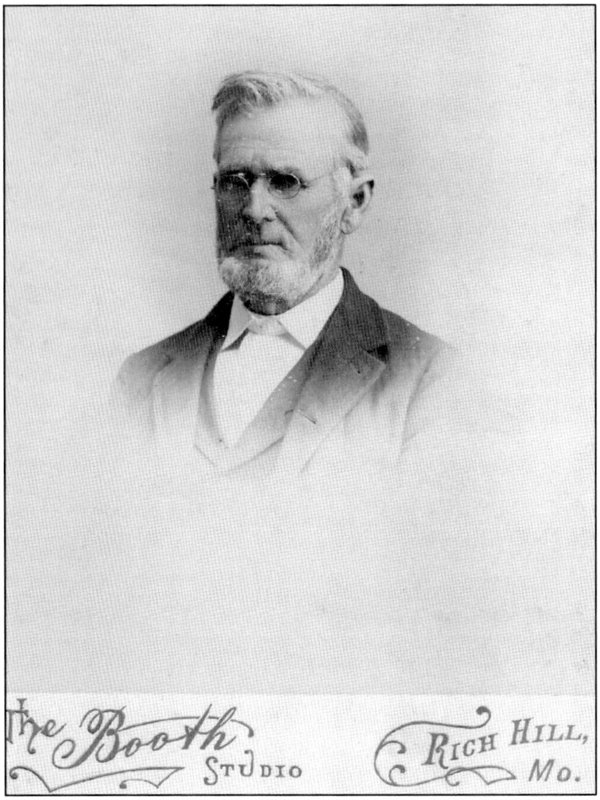

In 1869, Bates County experienced a settlement boom. H.P. Robinson arrived that year, taking up residence in Osage township in the vicinity of what later became the community of Rich Hill. A farmer by trade, by the turn of the 20th century, Robinson had amassed an estate of 1,200 acres sitting on one of the county's richest coal deposits. (Courtesy of the Bates County Historical Society.)

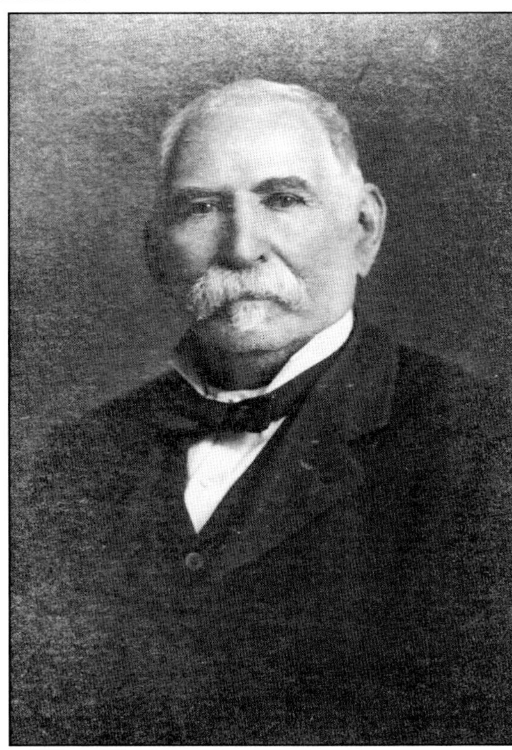

Aaron Hart, a German immigrant, also arrived in Bates County in 1869 and opened a general store. One of the original Old Settlers, Hart was elected, along with Calvin Boxley, O.D. Austin, R.S. Catron, and Charles Radford, to serve on the organizing committee for the society's first annual meeting. (Courtesy of the Bates County Historical Society.)

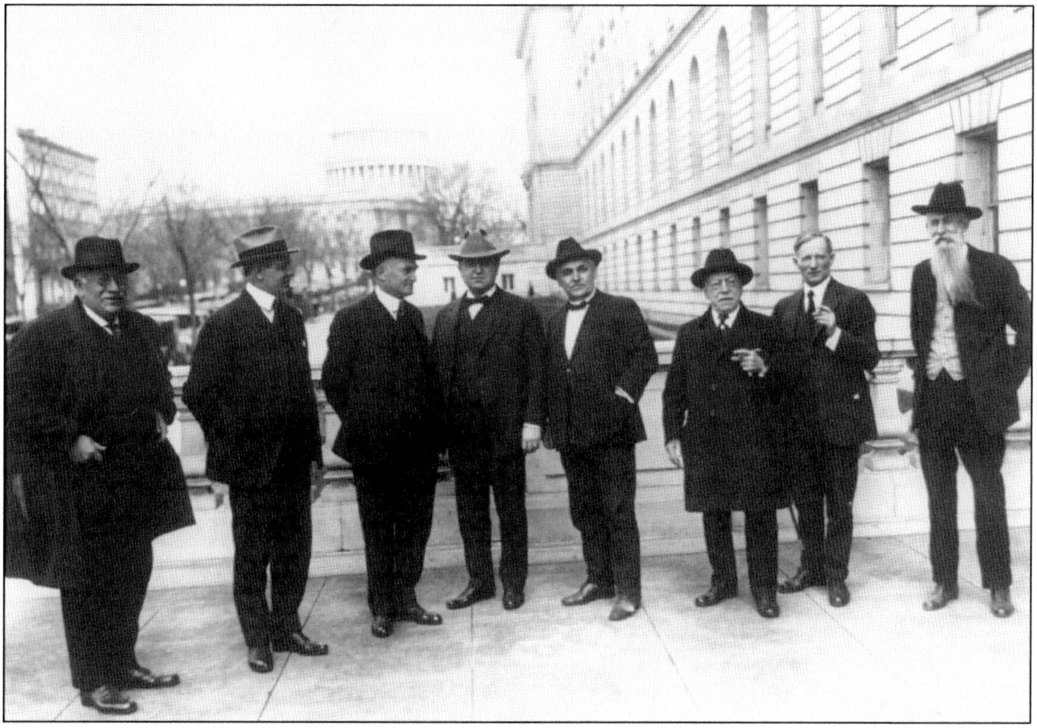

William Oscar Atkeson (far right), easily distinguishable by his Santa-like beard, was the Missouri 6th District's Republican representative in Congress from 1921 to 1923. He moved to Butler in 1889, where he acted as editor for both the *Butler Free Press* and the *Bates County Record*. More importantly, where historians are concerned, he wrote the massive, 983-page *History of Bates County, Missouri* in 1918. (Courtesy of the Library of Congress.)

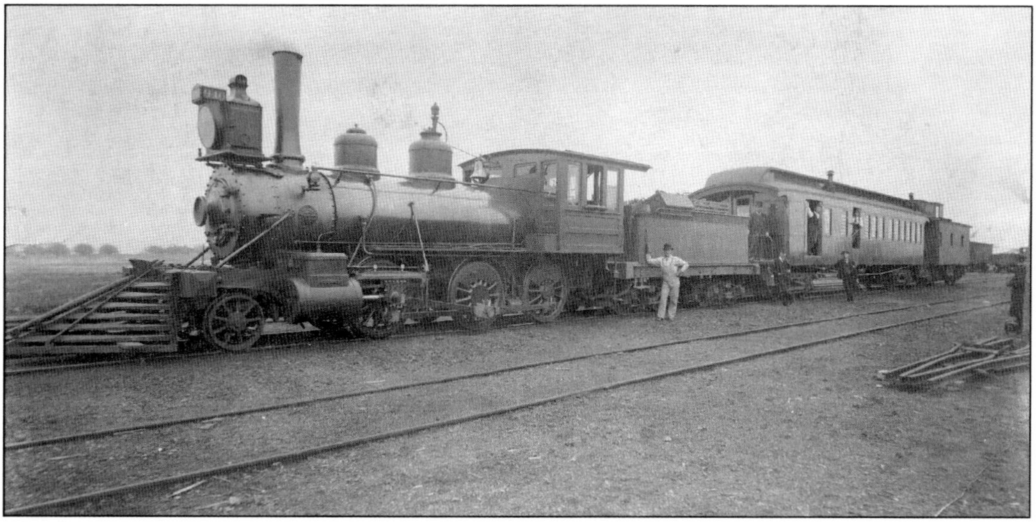

The first Missouri Pacific train steamed into Butler in 1879 after 13 years of unending wheeling, dealing, scheming, and scamming. New proposals surfaced and failed almost weekly. William Atkeson described it as a time when "railroad construction on paper was in the air, [and] the black smoke of the on-coming engines from all directions could be snuffed in the ozone of the atmosphere." (Courtesy of the Bates County Historical Society.)

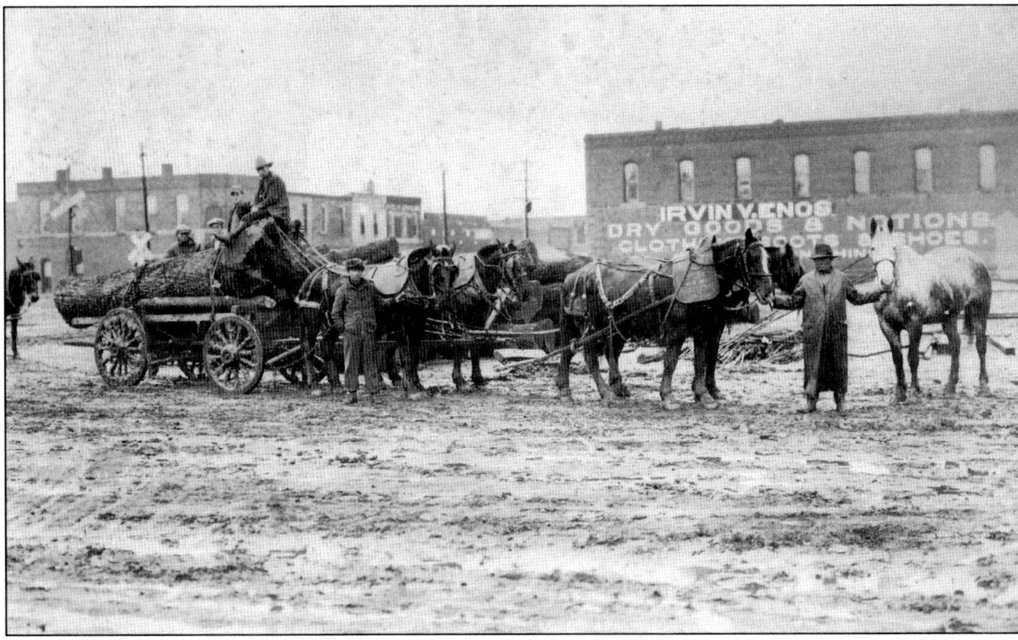

The advent of the railroad encouraged new business, but it also created new competition. Bustling towns began to grow up along its path where once there had been only prairie grass. Adrian, founded 10 miles north of Butler in 1880, was one of these. Here, Nimrod Underwood leads a team hauling walnut logs through the town alongside the tracks around 1927. (Courtesy of the Bates County Historical Society.)

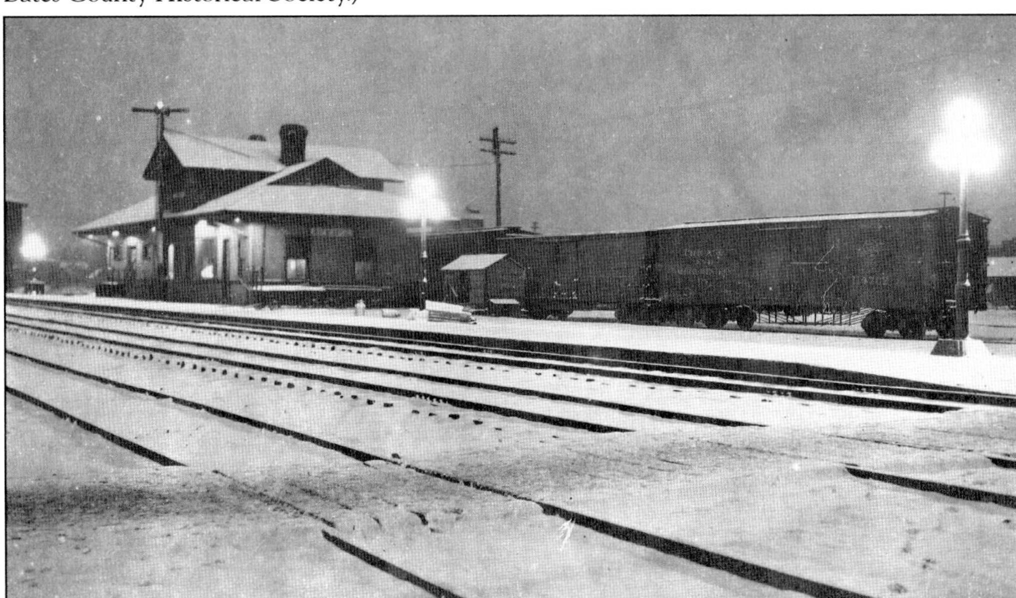

The Rich Hill depot, 10 miles south of Butler, basks in the winter moonlight. Home to two major coal-mining ventures and punctuated by two railroad lines, Rich Hill was another of the upstart "rail babies." Also established in 1880, the town grew so quickly that one journalist, a year after its founding, wondered if it had sprung complete from Aladdin's magical lamp. (Courtesy of the Bates County Historical Society.)

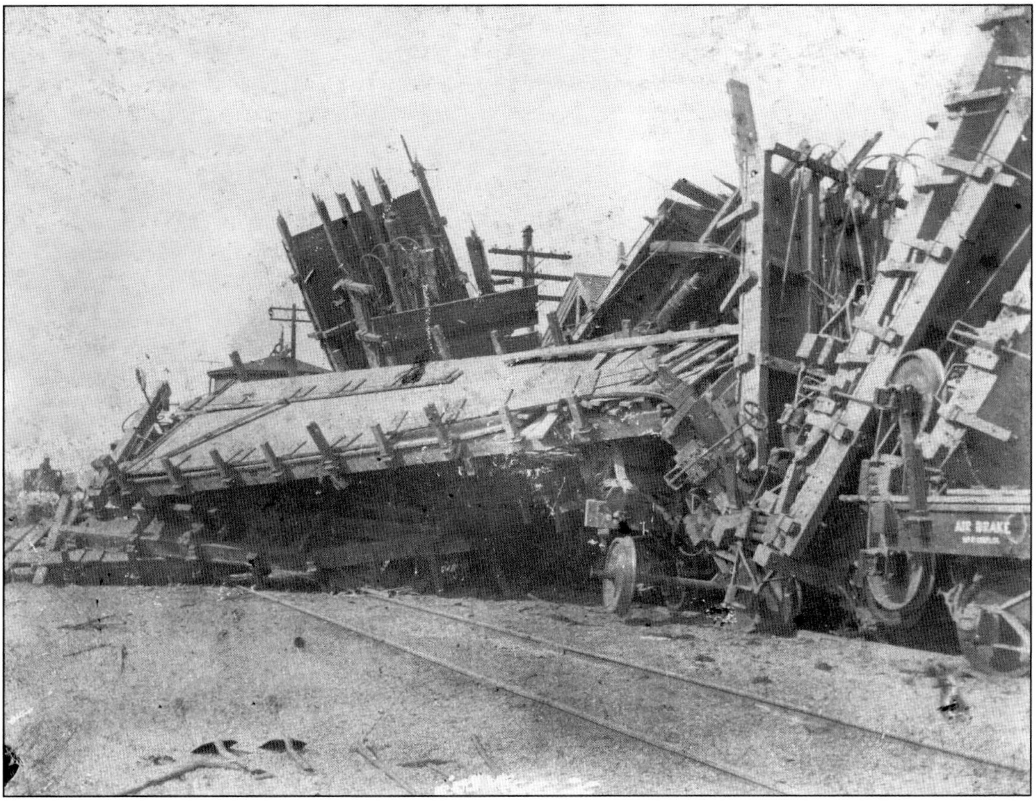

The utility of railroad transport sometimes came at a price. In the dark hours of a Saturday morning on June 21, 1901, a colossal train wreck occurred at the Butler Depot, tossing fragments of coal wagons around like matchsticks. No one was killed, but 11 cars were mangled beyond repair. As can be seen from the photograph below, rubbernecking was as much an American pastime then as it is now. Finely dressed women stroll hand in hand along the tracks, surveying the damage. The wreckage seems to have provided the ideal entertainment for a lazy weekend afternoon. (Both, courtesy of the Bates County Historical Society.)

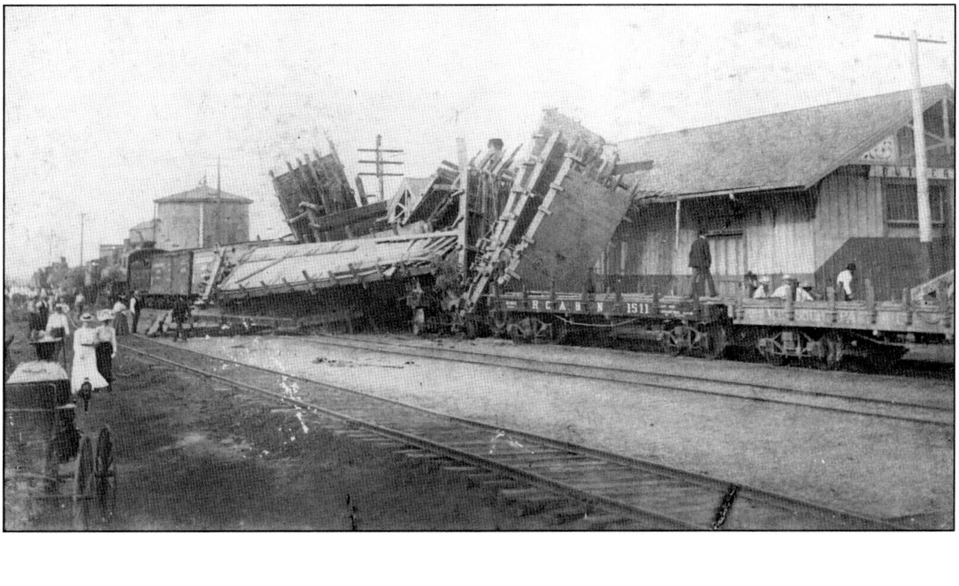

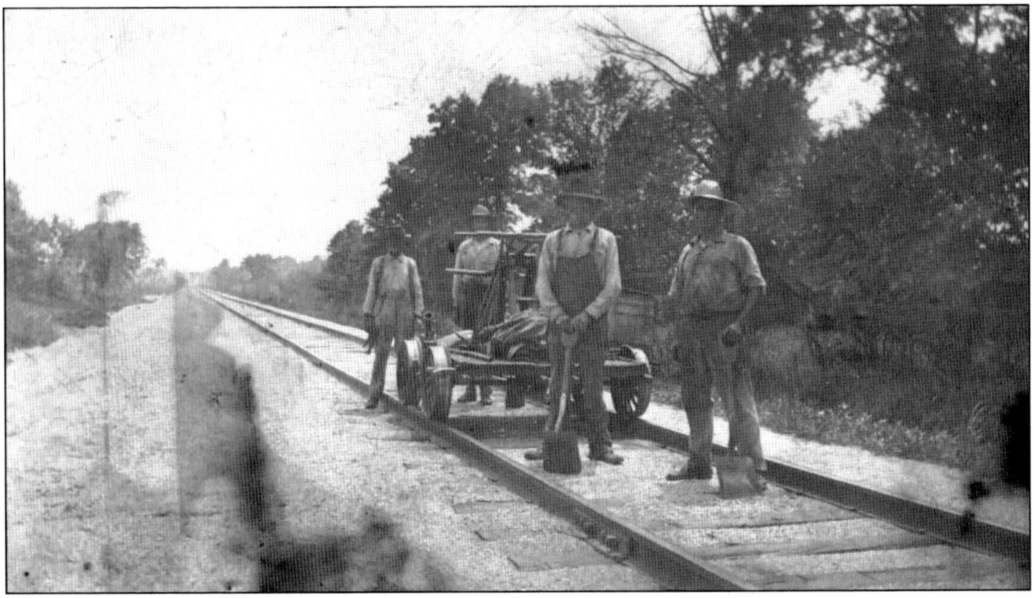

When the tracks finally did reach Butler, they brought along new employment opportunities. In this photograph, Dove Alkire (center, with shovel) works a stretch of road between Butler and Rich Hill. The railroad also altered old business routes significantly. Coal transport was the main issue, but cross-county cattle drives also became a thing of the past. From now on, merchandise would move straight from Butler to its market destination. (Courtesy of Barbara Herrell.)

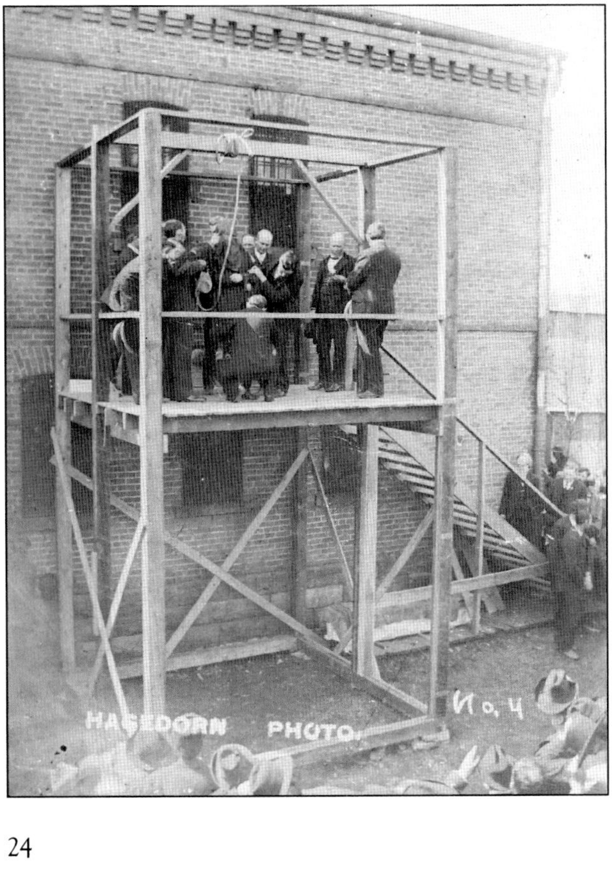

The privilege of rank often has a dark side. Papinville, in its days as county seat, discovered this in the case of the wife-killer Dr. Samuel Nottingham, victim of the first legal execution in Bates County. In its turn, Butler enjoyed the dubious honor of playing host to two fairly sensational hangings, including that of Dr. James Gartrell in 1903, pictured here. (Courtesy of the Bates County Historical Society.)

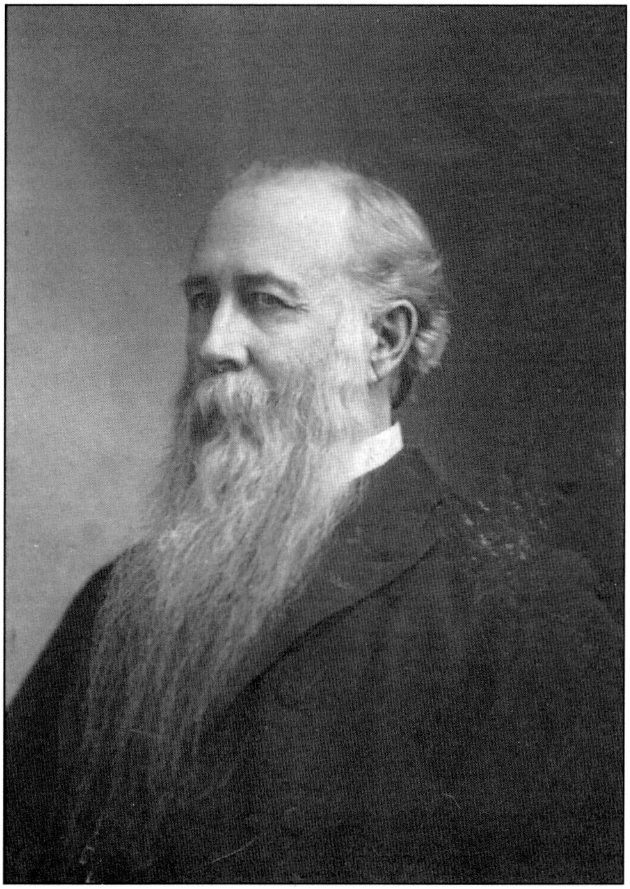

Dr. James L. Gartrell, former Texas legislator and probate judge of Refugio County, Texas, was hanged in Butler on April 17, 1903, for the murder of D.B. Donegan, a Colorado miner. Donegan's corpse was fished out of Mulberry Creek near Amoret, and the murder weapon, an ax, was found in the brush nearby. Gartrell's was the last legal hanging in Bates County. (Courtesy of the Bates County Historical Society.)

This invitation admitted one to the hanging of Noah "Bunk" McGinnis in Butler on December 20, 1900, for the shooting of a German farmer named Borcherding. As his last official act in office, Sheriff E.C. "Shelt" Mudd personally threw the lever that sent McGinnis to his death; Mudd would swear to his dying day that he was haunted by the young man's spirit. (Courtesy of the Bushwhacker Museum, Nevada, Missouri.)

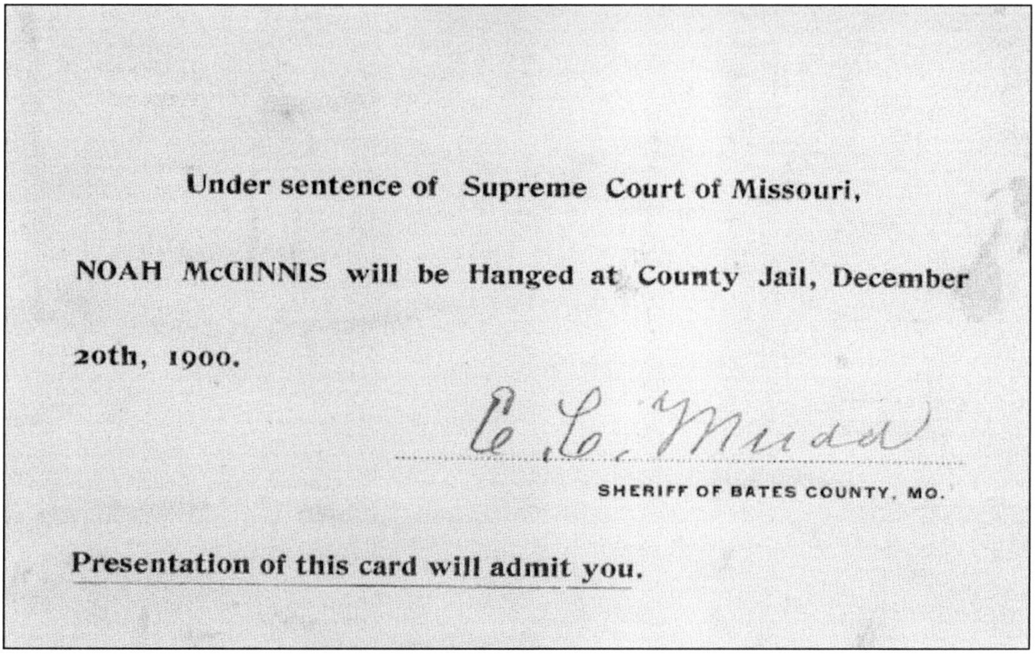

Under sentence of Supreme Court of Missouri,

NOAH McGINNIS will be Hanged at County Jail, December 20th, 1900.

E. C. Mudd

SHERIFF OF BATES COUNTY, MO.

Presentation of this card will admit you.

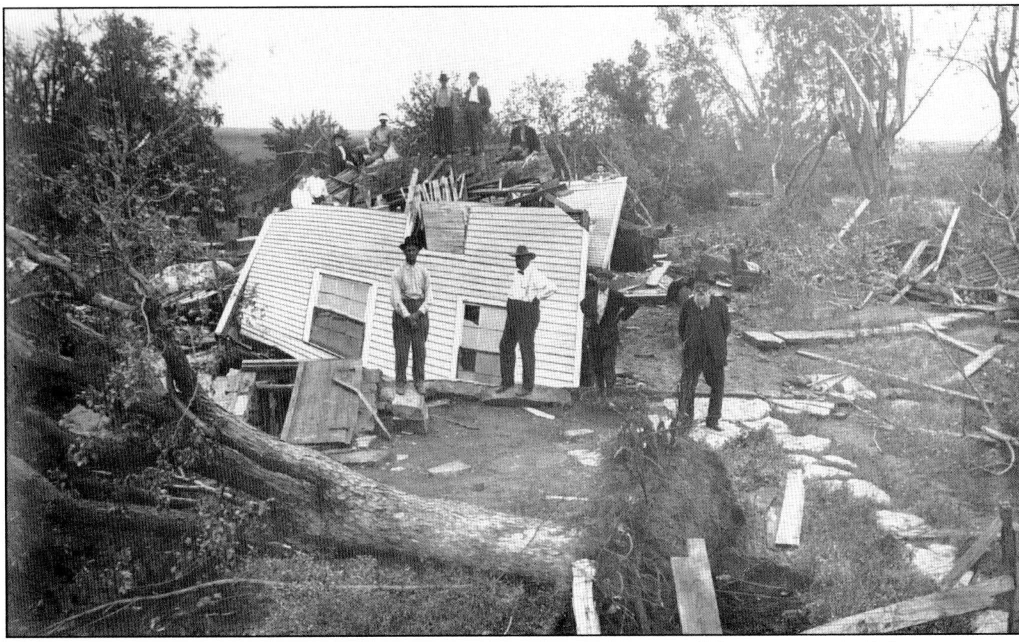

On June 15, 1912, a murderous cyclone tore across Bates County, blazing a trail of destruction as it went. H.L. Wright watched helplessly as it obliterated his family's home and possessions. He described to William Atkeson "a black, angry-looking, twisting cloud . . . sweeping down upon them from the west." In Amoret, Ada Stitt's brick home (the remains of which are pictured below) was all but ripped from the face of the earth. By a stroke of luck, the six people inside the house when the twister hit escaped unscathed, but not all were so lucky. The most poignant memorial of that dark day stands in the old West Point cemetery: a granite headstone marking the graves of Henry Cameron and Mary Belle, his wife, "killed by cyclone, June 15, 1912." (Both, courtesy of the Bates County Historical Society.)

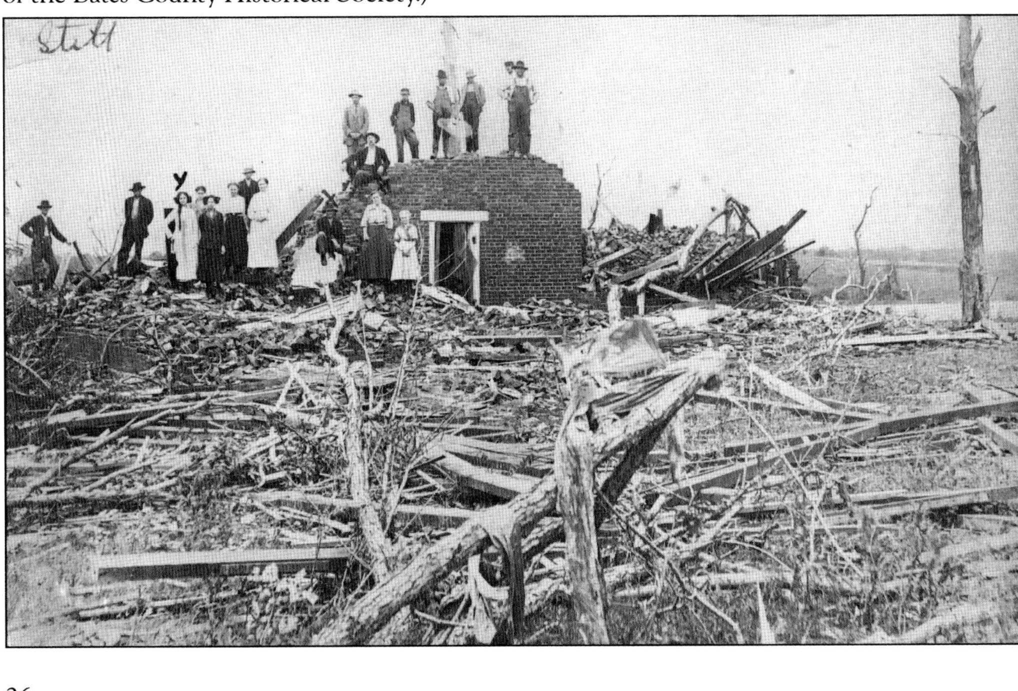

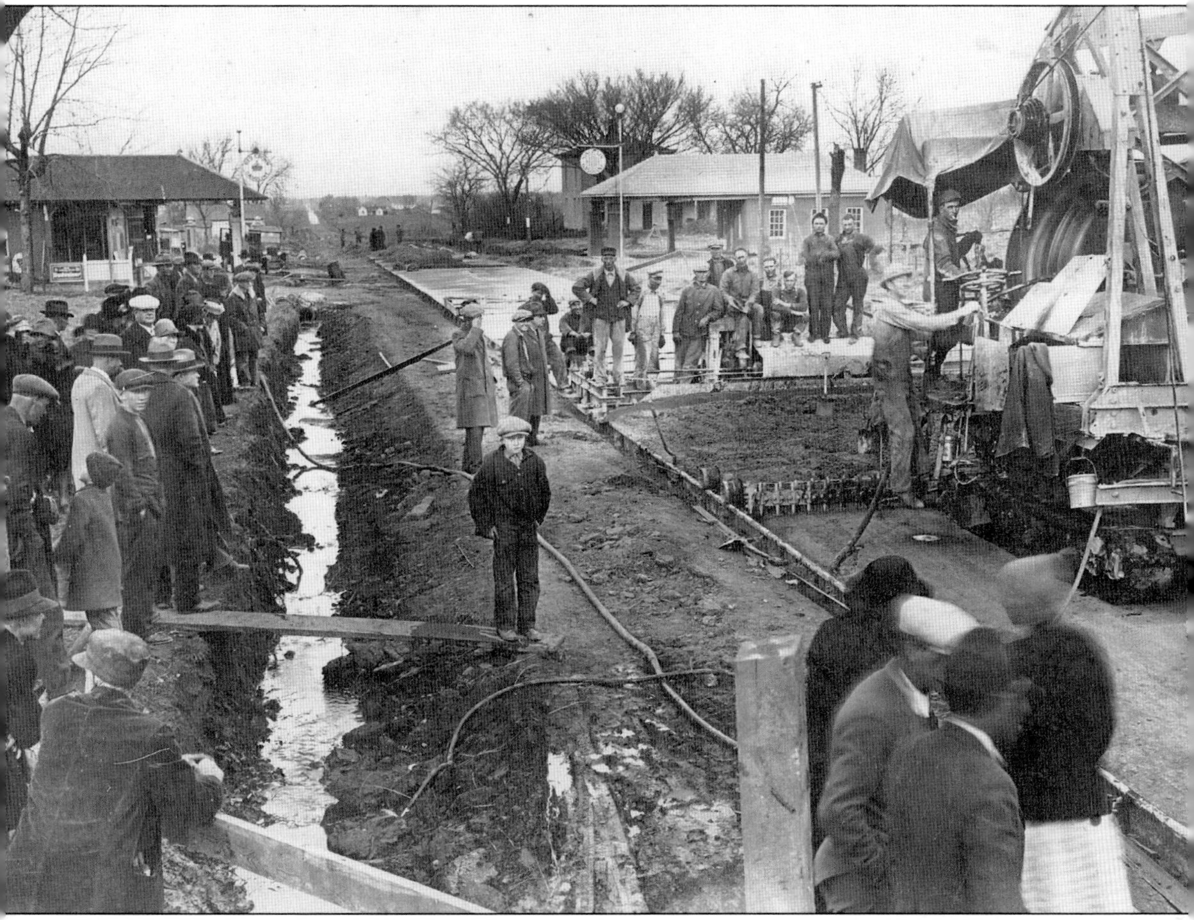

The paving of US 71 through Rich Hill in 1926 was, like so many similar events, a community affair. Work to divert and widen the highway to four lanes began in 1969 or 1970, but stretches of "Old 71" may still be found scattered up and down Bates County, a reminder of a time when travel ran through small-town life instead of around it. (Courtesy of the Bates County Historical Society.)

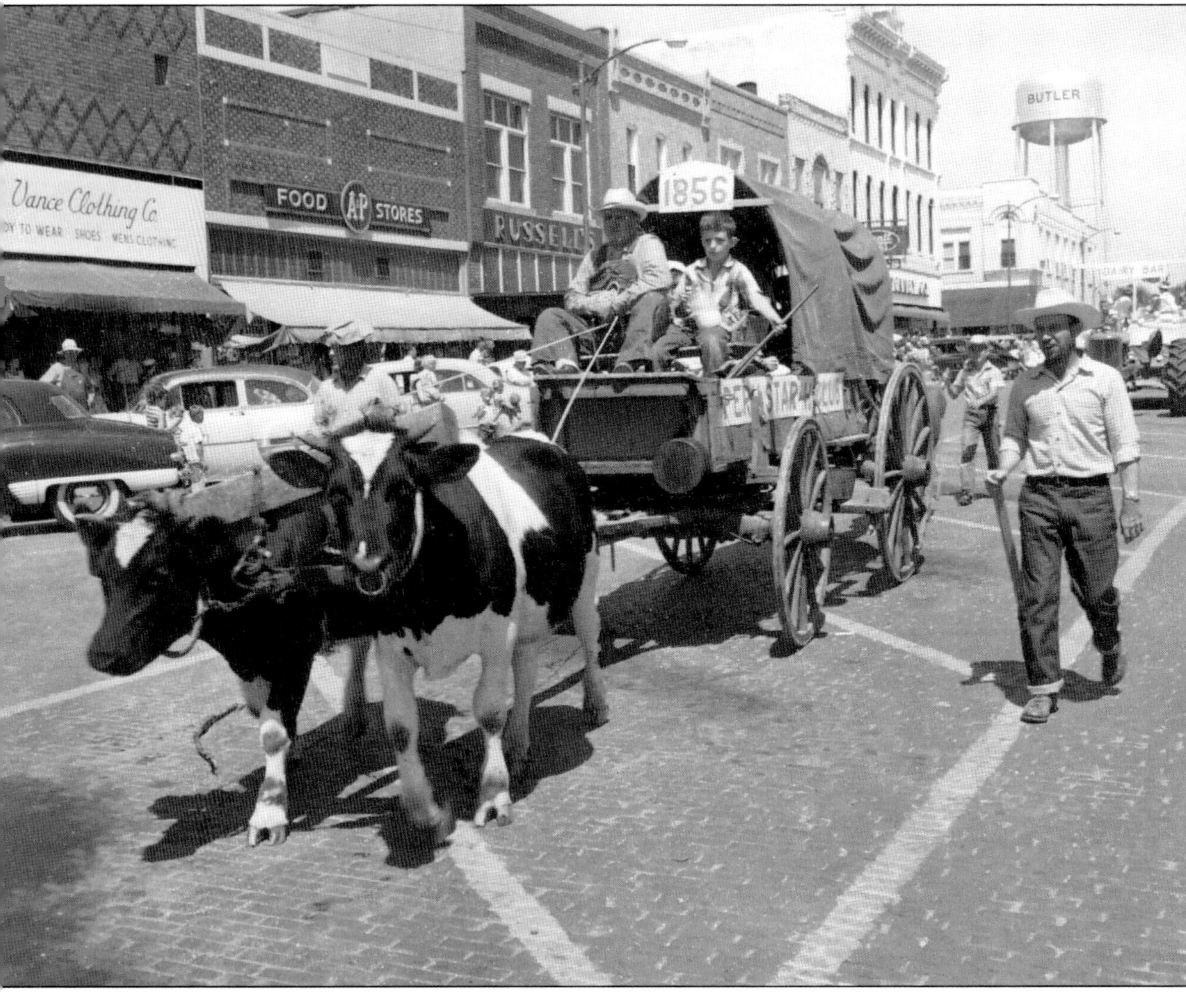

Butler celebrated its 100th birthday from August 31 to September 4, 1956. The festivities included four performances of a 13-scene pageant, *General Butler Rides Again*, featuring Clifford Bruner as Gen. William O. Butler of Kentucky, for whom the town was named. Other events included a tractor-tipping safety demonstration and fresh egg, greased pig, and rooster catching contests. (Courtesy of the Bates County Historical Society and the Eddie Herrman Collection.)

Two

Electric City

Trade and innovation have been an integral part of the Butler community since the arrival of the first settler, John C. Kennett, in 1845. Noting the steady stream of forty-niners passing through the area on their way to the California gold mines, Kennett opened a trading post four years after his arrival, hoping to cash in on a ready market for, among other things, smoke and drink. By 1853, Kennett had sold out to the second settler, John W. Montgomery, and joined the gold rush himself, but the die was cast; Butler was to be a city of commerce.

It was to become a cultural center, as well. A newspaper article from the late 1800s described the people of Butler as "progressive, wide-awake, enterprising, and hospitable," and the attention given to the patronage of the arts underlines these characteristics. From William Walton's original opera house to the Lyceum Course headed by Charles Fisk to the connection to the activities of the wider world provided by the film reels of Fisk's Theatre, Butler proved itself both worthy of and attractive to the great talents of the day. It also supplied some of those talents, as with Charlie Fisk's Orchestra in the 1940s and 1950s.

The arrival of the railroad in 1880, fueled by the county's abundance of coal, prompted an explosion in the city's infrastructure. In 1881, though, came the moment that cemented the town's position as the feather in Bates County's cap and as a cosmopolitan center in her own right: the lights went on. From the square to the train depot, a line of glass globes marched down Ohio Street, Butler's Great White Way. Four more lights shone from the cupola of the courthouse, visible, according to the Old Settlers, from a distance of 15 to 20 miles. If true, this measurement encompasses almost the entire county. Flavius Tygard's construction of the power plant responsible for all this acquired brilliance made Butler one of the first cities in the United States to generate its own electricity. With this achievement, Butler, Missouri, became the "Electric City."

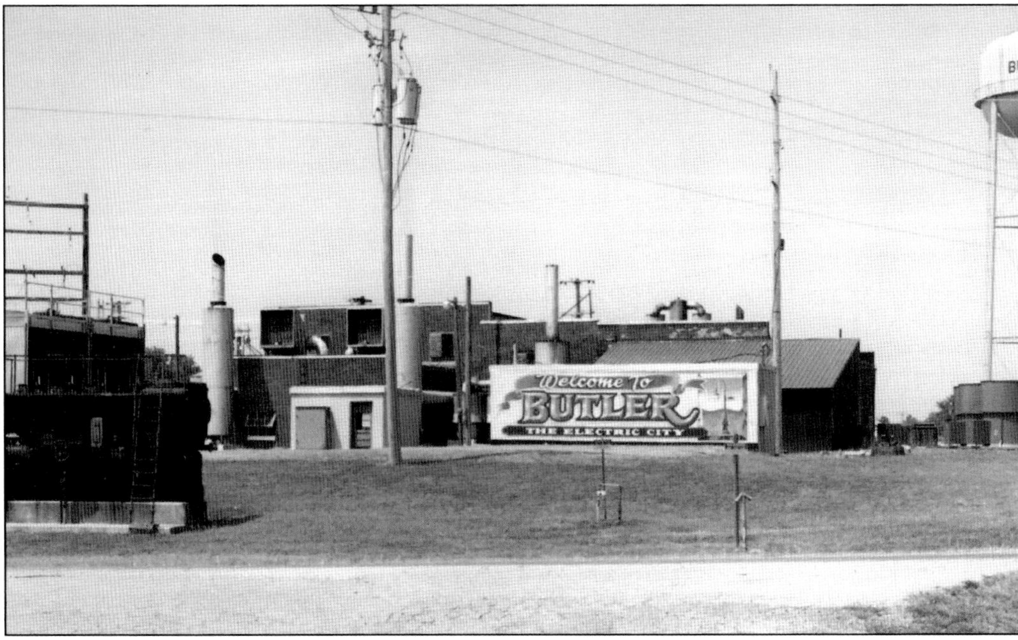

At the intersection of Mill Street and Old 71, one of the town's original electric generators (front left) welcomes visitors to the Electric City. The brainchild of Capt. Flavius J. Tygard who, in Eddie Herrmann's words, "saw the light" while attending the 1876 Philadelphia Centennial Exposition, the Brush Electric Light and Power Company of Butler incorporated in 1881. Butler's power system, municipally owned since 1900, is the oldest in continuous operation in the United States: the town lit up on December 6, 1881, nine months before Thomas Edison's Pearl Street Station went online in Manhattan. (Both, courtesy of the Bates County Historical Society and the Eddie Herrman Collection.)

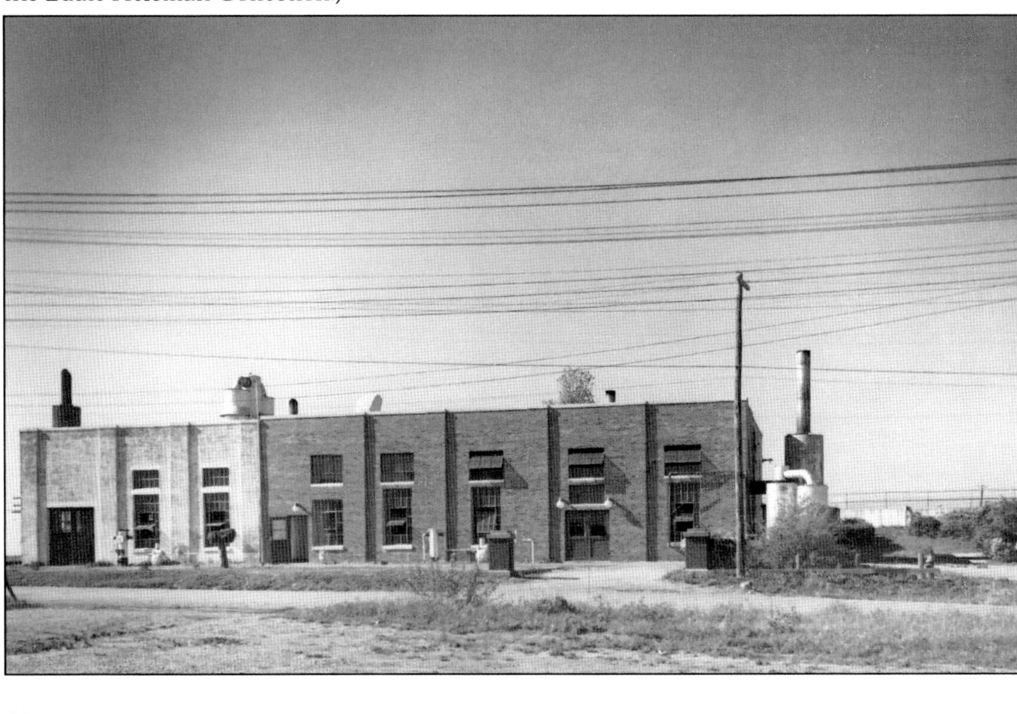

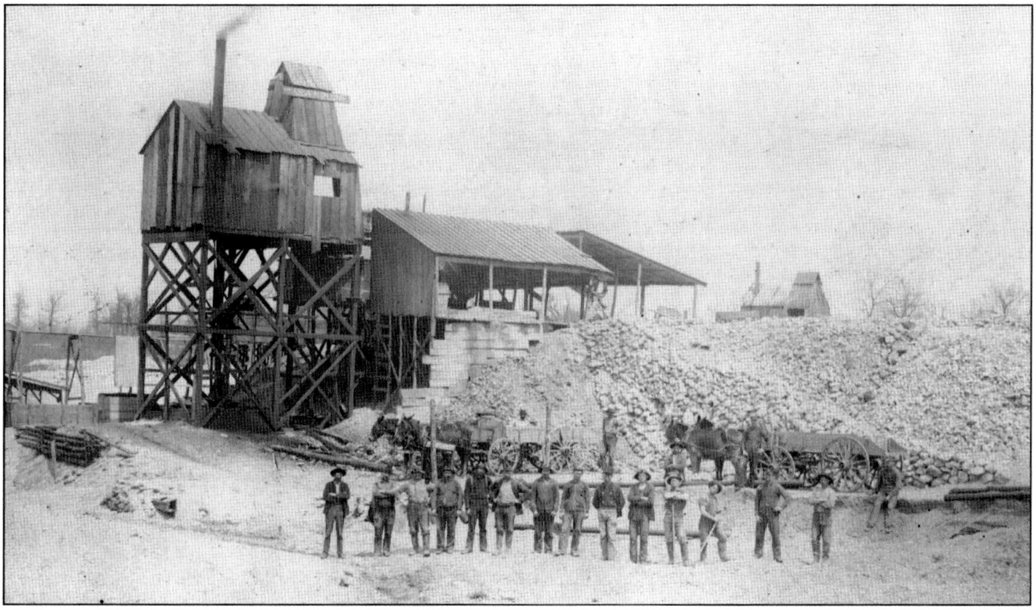

In the 1880s, coal exploded to the forefront of the Bates County economy. Centered in Rich Hill, coal mining at its height employed around 1,000 men and paid out nearly $300,000 annually for labor. In 1889, Bates County reached a record output of 730,000 tons; by 1898, it ranked second in coal production in the state of Missouri. (Courtesy of the Bates County Historical Society.)

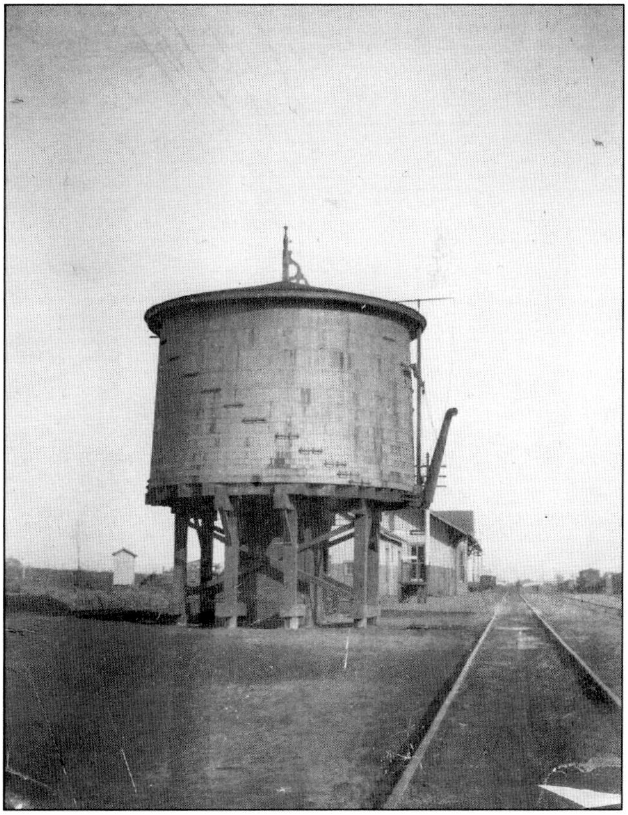

The rise of the coal mine both increased demand and offered greater incentives for rail construction through Bates County. By late 1880, Missouri Pacific trains frequented water stations like this one as they carried shipments of coal from Rich Hill and Butler along the Kansas City, Fort Scott & Gulf and Kansas City & Southern lines. (Courtesy of the Bates County Historical Society.)

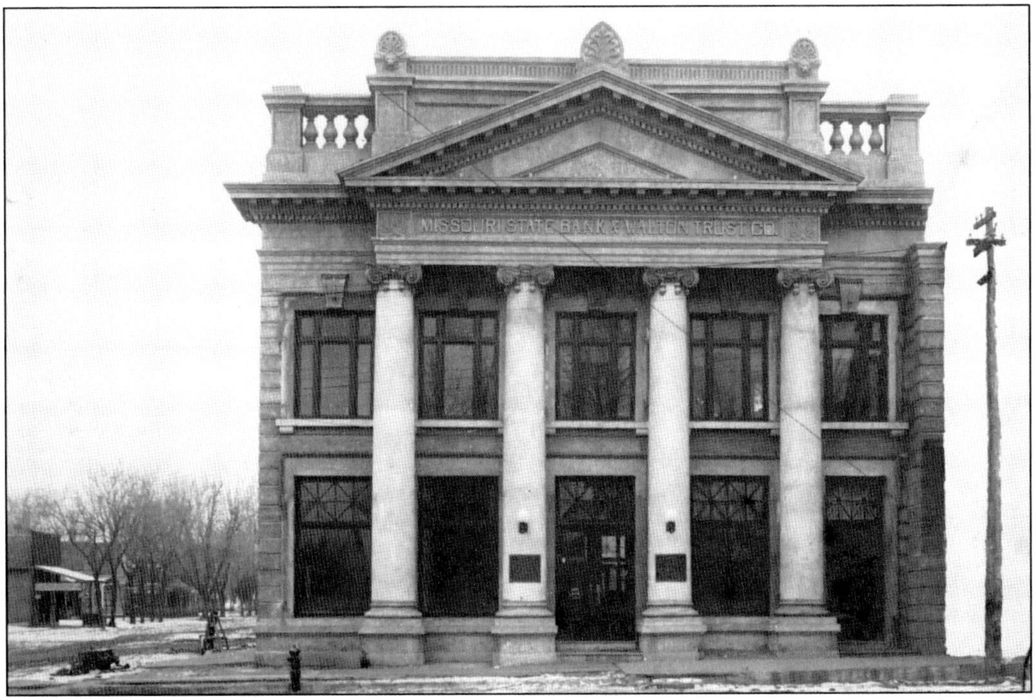

The Missouri State Bank opened for business in December 1880, continuing a pattern begun in 1868 by C.B. Dunbaugh that would define Bates County as a focus of Midwest finance. By 1918, the county boasted 15 banks and two trust companies funding farm ventures in three states, a remarkable statistic for a county with such strong agricultural inclinations. (Courtesy of the Bates County Historical Society and the Eddie Herrman Collection.)

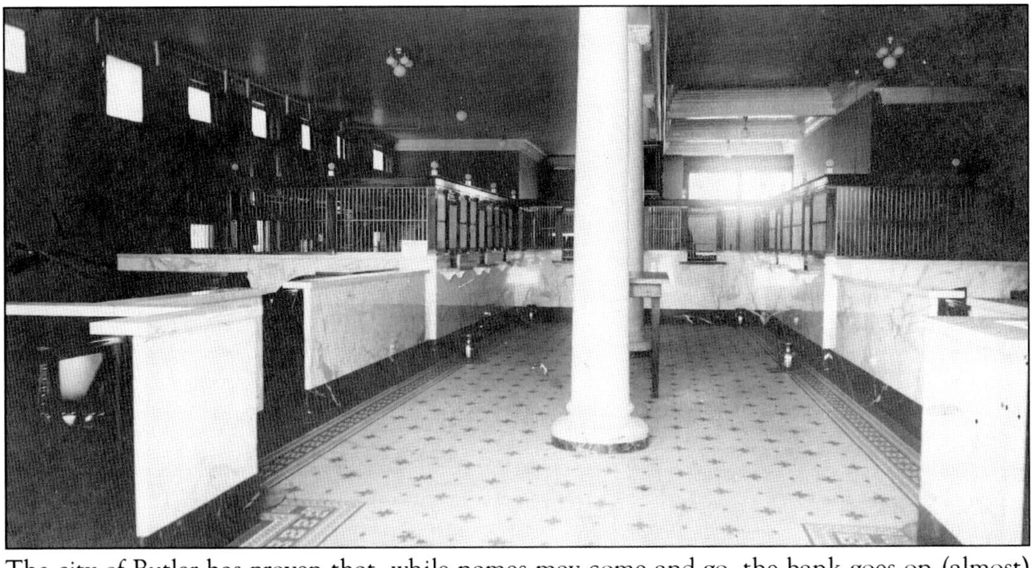

The city of Butler has proven that, while names may come and go, the bank goes on (almost) forever. Missouri State Bank (pictured here) failed in 1931 and was replaced by Butler State Bank in 1947, then subsequently by Charter, Boatmen's, and finally by NationsBank in 1997. It was updated to house city hall in 2005. (Courtesy of the Bates County Historical Society and the Eddie Herrman Collection.)

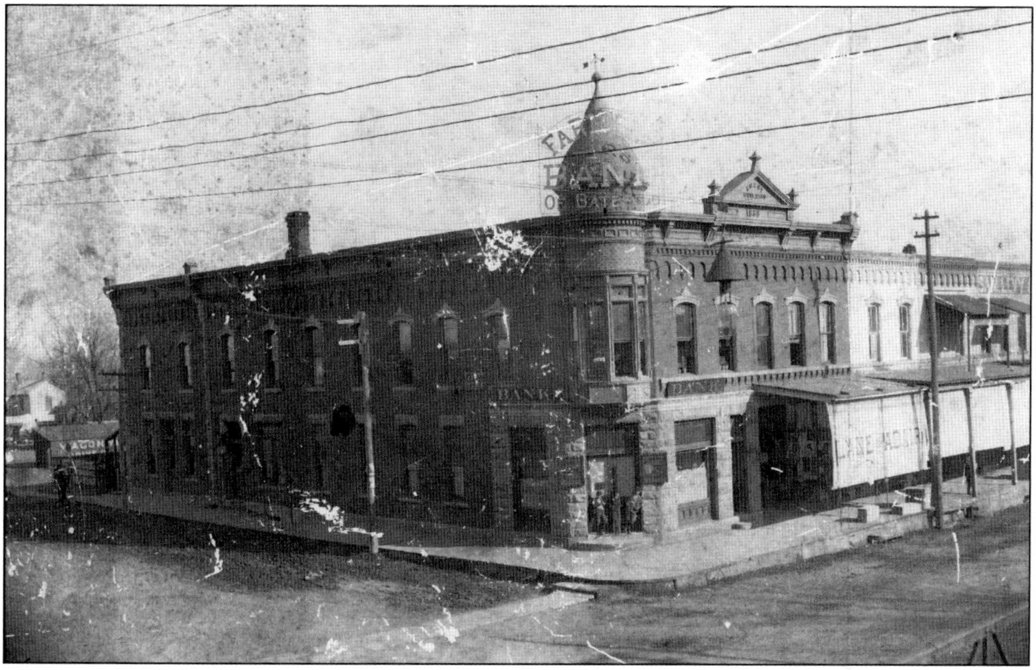

In 1889, a bank for farmers, by farmers opened in Butler under the predictable name of Farmers Bank of Bates County. Two of its principal sponsors, D.N. Thompson and James J. McKee, came to Butler in 1869. Thompson worked cattle drives between Butler and Appleton City; McKee grew apples, his favorites being Mammoth Black Twig and Early Harvest. (Courtesy of the Bates County Historical Society and the Eddie Herrman Collection.)

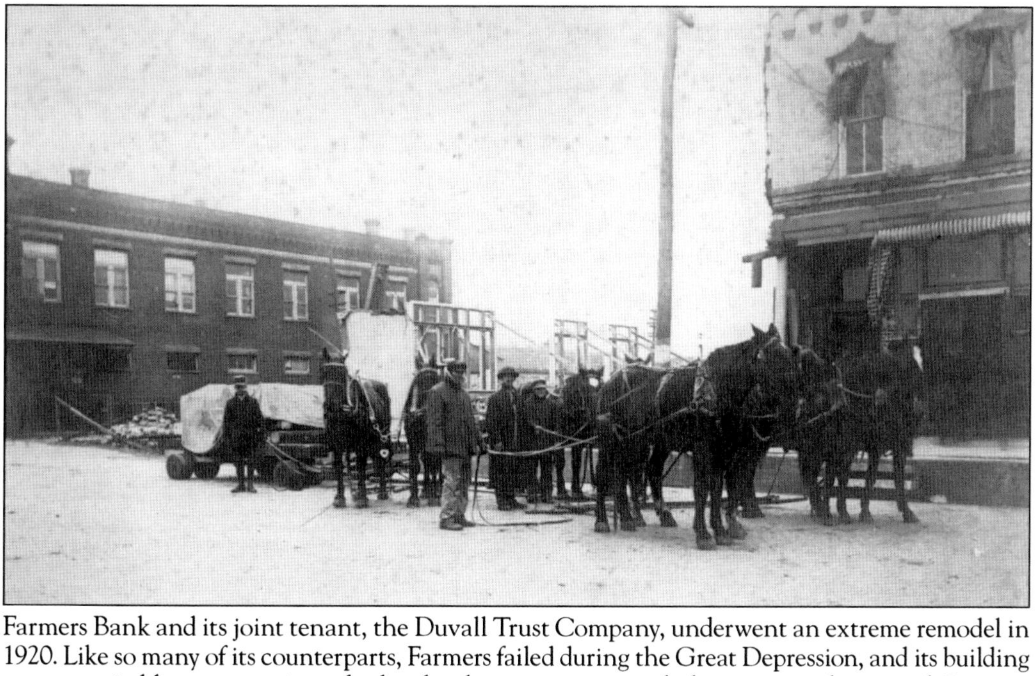

Farmers Bank and its joint tenant, the Duvall Trust Company, underwent an extreme remodel in 1920. Like so many of its counterparts, Farmers failed during the Great Depression, and its building was occupied by a succession of other banking ventures, including a recently opened Security Bank. (Courtesy of the Bates County Historical Society and the Eddie Herrman Collection.)

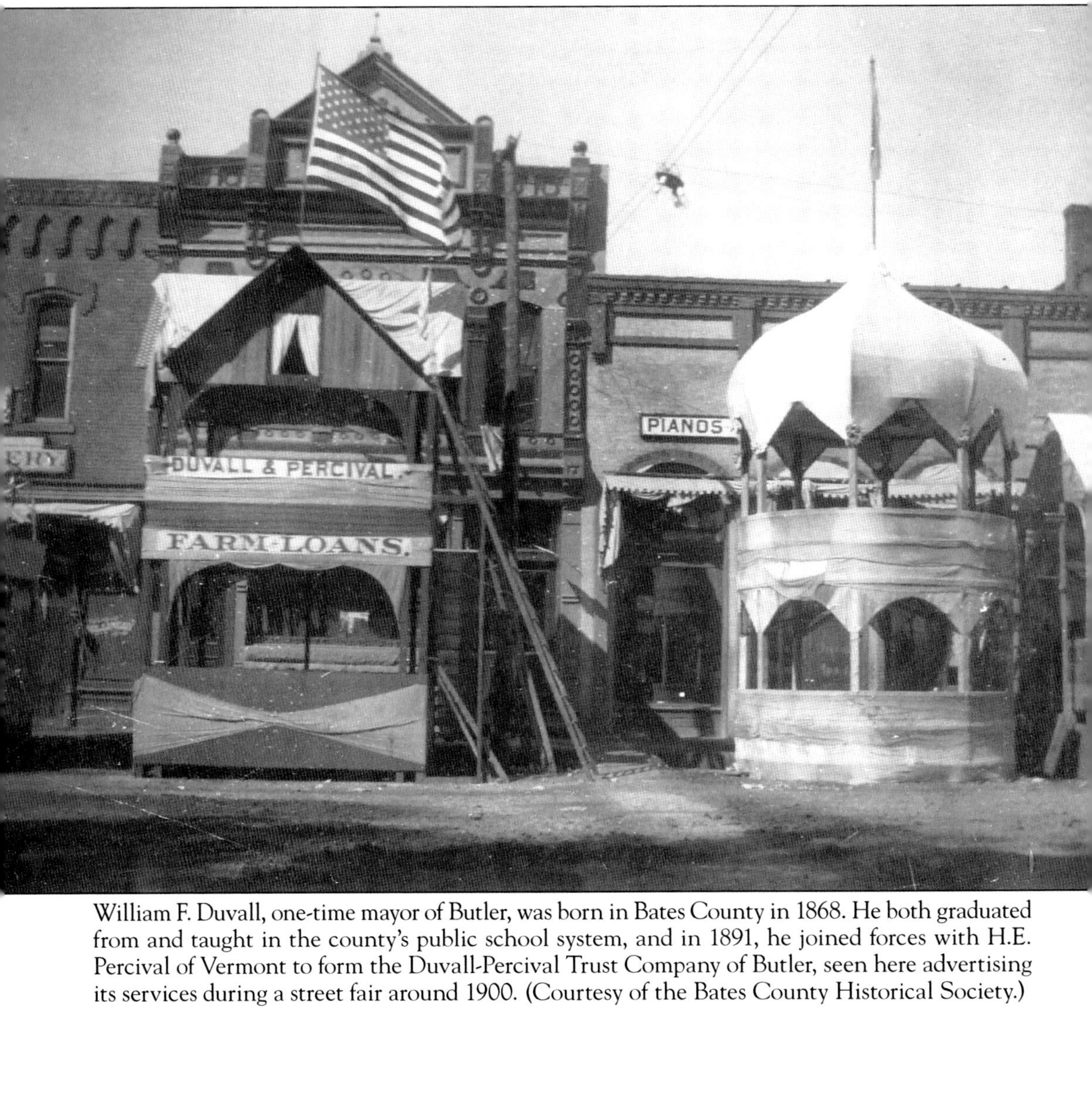

William F. Duvall, one-time mayor of Butler, was born in Bates County in 1868. He both graduated from and taught in the county's public school system, and in 1891, he joined forces with H.E. Percival of Vermont to form the Duvall-Percival Trust Company of Butler, seen here advertising its services during a street fair around 1900. (Courtesy of the Bates County Historical Society.)

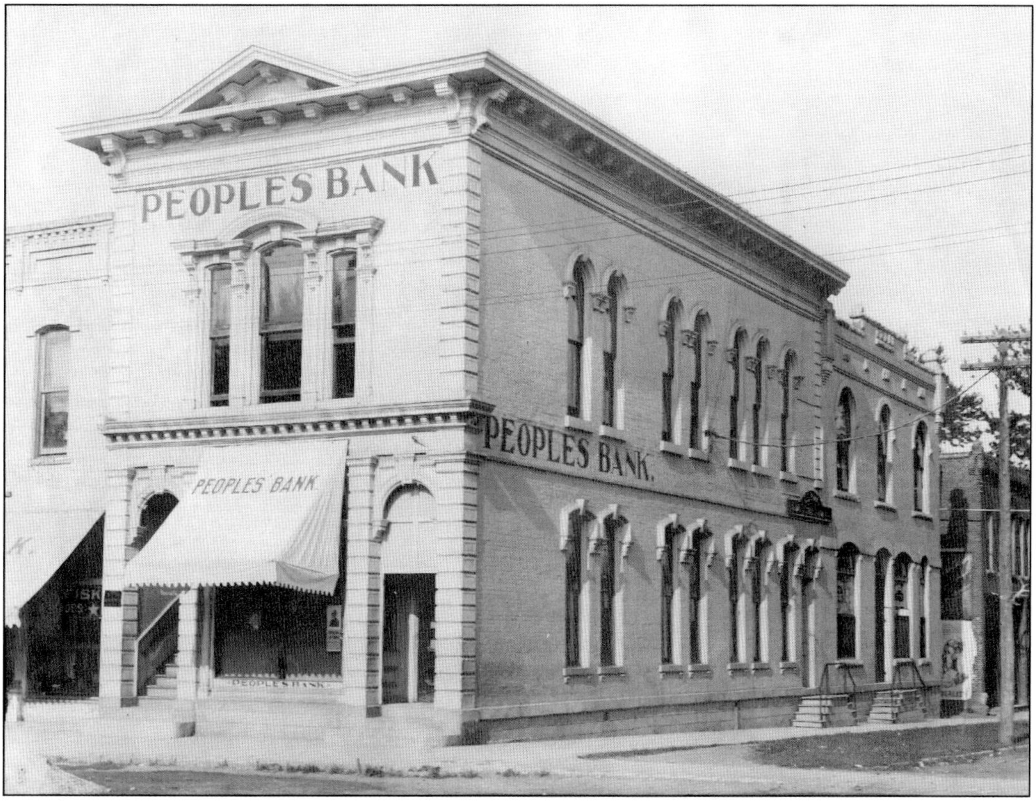

People's Bank of Butler was chartered on July 27, 1908, under the auspices of J.R. Jenkins, president, and Wesley Denton, cashier. Situated on the northwest corner of the square, the bank failed during the Depression, despite William Atkeson's praise a decade earlier of its starring role in ensuring the financial stability of Bates County. (Courtesy of the Bates County Historical Society and the Eddie Herrman Collection.)

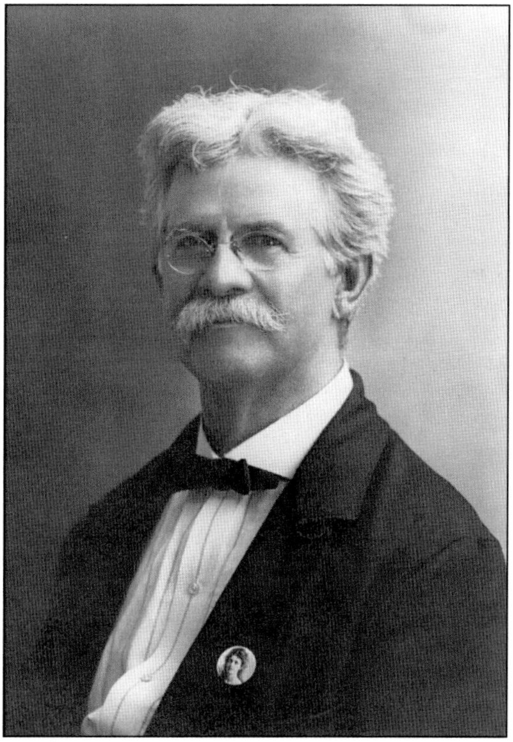

J.R. Jenkins acted as president of the People's Bank of Butler from its establishment in 1908 until 1918, throughout which period he was to be found perennially at his desk, engaged in his work with "careful exactness and keen interest." Jenkins was also a founding member of Butler's Christian Science congregation. (Courtesy of the Bates County Historical Society and the Eddie Herrman Collection.)

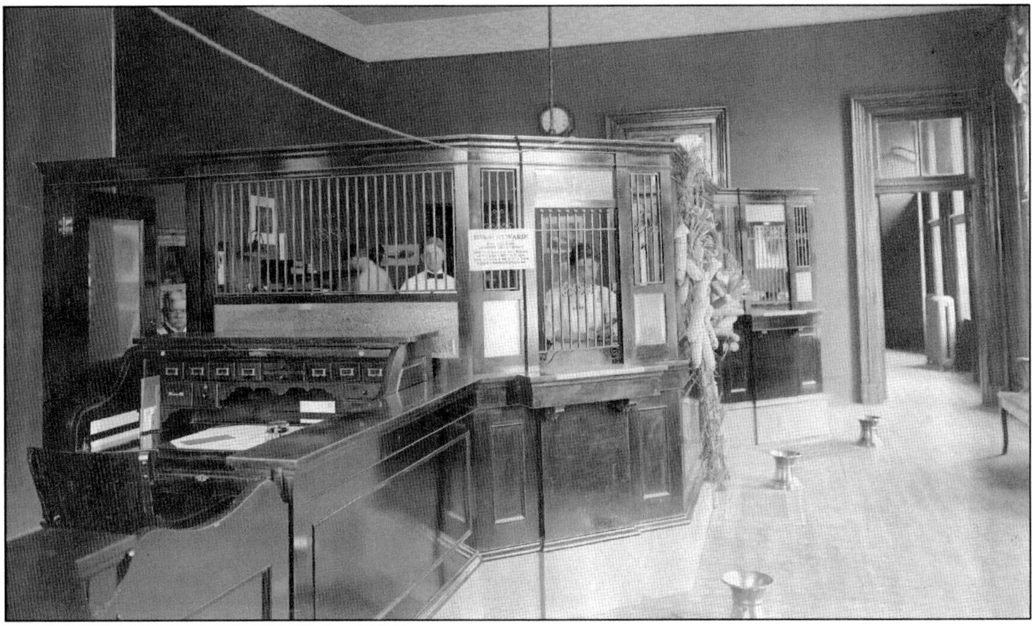

Inside the People's Bank lobby, placed as conspicuously as possible, hung a notice from the Missouri Bankers Association offering a $500 reward for the apprehension of anyone attempting to burglarize the premises, a warning to anyone with bright ideas. (Courtesy of the Bates County Historical Society and the Eddie Herrman Collection.)

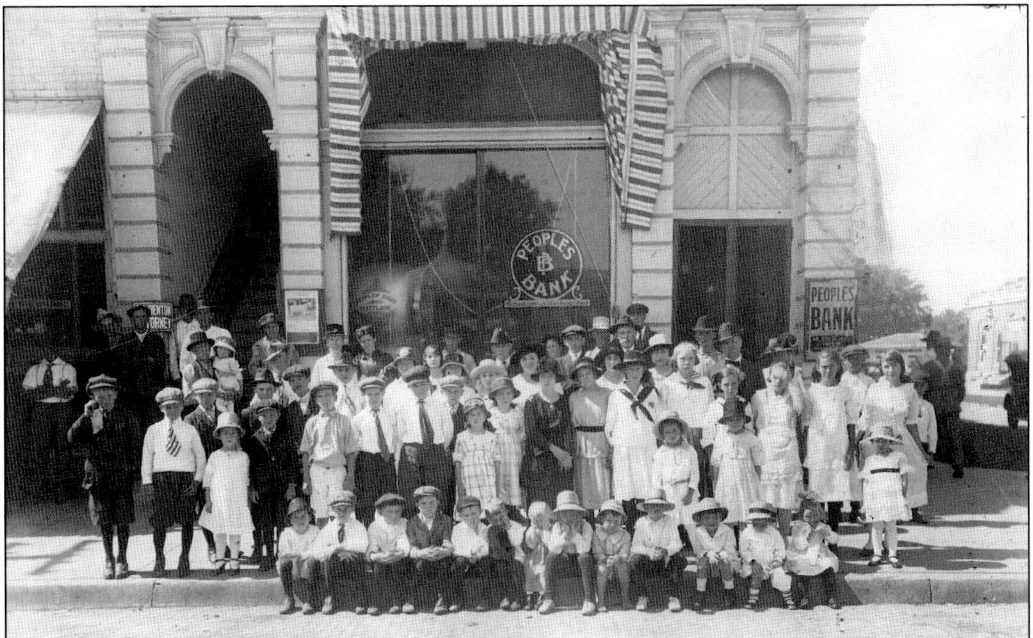

The connection between business and community in Butler has always been strong, and in its day, People's Bank ("the bank on which you can always bank") set the gold standard. From president Wesley Denton's Calf Club initiative to the bank's Children's Day, pictured here, People's Bank showed a constant concern for the welfare of future generations. (Courtesy of the Bates County Historical Society and the Eddie Herrman Collection.)

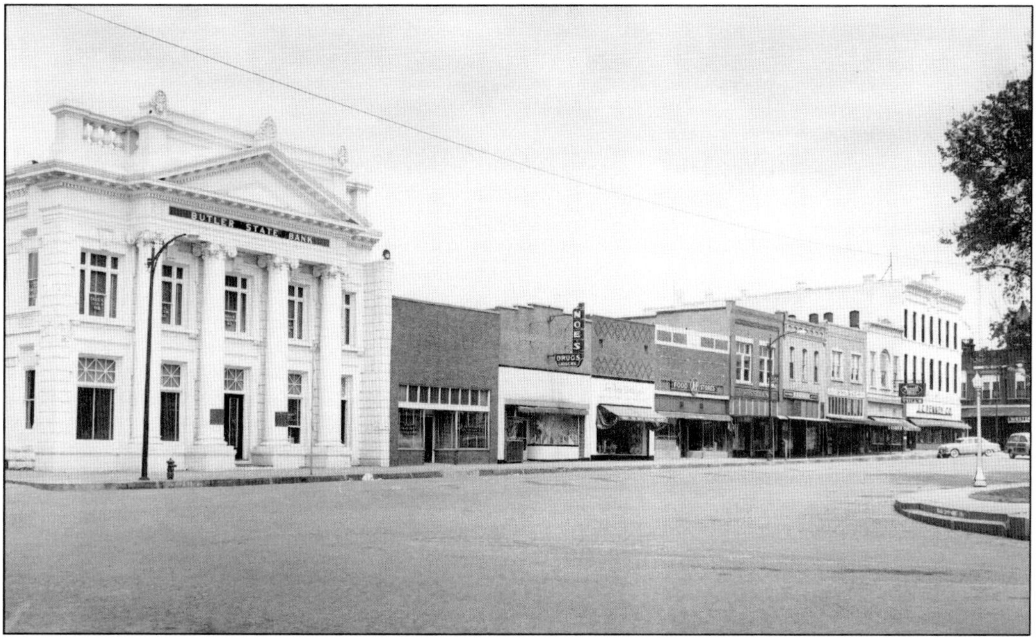

In the 1950s, the Butler square was crowded with business, as evidenced by this photograph of its north side. From the left, these establishments included the Butler State Bank, Walton Real Estate, Noe's Drug, Tom Vance Clothing, the A&P Grocery, Russell's Five-and-Dime, Kroger Grocery, the *Bates County Democrat* newspaper, Tull's Drug, and J.C. Penney. (Courtesy of the Bates County Historical Society and the Eddie Herrman Collection.)

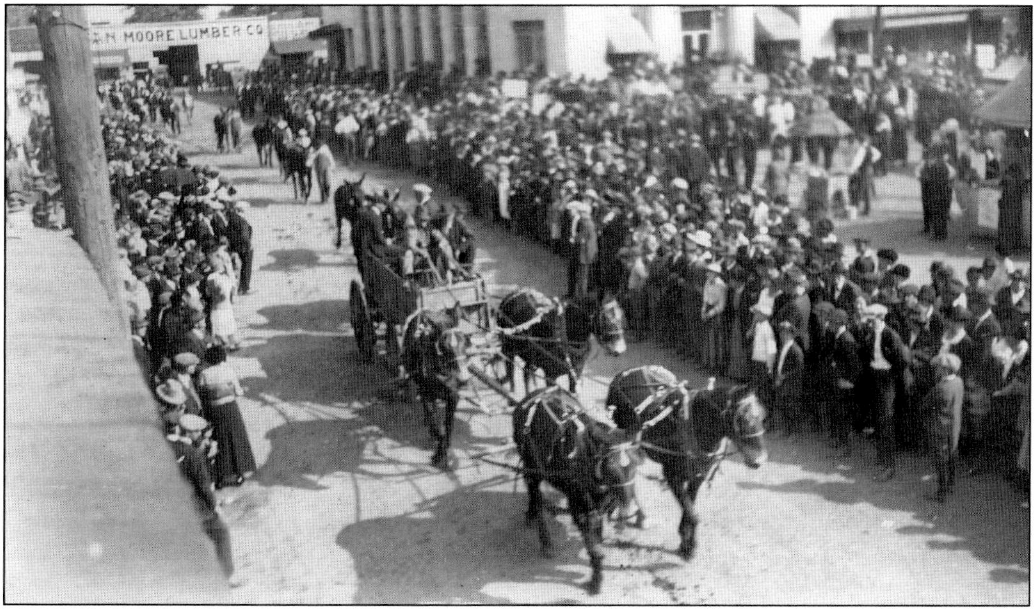

The 1923 Bates County Fair parade rounds the square, headed west on Ohio Street. In the background, the corner of the Farmers Bank and Duvall Trust building shadows the procession, and at the far end of the street stands the Logan-Moore Lumber Company, a site taken over in 1956 by Butler City Hall. (Courtesy of the Bates County Historical Society and the Eddie Herrman Collection.)

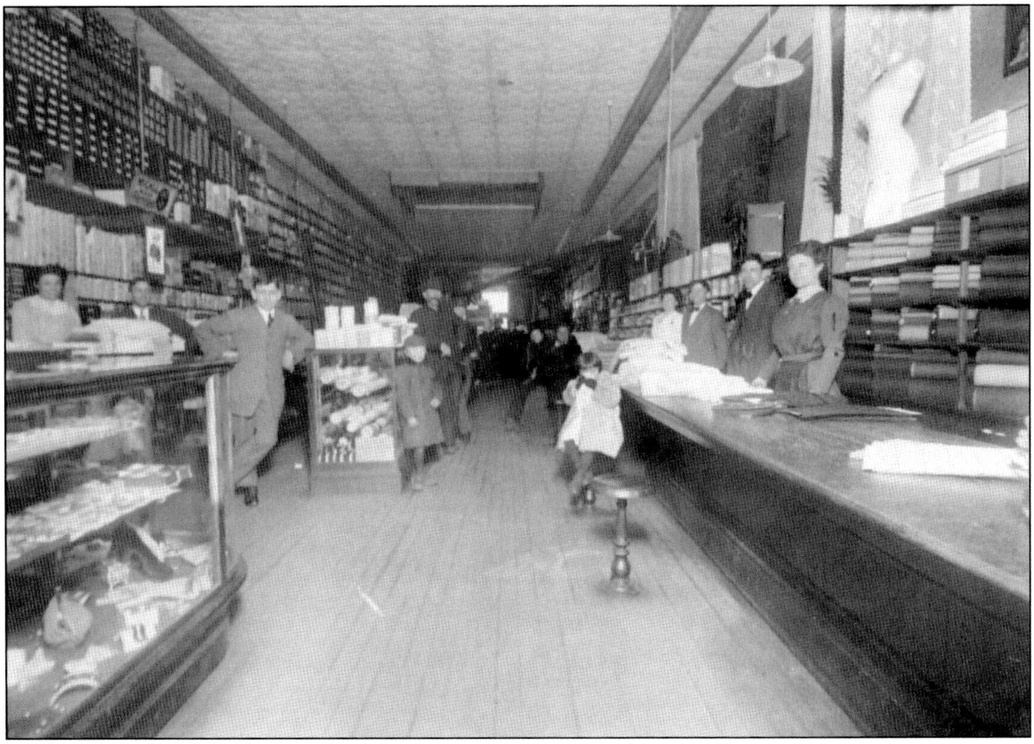

In 1876, German immigrant Samuel Levy opened the eponymous Levy Mercantile Company in Butler. The largest and oldest department store in the area, Levy's specialized in personalized service; they knew their customers, and their customers loved them. When Levy's doors closed in 2002, after 120 years of service, it seemed to some like the town square closed with them. (Courtesy of the Bates County Historical Society.)

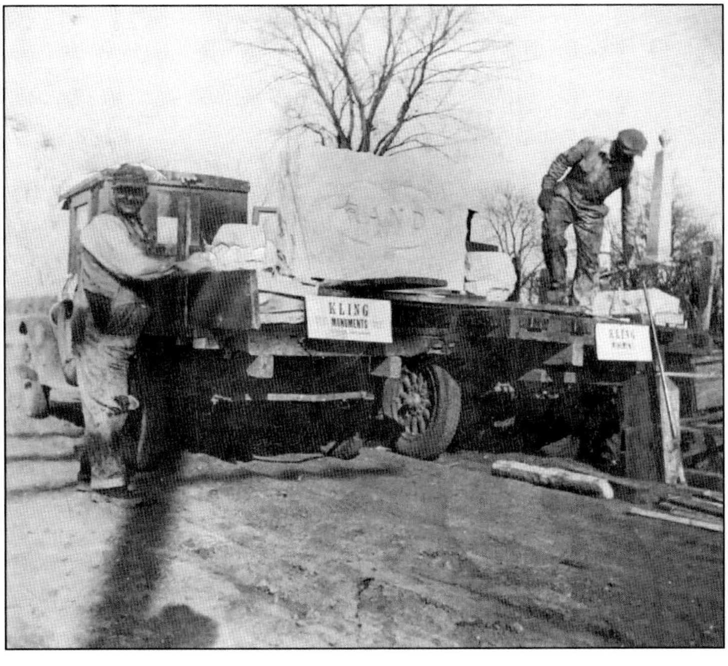

The men of Kling Memorials, photographed setting a headstone at Oak Hill Cemetery, represent one of the oldest businesses in Butler. Founded in 1888 in Nevada, Missouri, by German immigrant Charles Kling, the firm—now the Butler Monument Company—moved to Butler in 1925. (Courtesy of the Bates County Historical Society and the Eddie Herrman Collection.)

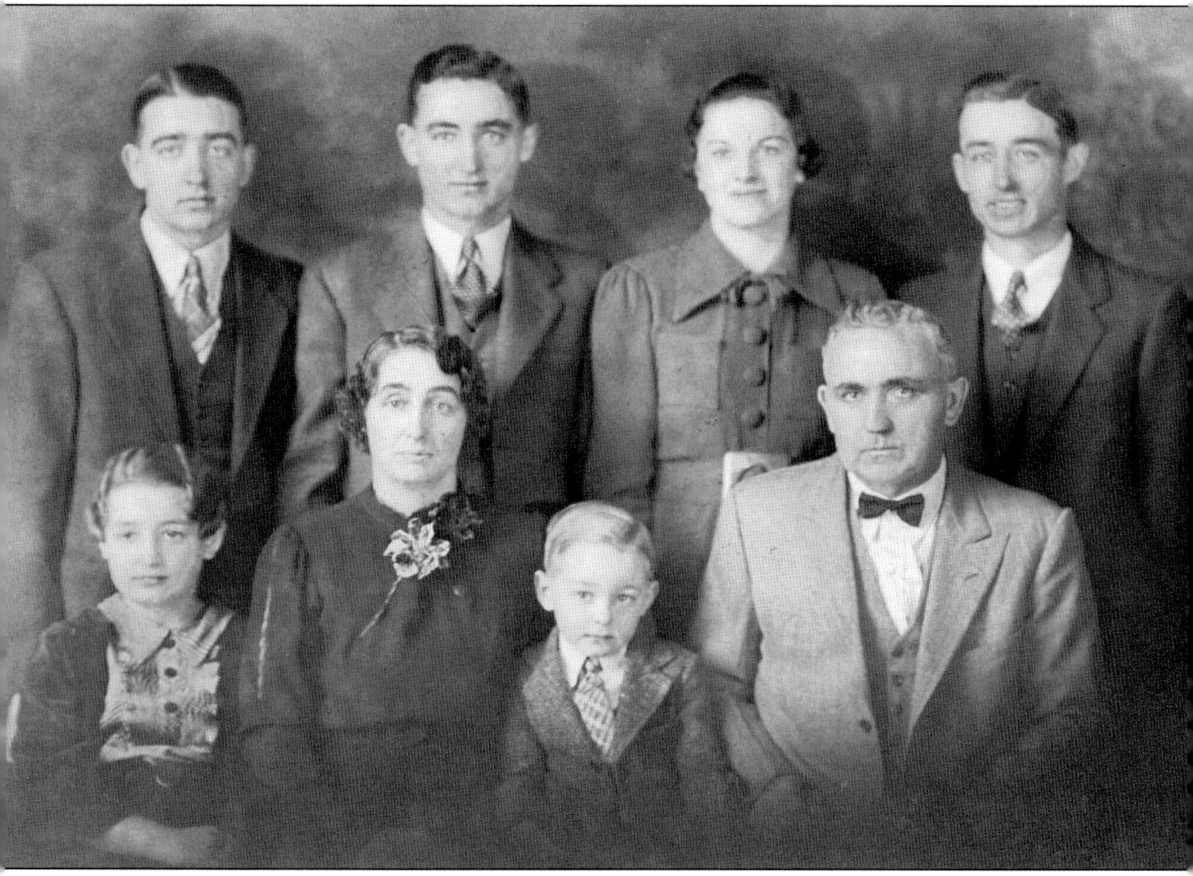

The Jennings family moved their market to Butler from the small community of Virginia, Missouri, in 1935. Arthur (first row, far right) was the original proprietor; with him are, from left to right, (first row) Alice May, Molly (Arthur's wife), and Wilbur; (second row) Harold, Orville, Marie, and George. Theirs was a truly traditional business, honoring requests to "put it on the tab" right up until the store closed in 2008. (Courtesy of Eileen Vannatta.)

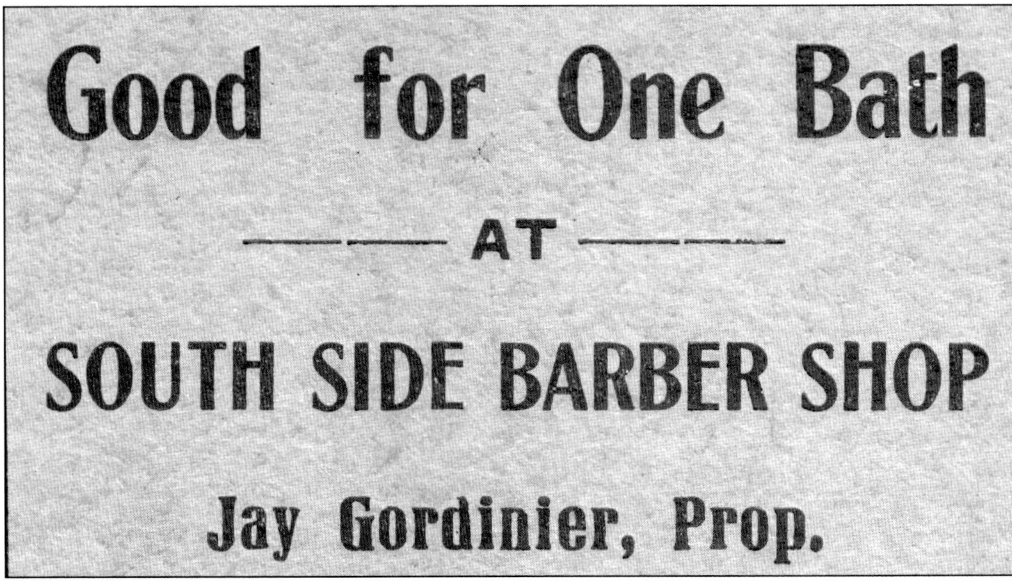

South Side Barbershop opened in 1900 in its current location and was a destination for the young men of the town to come for a bath (the shop's amenities included three bathtubs), shave, cut, and tonic before going out for a Saturday night on the town. In 1950, when current barber Lowell Logan began working there, baths and shaves cost 50¢, and haircuts, 65¢. (Courtesy of Lowell Logan.)

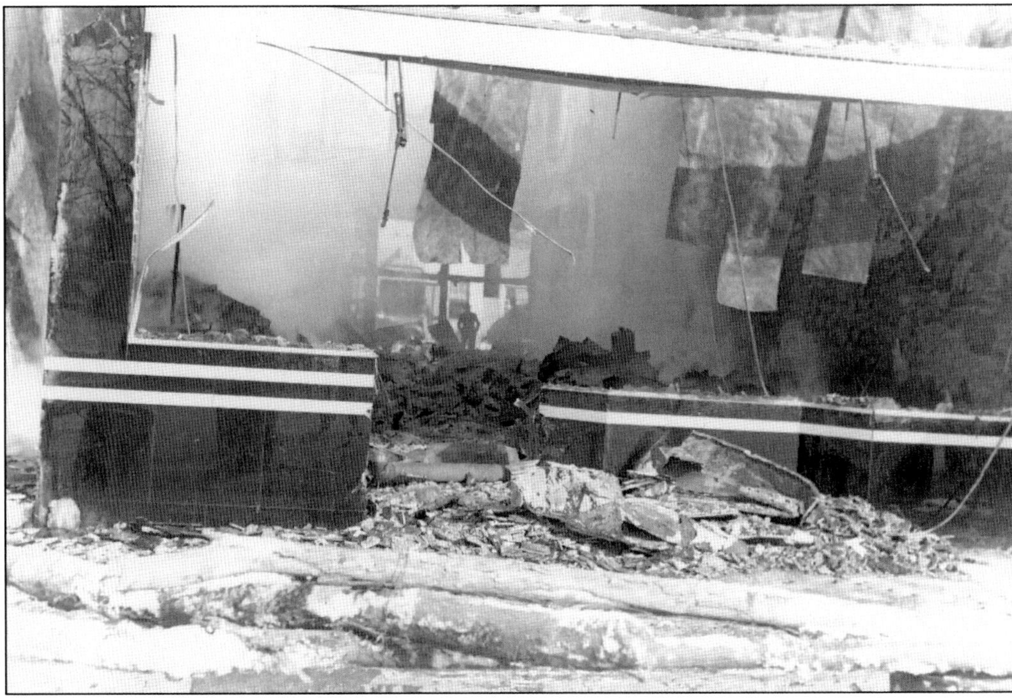

It often seems as if no structure in the town of Butler escaped fire damage of some sort. Noe's Drug, a favorite destination of children and teenagers—thanks to a well-stocked soda fountain—added its name to the list of casualties in 1940. (Courtesy of the Bates County Historical Society and the Eddie Herrman Collection.)

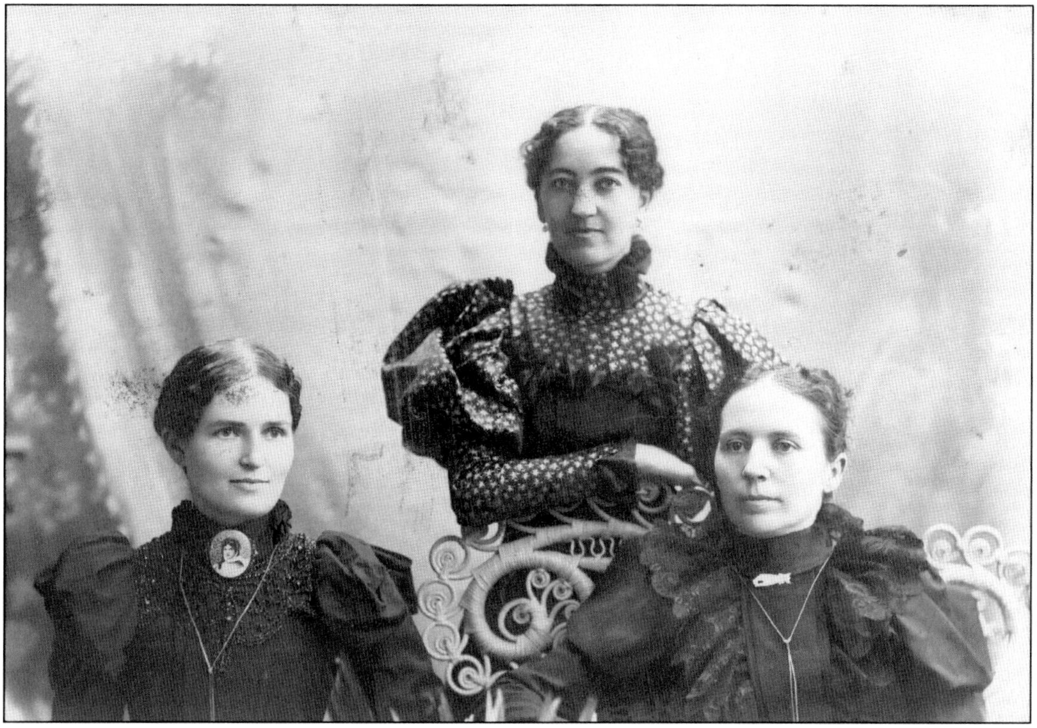

From left to right, Nellie Ealy, Alice Van Hall (standing), and Mrs. Charley Lewis sit for a portrait around 1900. Alice's husband, Gustave, was a Butler druggist at the turn of the century, as well as a minor celebrity. Newspapers from Iowa to Oklahoma featured his endorsement of a popular tonic: "We have great luck with Beggs Blood Purifier!" (Courtesy of the Bates County Historical Society and the Eddie Herrman Collection.)

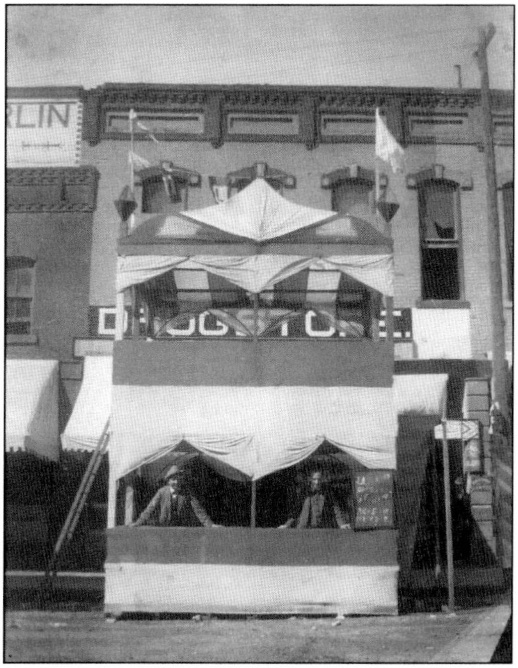

Jess Trimble (right) advertises his pharmaceutical wares during a street fair around 1900. Another widely known Butler merchant, Trimble served multiple terms on the governing body of the Missouri Pharmaceutical Association (MPA) and, in 1917, participated in a protest against an eight percent manufacturer's tax enacted by Congress on proprietary medicines. His wife also served in 1917 and 1918 as president of the women's branch of the MPA. (Courtesy of the Bates County Historical Society.)

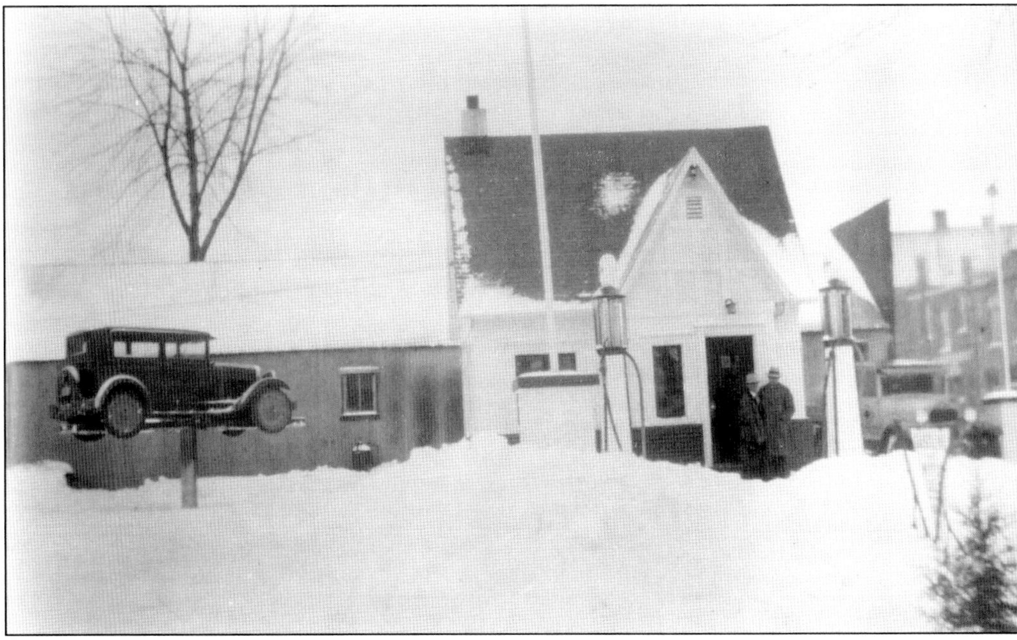

In addition to his drugstore, Gustave Van Hall also owned a filling station at the intersection of Chestnut and Delaware Streets. In the 1930s and early 1940s, the station was managed by a World War I veteran named Wesley Black. In the 1950s, it was purchased by Tom Mefford, whose gasoline of choice was Sinclair. (Courtesy of the Bates County Historical Society.)

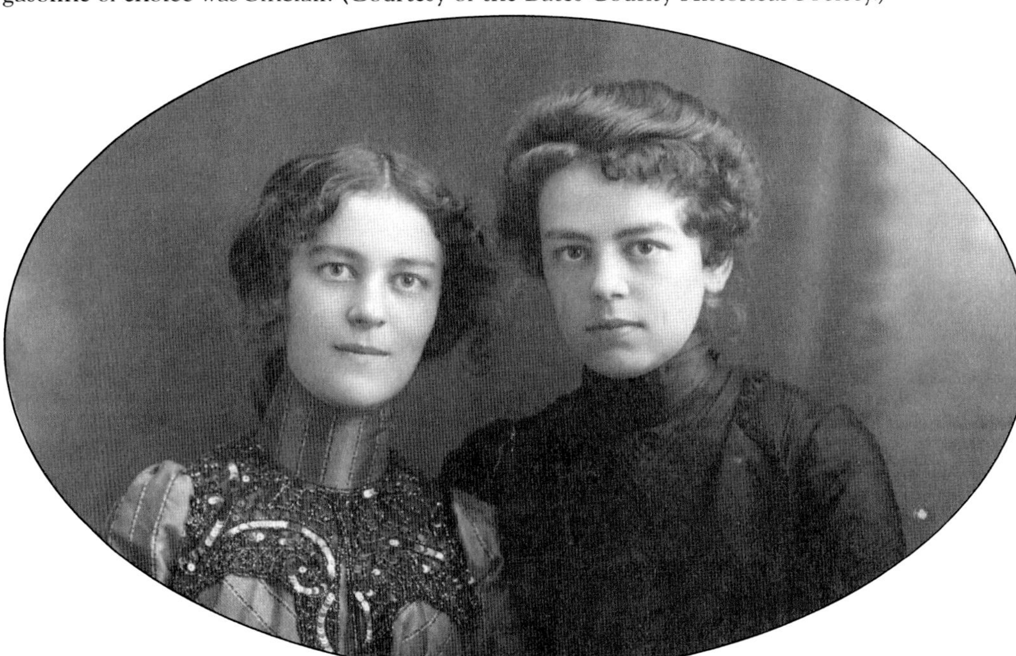

Louise (left) and Clara Endres were daughters of John Endres, a leader among Bates County bakers. In 1901, Louise married W.H. Smith, proprietor of the Red Ball Garage on South Main Street, whom William Atkeson memorialized as "a wide-awake salesman, an expert mechanician, and a 'hustler,'" greatly deserving of his success. (Courtesy of the Bates County Historical Society.)

Edward Bruglar Childs was born in 1874, five years after his family relocated to Butler from Salt Lake City. His father, Thomas, was a grocer, a dealer in farm implements, and vice president of the Butler National Bank. Young Ed entered the oil trade and eventually left Butler for Kansas City, where he became a traveling salesman for Kansas City Oil. (Courtesy of the Bates County Historical Society.)

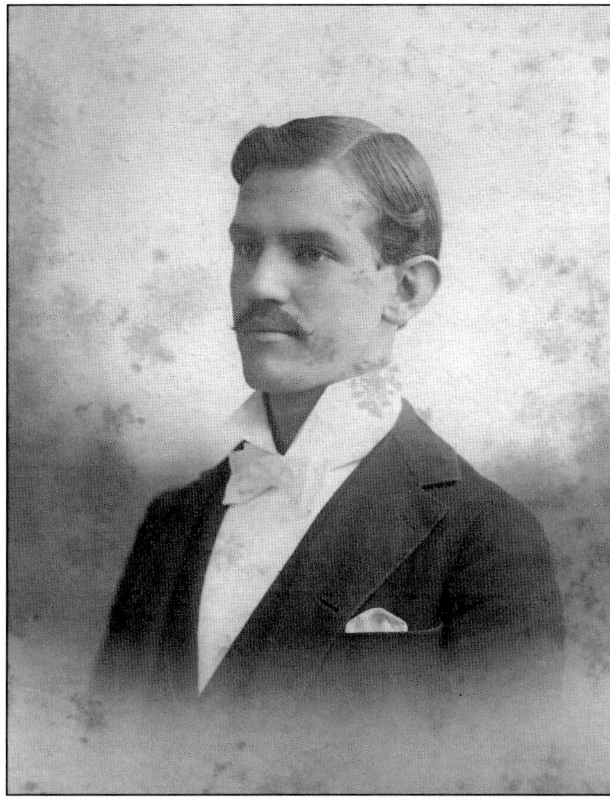

Thomas L. Pettys, orphaned at a young age, first visited Butler in the late 1860s during the period of reconstruction following the Civil War. In the 1870s, Pettys worked for Levy Mercantile, and in 1885, he established his own grocery on the Butler square. In 1889, he moved into these premises, where his candy counter apparently captured someone's attention. (Courtesy of the Bates County Historical Society.)

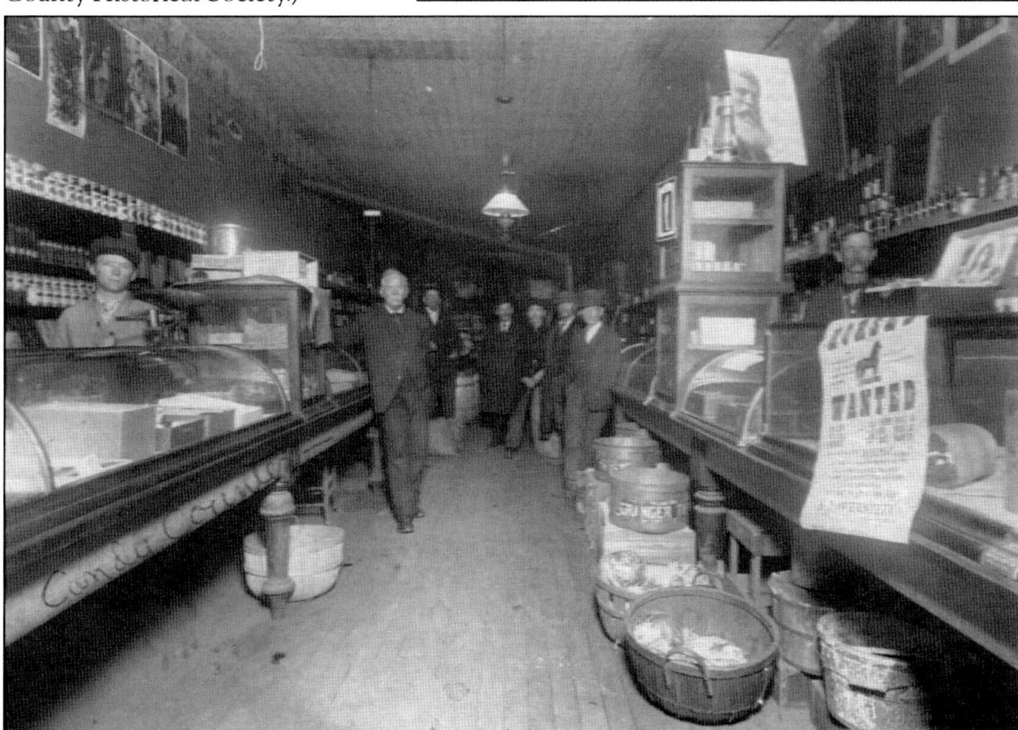

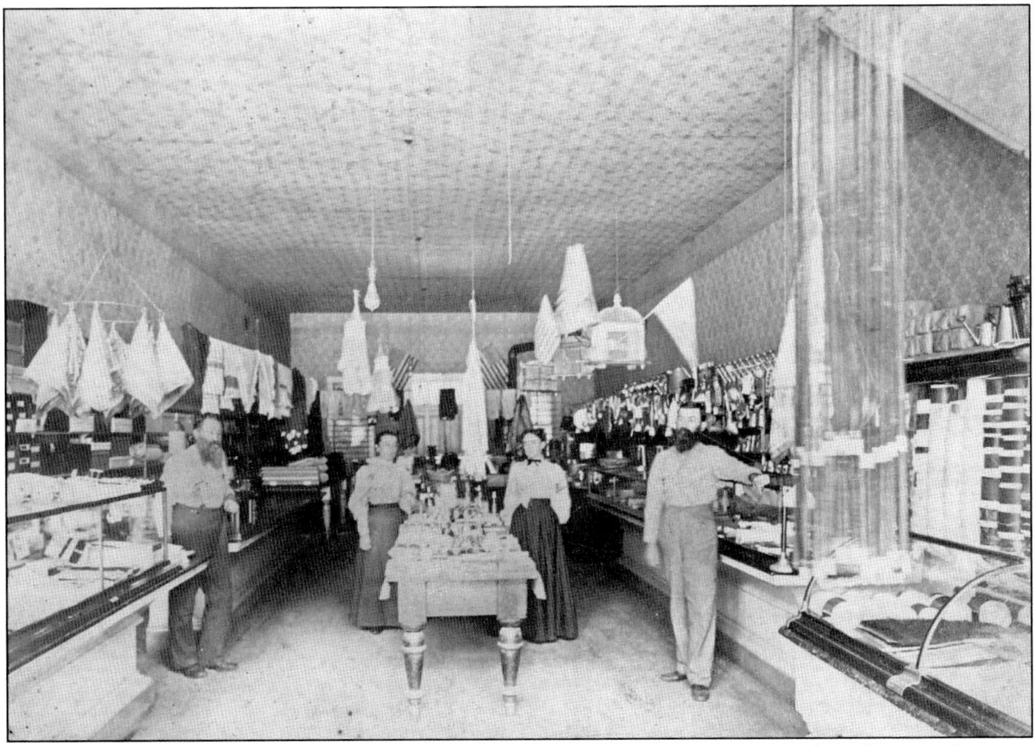

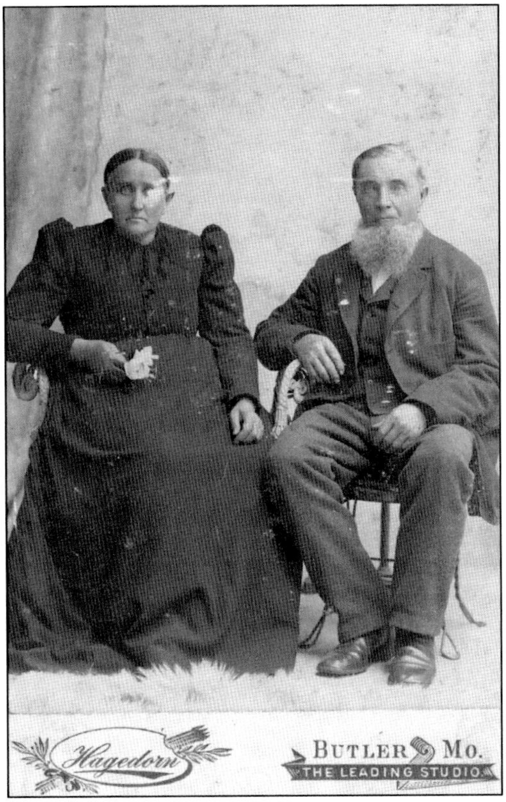

Birdcages, watering cans, handkerchiefs, and American flags were among the many things a person could purchase at the Bazar, "the great bargain house of Bates County." The owners also had a penchant for commemoratives, producing items ranging from teacups to cream pitchers in honor of important local events, like the completion of the new high school in 1912. (Courtesy of the Bates County Historical Society and the Eddie Herrman Collection.)

"Aunt" Martha and "Uncle" Clem Slayback sit for a portrait at the Hagedorn art studio, one of the finest in the state in its time. J.C. Hagedorn, German by birth, set up shop in Butler in 1881. Besides being a top-notch photographer, Hagedorn is remembered as a scholarly gentleman, fond of a good hunt in the company of good friends. (Courtesy of the Bates County Historical Society.)

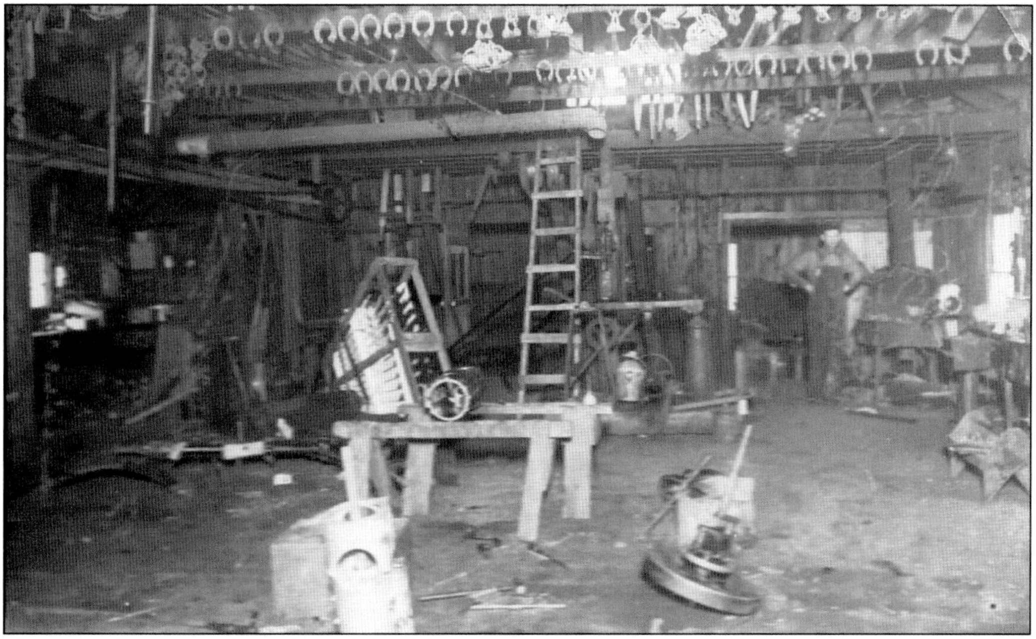

Cevanus Vantrees joined his father at the forge as a teenager and, after mastering the craft, entered an apprenticeship at a carriageworks in Clinton, Missouri, in 1881. Five years later, with a second trade under his belt, Vantrees came to Butler and opened a smithy of his own. William Atkeson praised him as "one of the best, most skilled workmen in the county." (Both, courtesy of the Bates County Historical Society.)

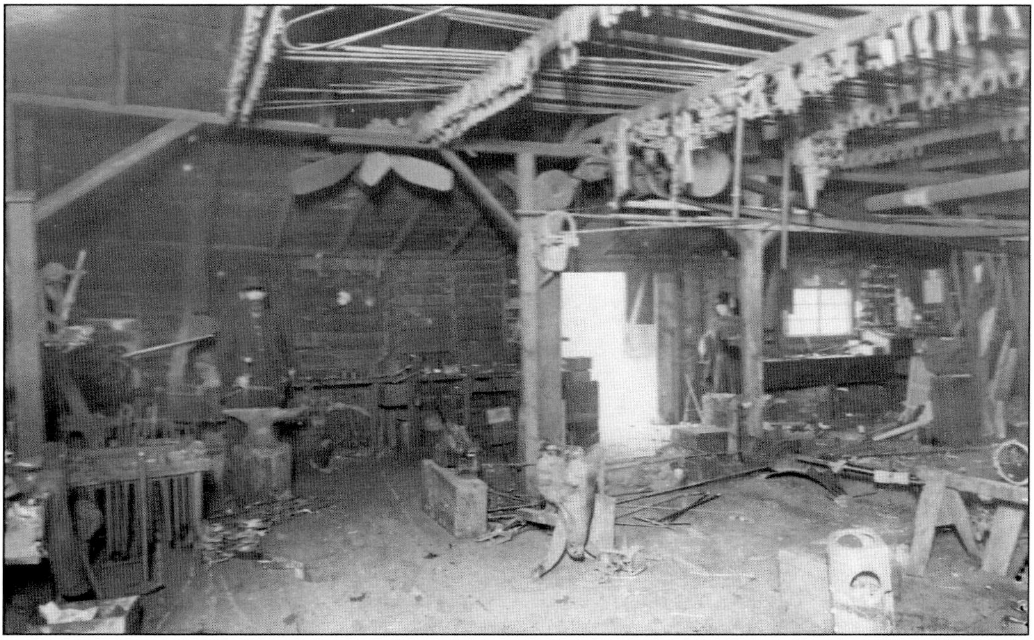

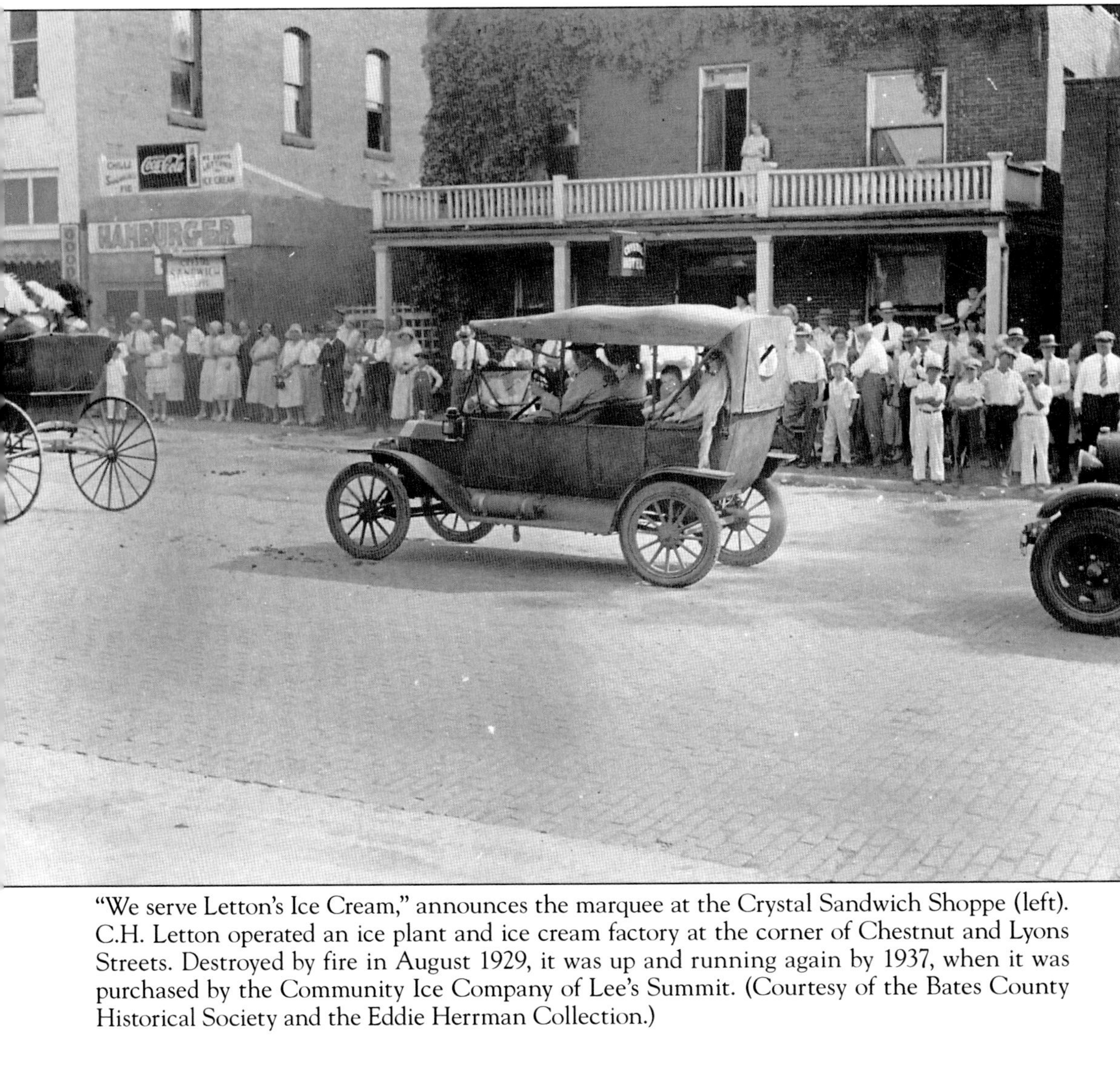

"We serve Letton's Ice Cream," announces the marquee at the Crystal Sandwich Shoppe (left). C.H. Letton operated an ice plant and ice cream factory at the corner of Chestnut and Lyons Streets. Destroyed by fire in August 1929, it was up and running again by 1937, when it was purchased by the Community Ice Company of Lee's Summit. (Courtesy of the Bates County Historical Society and the Eddie Herrman Collection.)

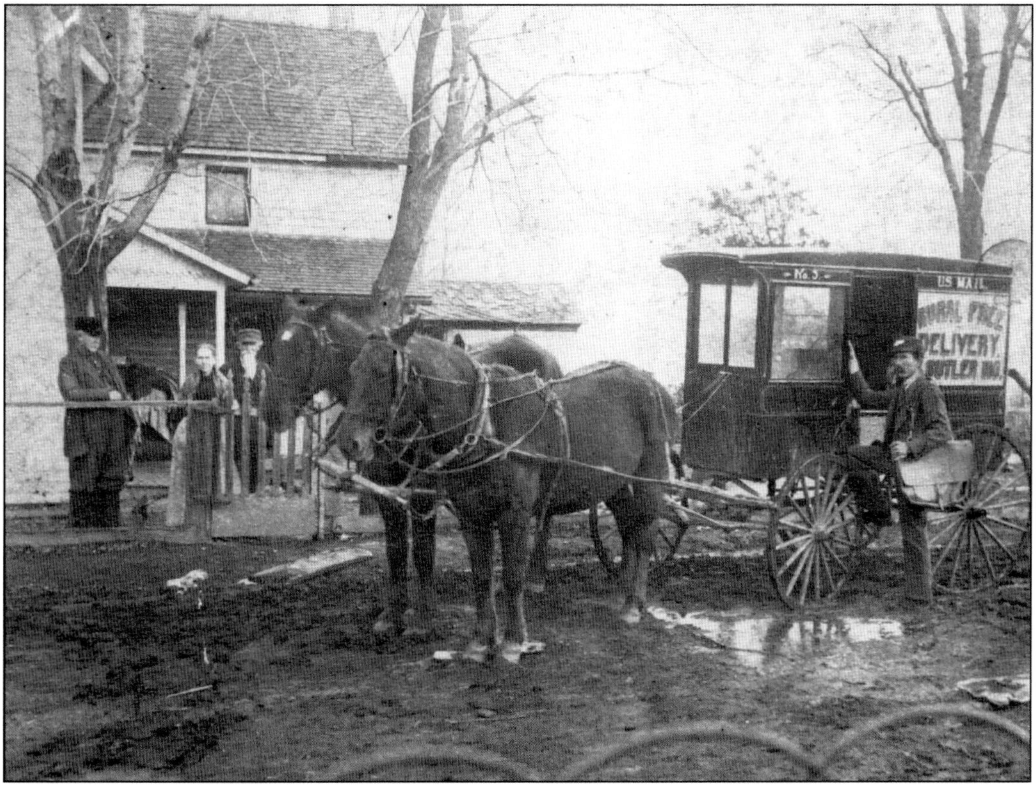

On a muddy day in the 1920s, Thomas Wainwright arrives with the mail. For many years, the Butler post was operated out of a rental property on the square, but in 1918, a fine new post office (pictured below) opened on Ohio Street at a location formerly occupied by the Ohio Street Baptist Church. One of Butler's most prominent postmasters was O.D. Austin, whose claim to fame was having been a spectator at Ford's Theatre on the night Abraham Lincoln was shot. (Both, courtesy of the Bates County Historical Society.)

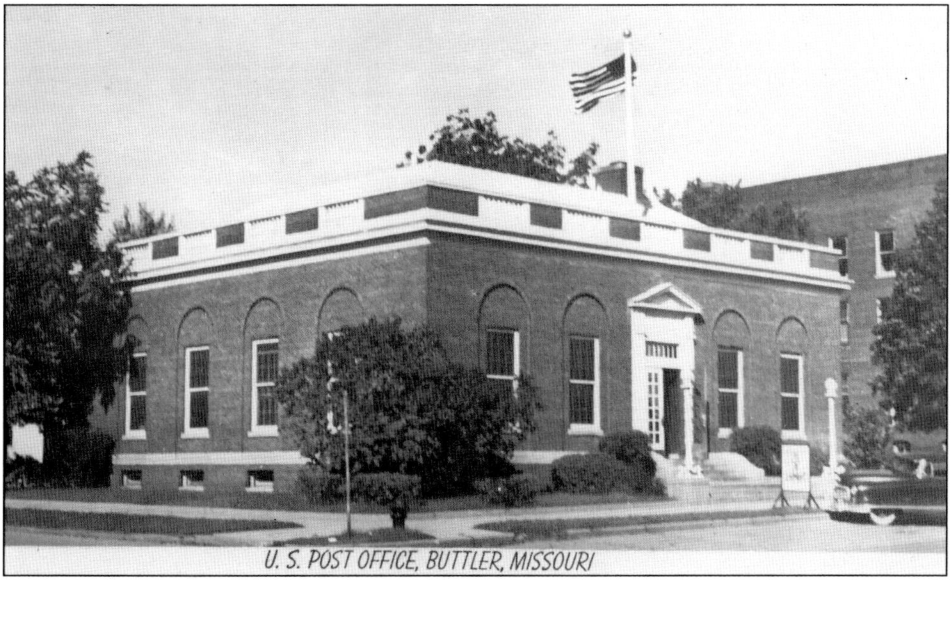

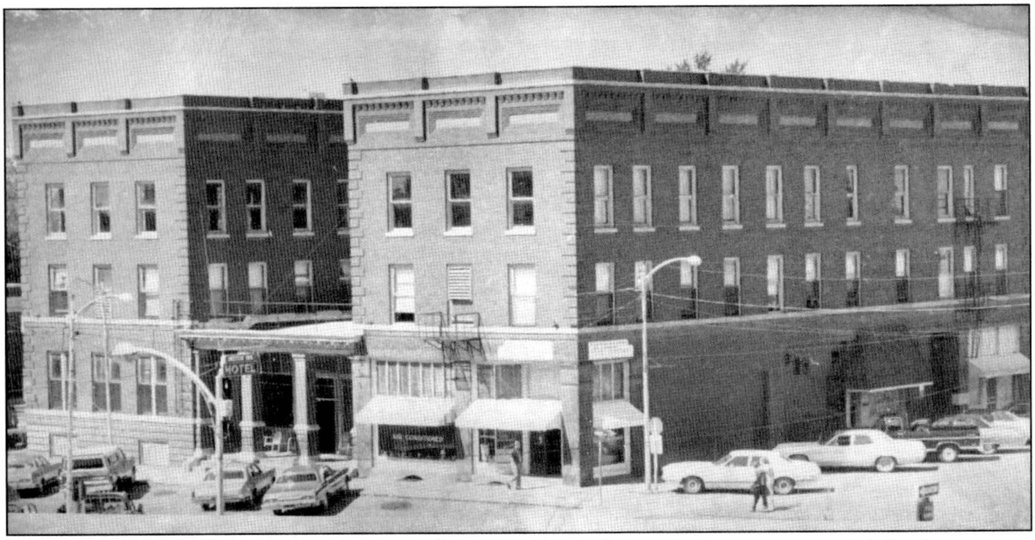

The Pennell Hotel opened on the northwest corner of the Butler square in 1907, the project of one E.M. Pennell. In the 1960s, the structure, which now houses a restaurant and meeting space, was home to the Motor Inn Hotel, charging its patrons nightly and weekly rates starting at $2 and $8, respectively. (Courtesy of the Bates County Historical Society and the Eddie Herrman Collection.)

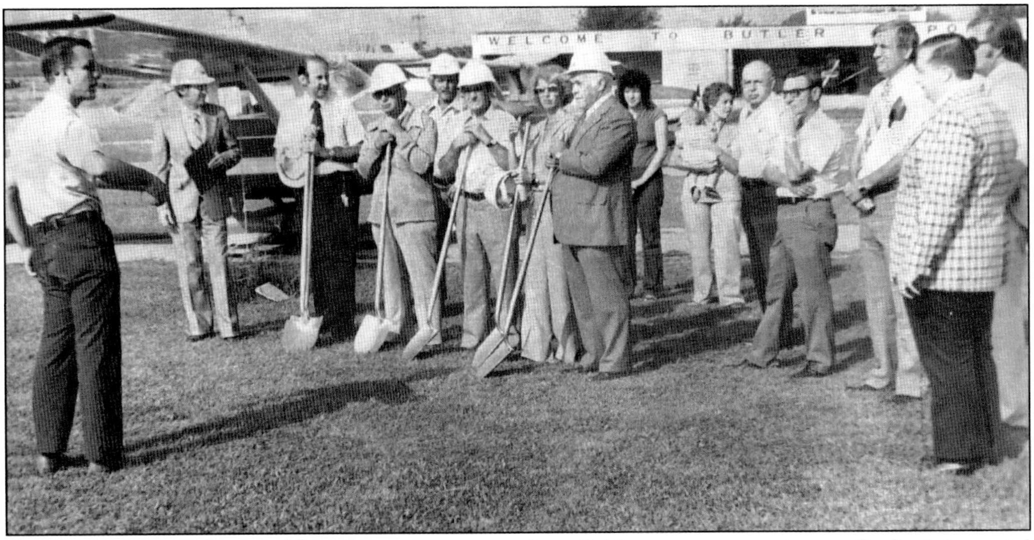

City officials attend ground-breaking ceremonies for a 1979 expansion project at Butler Memorial Airport, north of town on Old 71. Opened in 1946, the field was purchased by the city in 1963 and dedicated to the memory of local servicemen and women. The airport is home to Spencer Aircraft, a repair and maintenance outfit, and also houses a professional skydivers' training facility. (Courtesy of the Bates County Historical Society.)

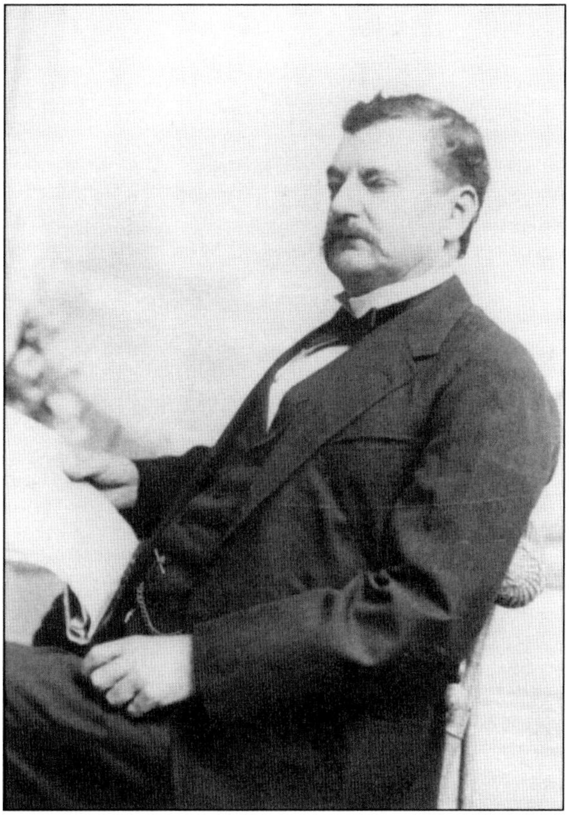

William E. Walton, an 1870 arrival, must be recognized as the godfather of Butler businessmen. Cashier and president of Missouri State Bank and the Walton Trust Company, he was a paragon of ethical business who always put the patron's welfare first. In addition to commerce, he also loved culture, as evidenced by Walton's Opera House, which ran from 1882 to 1889. (Courtesy of the Bates County Historical Society and the Eddie Herrman Collection.)

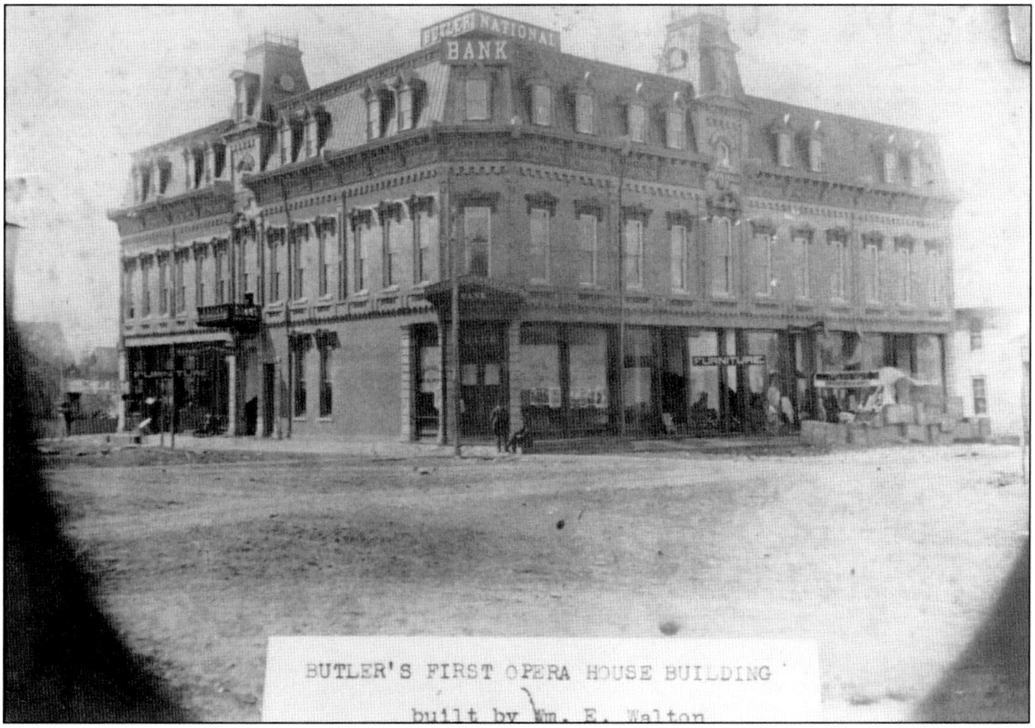

The curtain rose for the first time at Walton's Opera House on the night of December 11, 1882, with W.S. Gilbert's *Engaged*, a romantic comedy revolving around a series of matrimonial misunderstandings. Seating 1,000 and occupying the third floor of Butler National Bank's premises, the theater's success was cut short by a fire in February 1889. (Courtesy of the Bates County Historical Society and the Eddie Herrman Collection.)

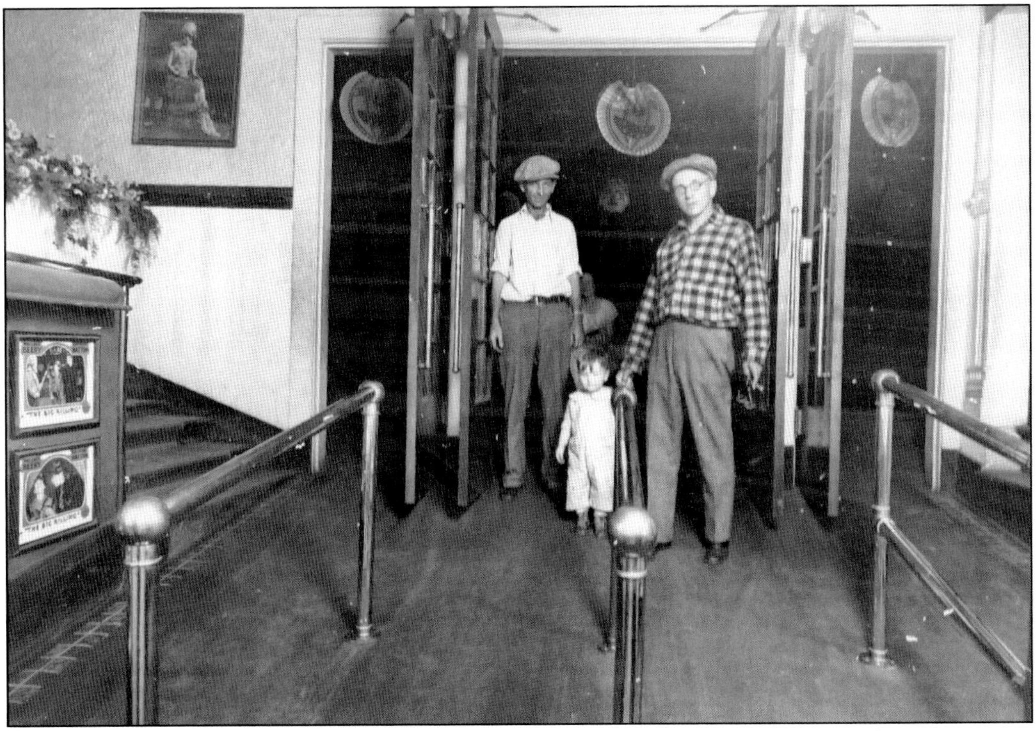

Charles Fisk (right) stands at the entrance of Fisk Theatre with his young son Joe and Boyd Guyton. Dubbed "the head of the amusement business in Butler" by William Atkeson, Fisk managed (and eventually purchased) the Butler Opera House in addition to directing the Butler Municipal Band. In his capable hands, the band won six first prizes in major competitions. (Courtesy of the Bates County Historical Society and the Eddie Herrman Collection.)

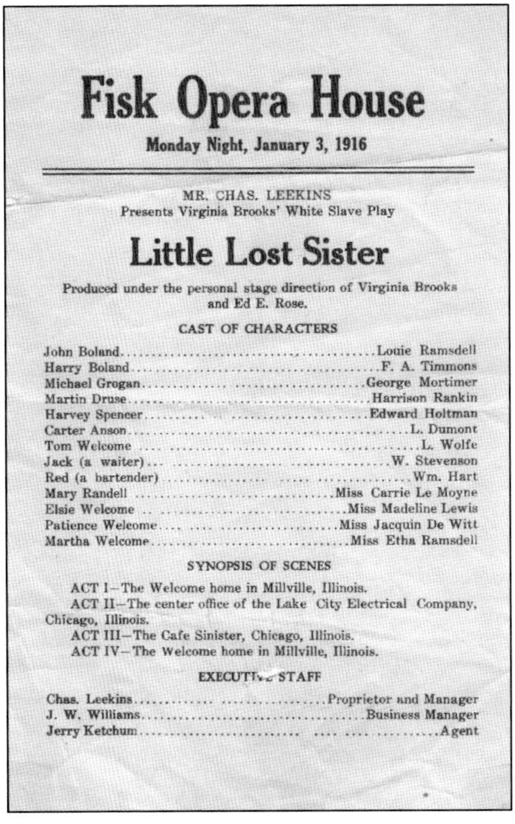

Fisk Opera House

Monday Night, January 3, 1916

MR. CHAS. LEEKINS
Presents Virginia Brooks' White Slave Play

Little Lost Sister

Produced under the personal stage direction of Virginia Brooks and Ed E. Rose.

CAST OF CHARACTERS

John Boland.......Louie Ramsdell
Harry Boland.......F. A. Timmons
Michael Grogan.......George Mortimer
Martin Druse.......Harrison Rankin
Harvey Spencer.......Edward Holtman
Carter Anson.......L. Dumont
Tom Welcome.......L. Wolfe
Jack (a waiter).......W. Stevenson
Red (a bartender).......Wm. Hart
Mary Randell.......Miss Carrie Le Moyne
Elsie Welcome.......Miss Madeline Lewis
Patience Welcome.......Miss Jacquin De Witt
Martha Welcome.......Miss Etha Ramsdell

SYNOPSIS OF SCENES

ACT I—The Welcome home in Millville, Illinois.
ACT II—The center office of the Lake City Electrical Company, Chicago, Illinois.
ACT III—The Cafe Sinister, Chicago, Illinois.
ACT IV—The Welcome home in Millville, Illinois.

EXECUTIVE STAFF

Chas. Leekins.......Proprietor and Manager
J. W. Williams.......Business Manager
Jerry Ketchum.......Agent

Fisk (Butler) Opera House, successor to William Walton's establishment, served as venue for the Lyceum Course, a $1,125 annual program dedicated to attracting premium theatrical and musical talent to the city of Butler. It also attracted other important figures: a 1917 band competition counted among its audience none other than former US president William H. Taft. (Courtesy of the Bates County Historical Society and the Eddie Herrman Collection.)

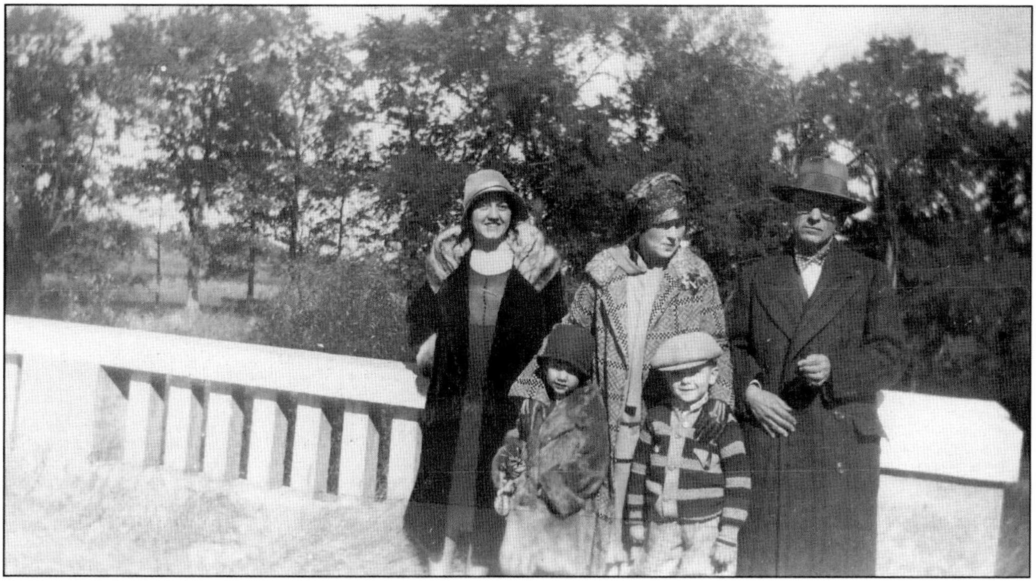

Charles Fisk (right) poses with his wife, Leta (center), and sons Joe and Charlie Jr. As a musician, Fisk earned a spot among the 12 best trouping bandleaders while with the Al G. Field Minstrel Show. As a theater operator in the 1930s, he earned a reputation as a rather salty reviewer of films. (Courtesy of the Bates County Historical Society and the Eddie Herrman Collection.)

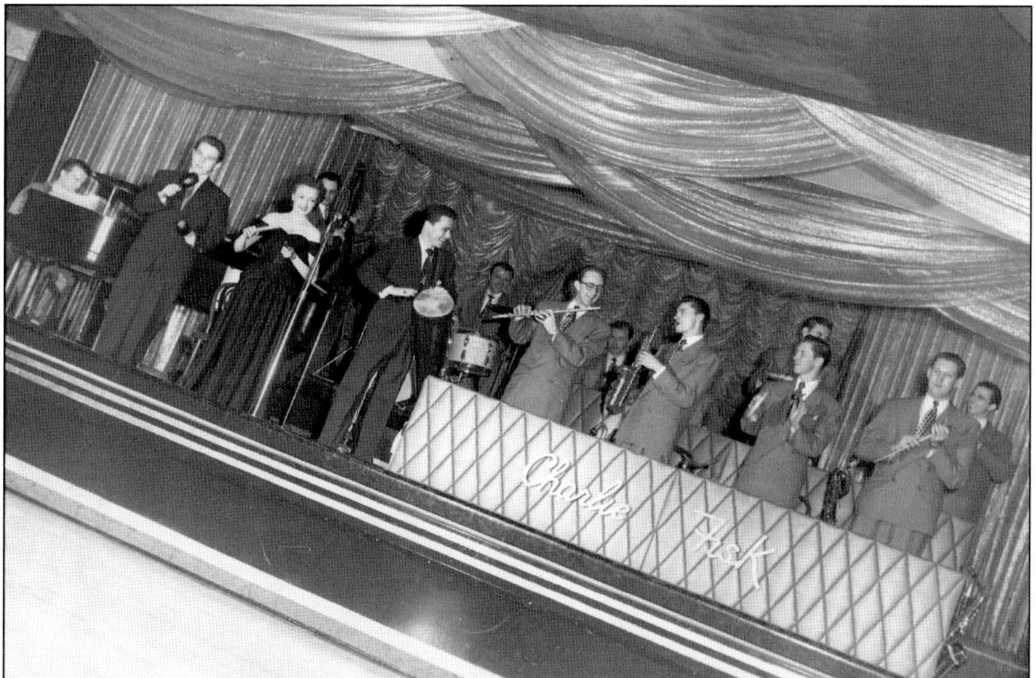

Butler boy Charlie Fisk Jr. plays the bongo with his orchestra, formed in the early 1940s. To his left is his wife, singer Ginny Coon. Fisk, who led the Butler Municipal Band as a high school student, toured the Midwest with the Charlie Fisk Orchestra for a decade from Port Arthur, Texas, to Youngstown, Ohio. (Courtesy of the Bates County Historical Association and the Eddie Herrman Collection.)

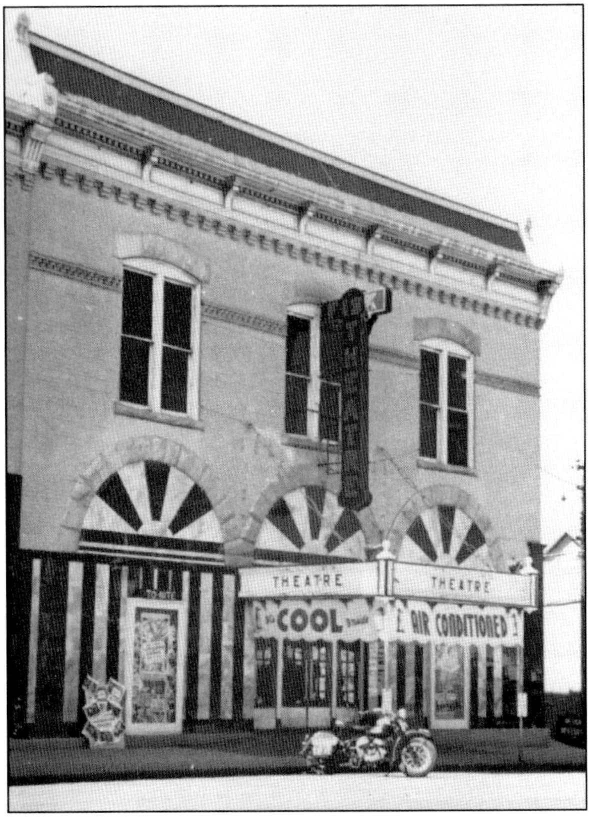

Fisk Theatre, remembered by John Swezy as a "magnificent movie palace," featured all manner of entertainment, from sporting events to popular serials like *Flash Gordon* and *Superman*. After a Butler High football victory over Kansas City's Pembroke Country Day School, it even hosted a rambunctious "snake dance." Fisk's burned in January 1951, and Jennings Market took its place. (Courtesy of the Bates County Historical Society and the Eddie Herrman Collection.)

For a short period before the 1951 fire, Charles Fisk's films faced a bit of competition from the Nu-Sho movie theater, which opened on Old 71 in 1949. The building, which also for a time housed Butler's bowling alley, was torn down in the 1970s to make way for a new Sonic Drive-In. (Courtesy of the Bates County Historical Society and the Eddie Herrman Collection.)

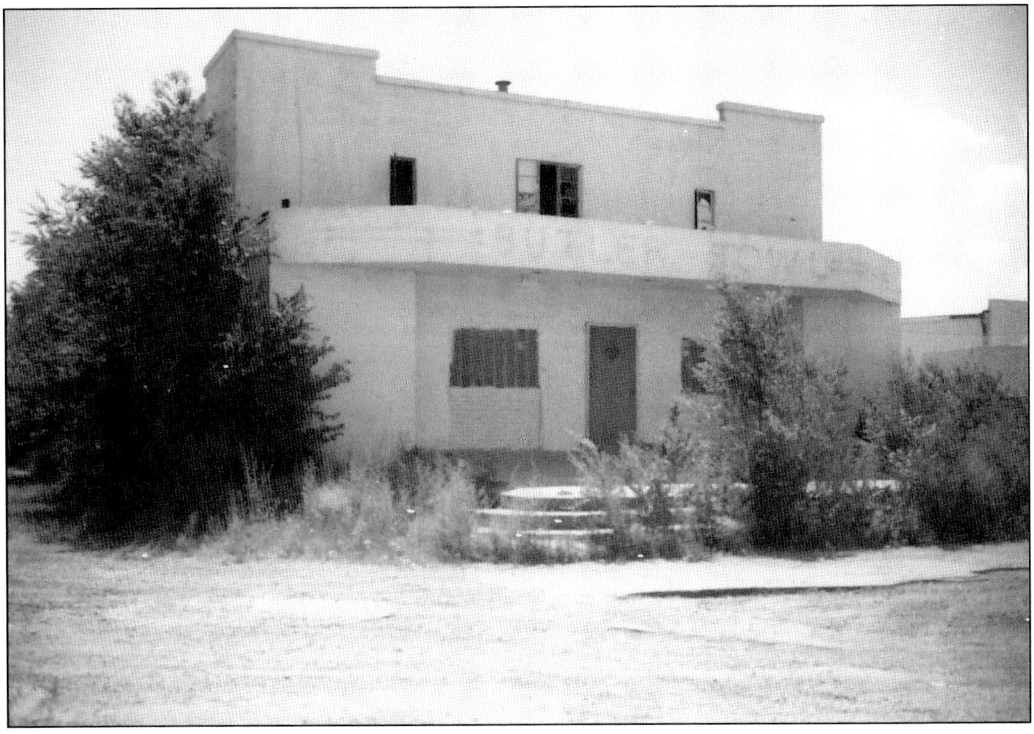

Three

Farm Living

Agriculture has always been at the heart of Bates County living, and it is, by all accounts, an area magnificently suited to the purpose. In his history, William Atkeson praised the diversity of crops amenable to the region, from grains to fruit orchards, and called on those engaged in production to embrace scientific methods newly available, believing there was no end to the demand Bates County farmers could supply. In 1918, he wrote:

> A circle drawn with Butler, the county seat of Bates county, as its center, and whose diameter is 200 miles and its radii 100, will inclose [*sic*] the richest and most productive area to be found on the face of the globe. . . . It might well be called a magic circle, for its agricultural possibilities are wonderful and its mineral resources marvelous; and if the diameter and radii of this circle should be doubled the same statements of its area would still be true. Such a circle would include the very heart of this country, and Bates [County] lies at its center.

Farming is a generational affair in this corner of the world. Of the 8,120 Century Farms (farms that have been owned and operated by the same family for 100 years or more) recognized by the State of Missouri, 83 are in Bates County. The oldest of these, the Charles Duncan farm, dates back to 1820. Children are encouraged to participate in the business of farm living, with formal and informal apprenticeships available in many forms, from 4-H to the local rodeo. It is not at all uncommon to see bale stackers protruding from the beds of pickup trucks in high school parking lots. In Bates County, they carry their forks with pride.

Farming and nostalgia go hand in hand in this place. Few are the area residents who cannot conjure up images of rickety old hay-barns and early morning jaunts in the old John Deere. Farms are the dwelling places of memory, and Bates County's memory is long.

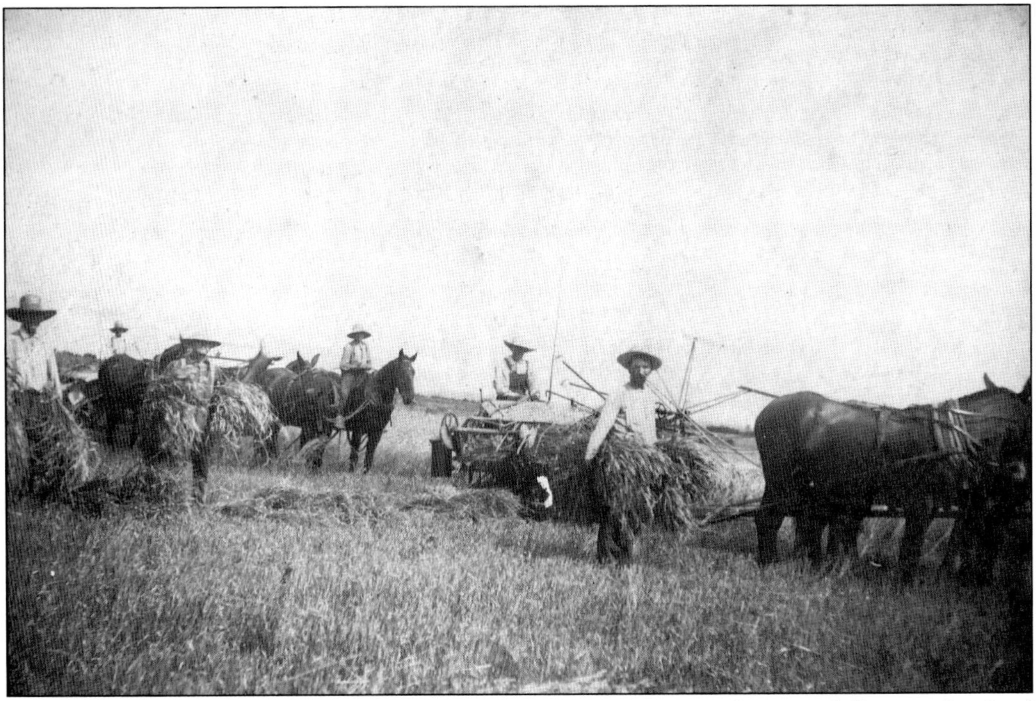

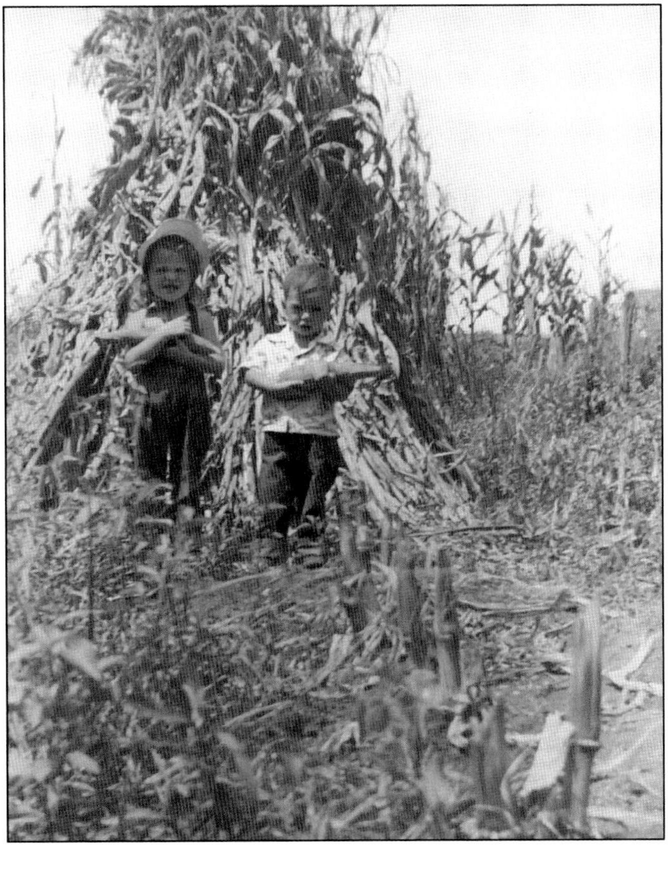

In the years following the Civil War, settlers began to flock to Bates County in droves, motivated by exceptionally low land prices in the area. Dr. Theodrick Boulware recalled that when he arrived in Butler in 1868, a farm could be purchased at $2 to $4 per acre. By century's turn, that price had risen to over $100 an acre. (Courtesy of the Bates County Historical Society.)

Barbara and Dave Alkire help with the corn harvest in their grandfather's garden. According to a report by the Missouri Pacific Railroad Company in 1898, the fertility of the soil in Bates County was unmatched west of the Mississippi, producing 40 to 70 bushels of corn per acre, and 15 to 30 bushels of wheat. (Courtesy of Barbara Herrell.)

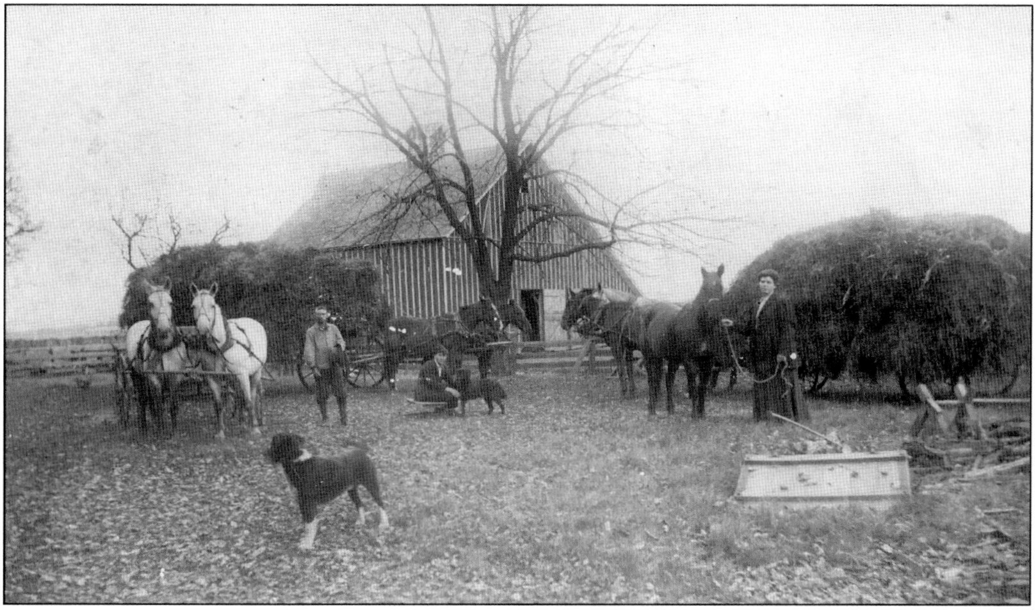

In earlier days, haying could be a risky affair. Rattlers, once plentiful, liked to hide under the sheaves. According to the Old Settlers, the only remedy for a rattlesnake attack was "to fill the victim with the very worst grade of whiskey obtainable and, if the whiskey did not kill him, the milder poison from the rattler [would give] up the job in disgust." (Courtesy of the Bates County Historical Society.)

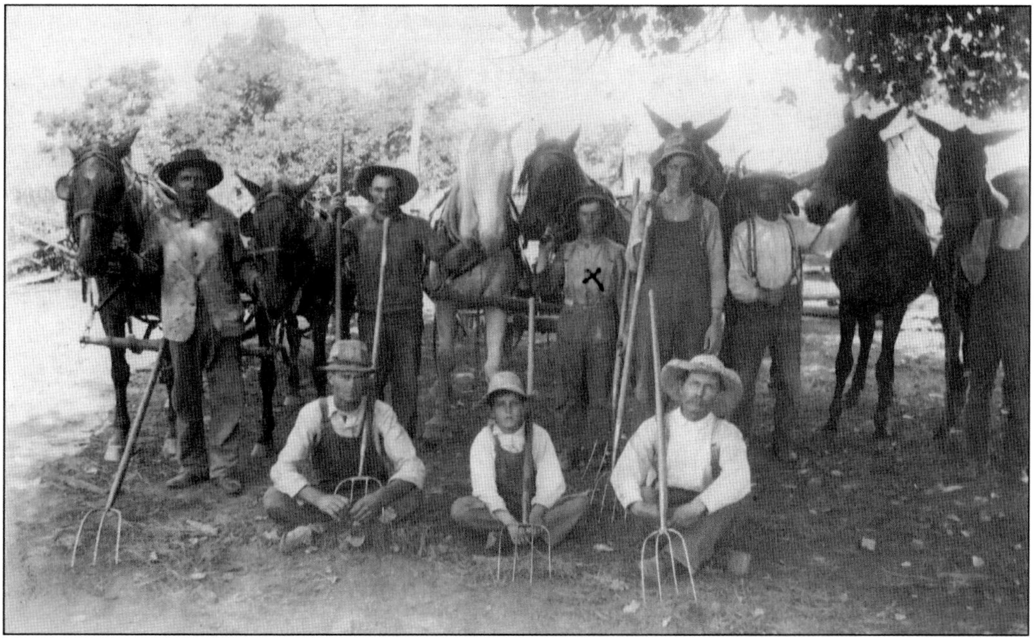

The farmhand was the linchpin of an agricultural economy like Bates County's. Without his help, the harvest season would have been much more challenging, and the farmer's living much more difficult to obtain. Most often, hired hands received room and board with the farm family as part of their pay. Those who did not received higher wages as compensation. (Courtesy of the Bates County Historical Society and the Eddie Herrman Collection.)

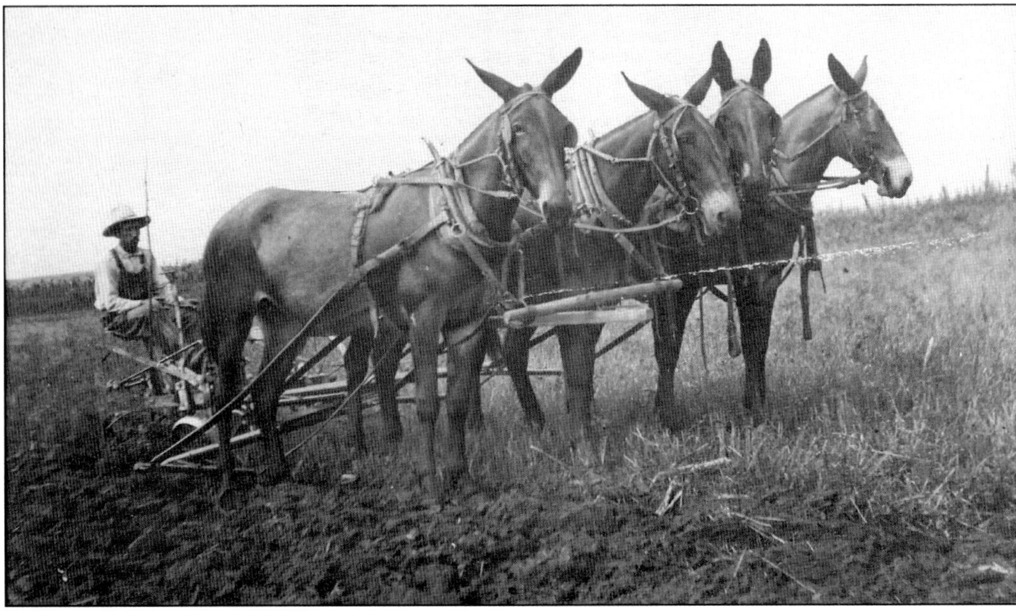

A team of Missouri mules—state animal since 1995—pull a plow on the James Walker farm. A sturdy and hard-working animal, the mule is a fitting symbol for the "Show Me State," whose people are of reputedly stubborn stock. Between 1870 and 1900, Missouri topped the charts in national mule sales, even supplying 115,000 to British troops during the Boer Wars. (Courtesy of the Bates County Historical Society.)

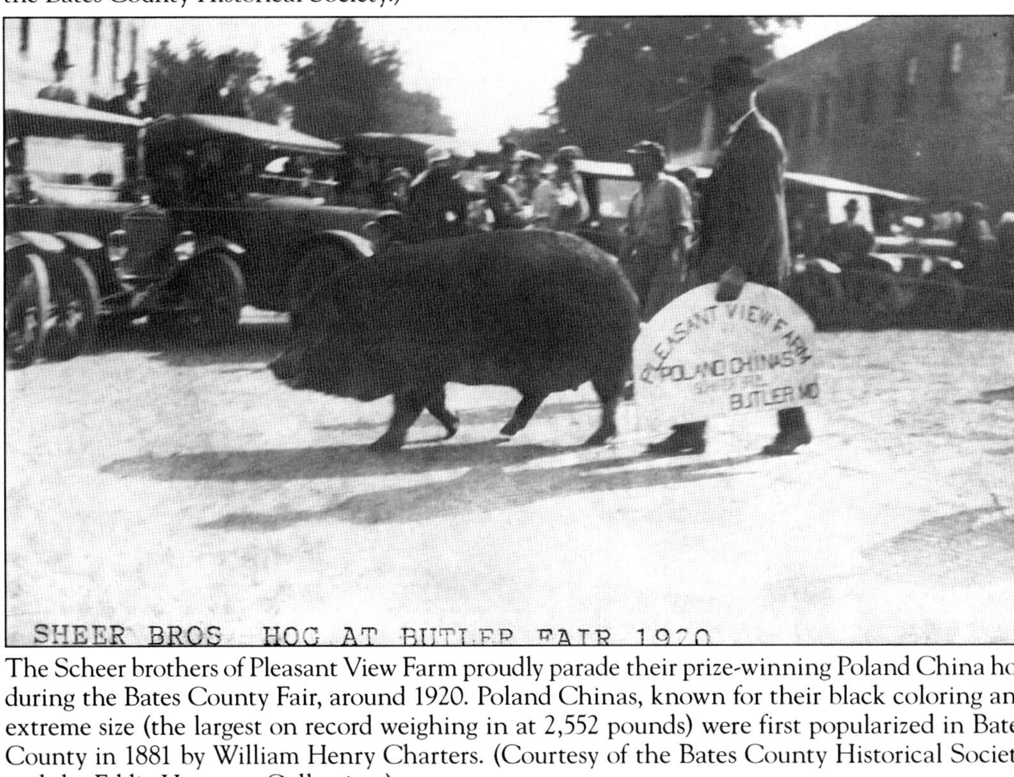

The Scheer brothers of Pleasant View Farm proudly parade their prize-winning Poland China hog during the Bates County Fair, around 1920. Poland Chinas, known for their black coloring and extreme size (the largest on record weighing in at 2,552 pounds) were first popularized in Bates County in 1881 by William Henry Charters. (Courtesy of the Bates County Historical Society and the Eddie Herrman Collection.)

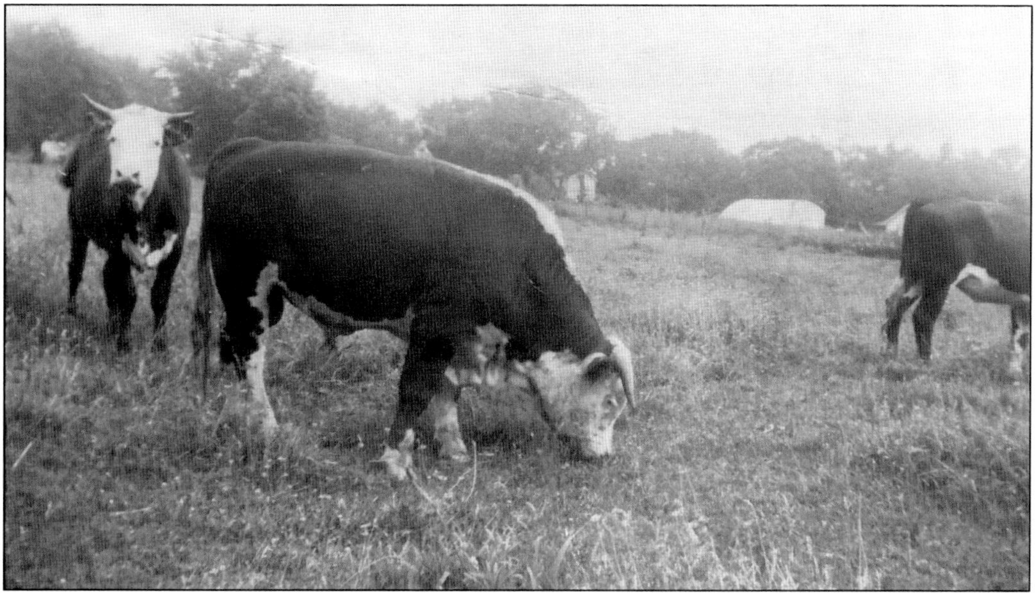

As this herd of Hereford will attest, beef farming has always been heavy industry in Bates County. According to the 2009 Missouri Beef Audit, Bates County remained in the top tier of beef producers in the state, ranking sixth in the percentage of head of cattle marketed in 2007 (1.89 percent) and netting in the process nearly $27 million. (Courtesy of the Durst family.)

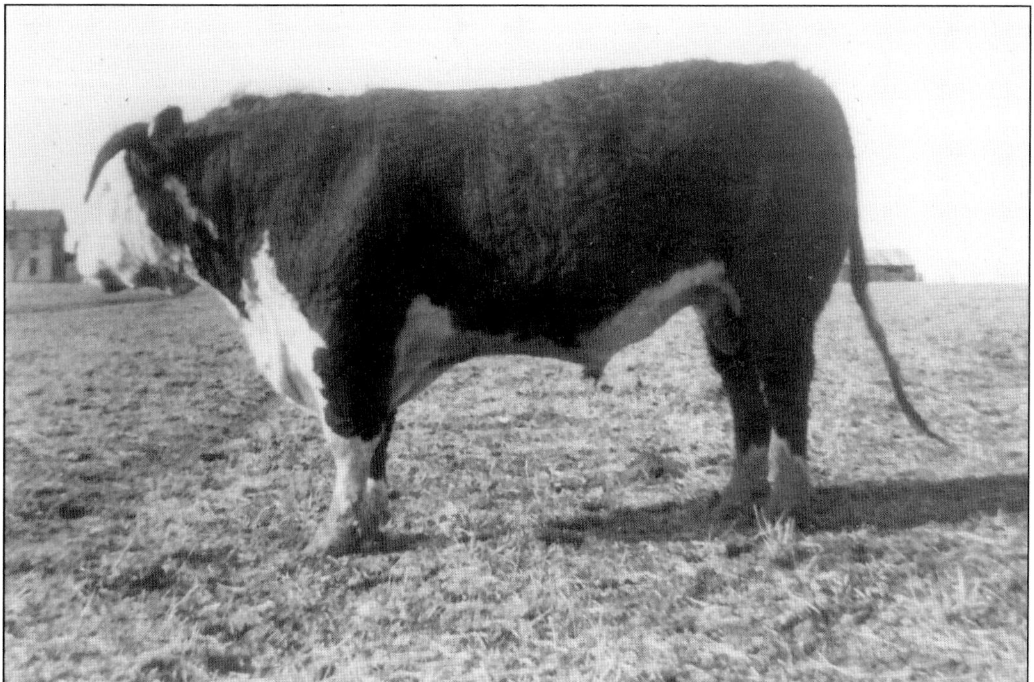

Ferdinand the bull, a massive Hereford, surveys his kingdom, otherwise known as the Durst Brothers' Farm. He was an unenlightened despot whose size, coupled with a mean temper, made him an object of fear. Sadly, Ferdinand's reign came to an unfortunate and untimely end when a local hunter mistook him for a deer. (Courtesy of the Durst family.)

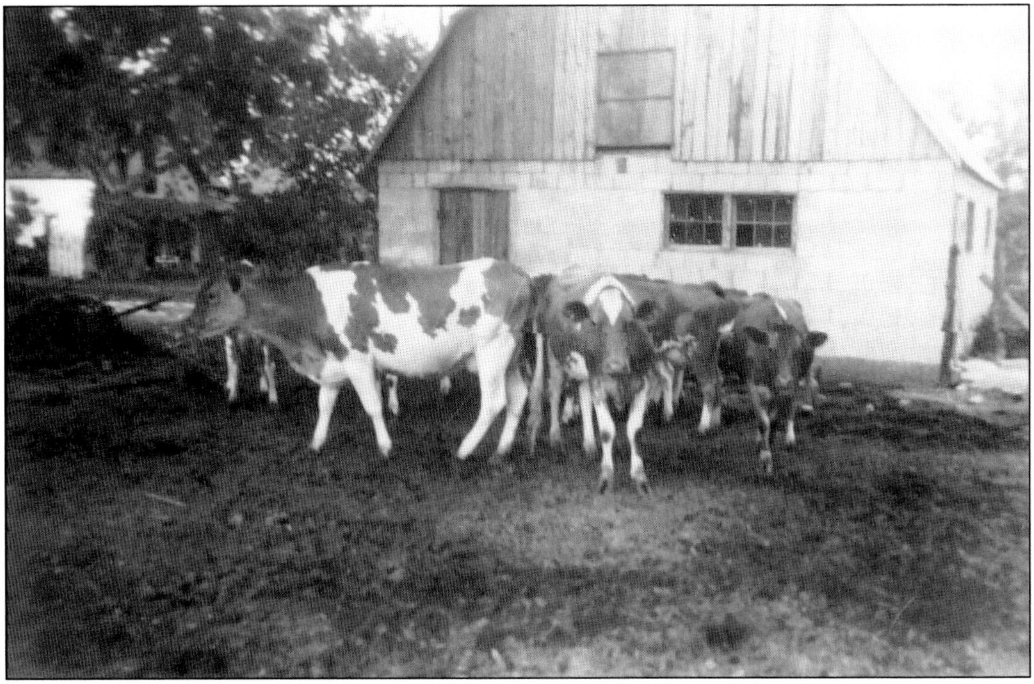

Guernseys, like these on the Erickson farm, were prized for the golden color and rich flavor of their milk. While large-scale dairies have always been part of the local economy, most farmers kept a few milking cows for family use and supplementary income. Small batches were set aside regularly to be collected by milkmen who, under contract with local bottlers, connected product to retailer. (Courtesy of Lucille Lindsay.)

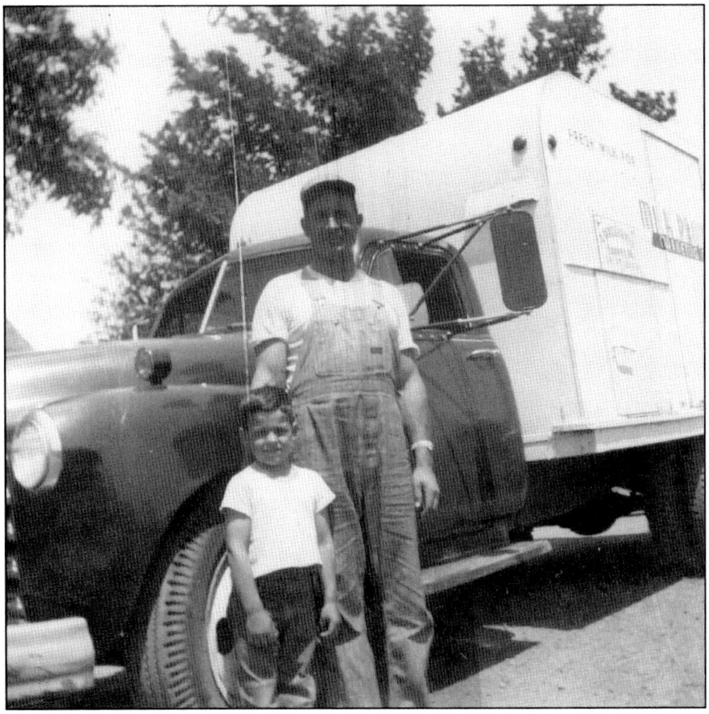

Young Jim Wackerman loved tagging along with his father, Albert, on milk runs. Jim remembers the old trick of dunking milk cans in basins of cool water to keep the milk from souring. He also remembers that it did not always work. Often, after inspection at the factory, cans of spoiled milk had to be delivered right back where they came from, if they did not explode first. (Courtesy of Vickie and Jim Wackerman.)

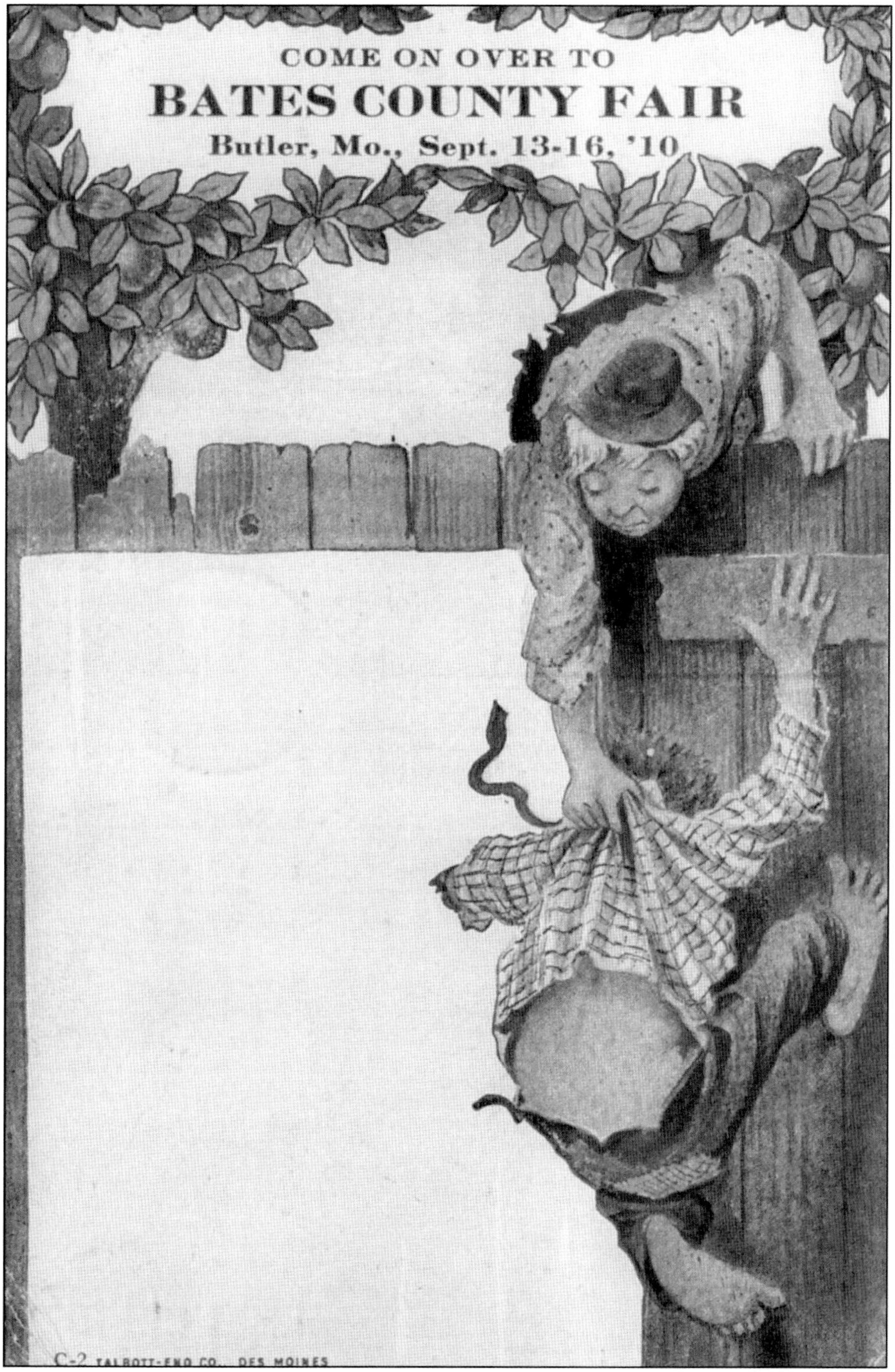

Quite probably, no one needed an invitation to the 1910 Bates County Fair. Although, lately, its popularity appears to be dwindling, it was once an occasion of high festivity. It was also a time for county farmers to shine. Exhibitions were held, and prizes were awarded for everything from produce to livestock. Blue ribbons conferred major bragging rights, at least until the following year's fair. (Courtesy of the Bates County Historical Society.)

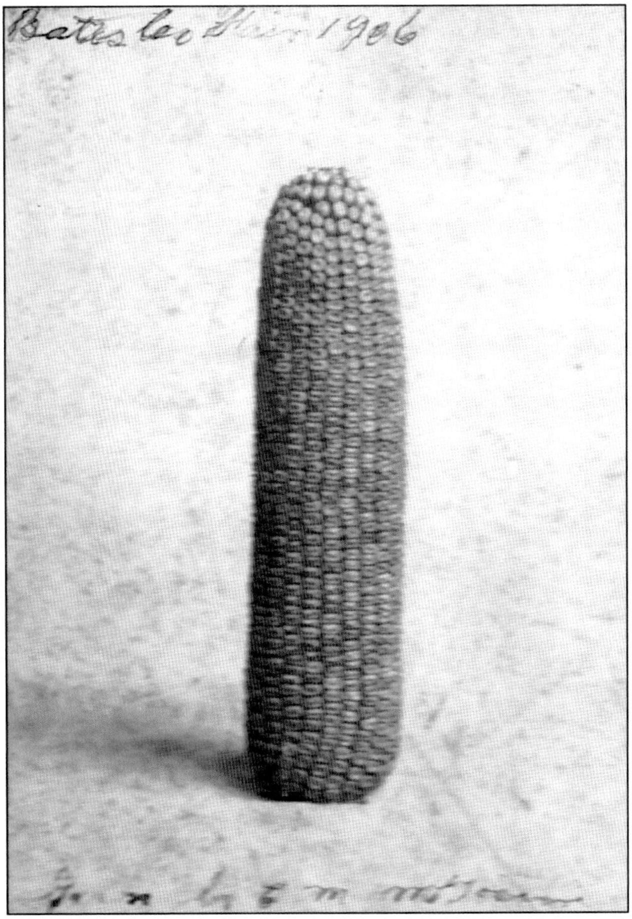

This ear of corn, representative of one of the area's major cash crops, was submitted by C.M. McGovern to the 1906 Bates County Fair. Corn is also a favorite Bates County meal. In 1915, Lucien Green of Hudson commented, "A choice ear of sweet corn, well-lubricated with butter and eaten from the cob—hog fashion—pleases the palate beyond the ability of words to explain." (Courtesy of the Bates County Historical Society.)

In this photograph, Abram Lewis, driving a horse-drawn buggy, inspects the day's haying while Elsie Lewis and Mag Thornbrugh look on. The men guiding the wagons are, from left to right, Russell Lewis, Strother Lewis, and an unidentified Thornbrugh. Abram's first farm was in his home state of Virginia. In 1870, he purchased these 160 acres in West Point Township and made them his home until his death in 1913. (Courtesy of Missie Good.)

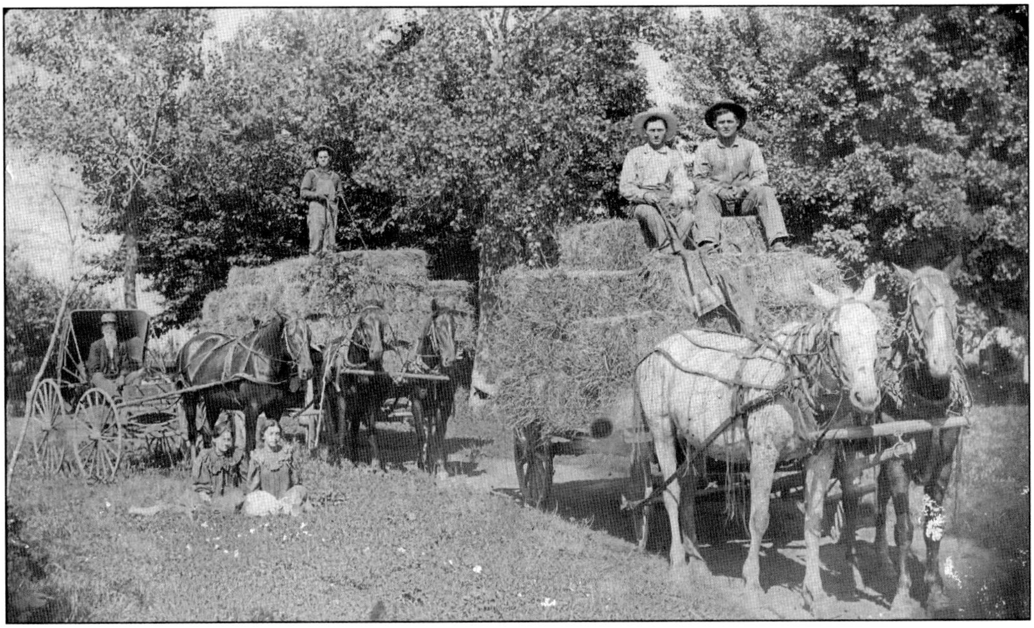

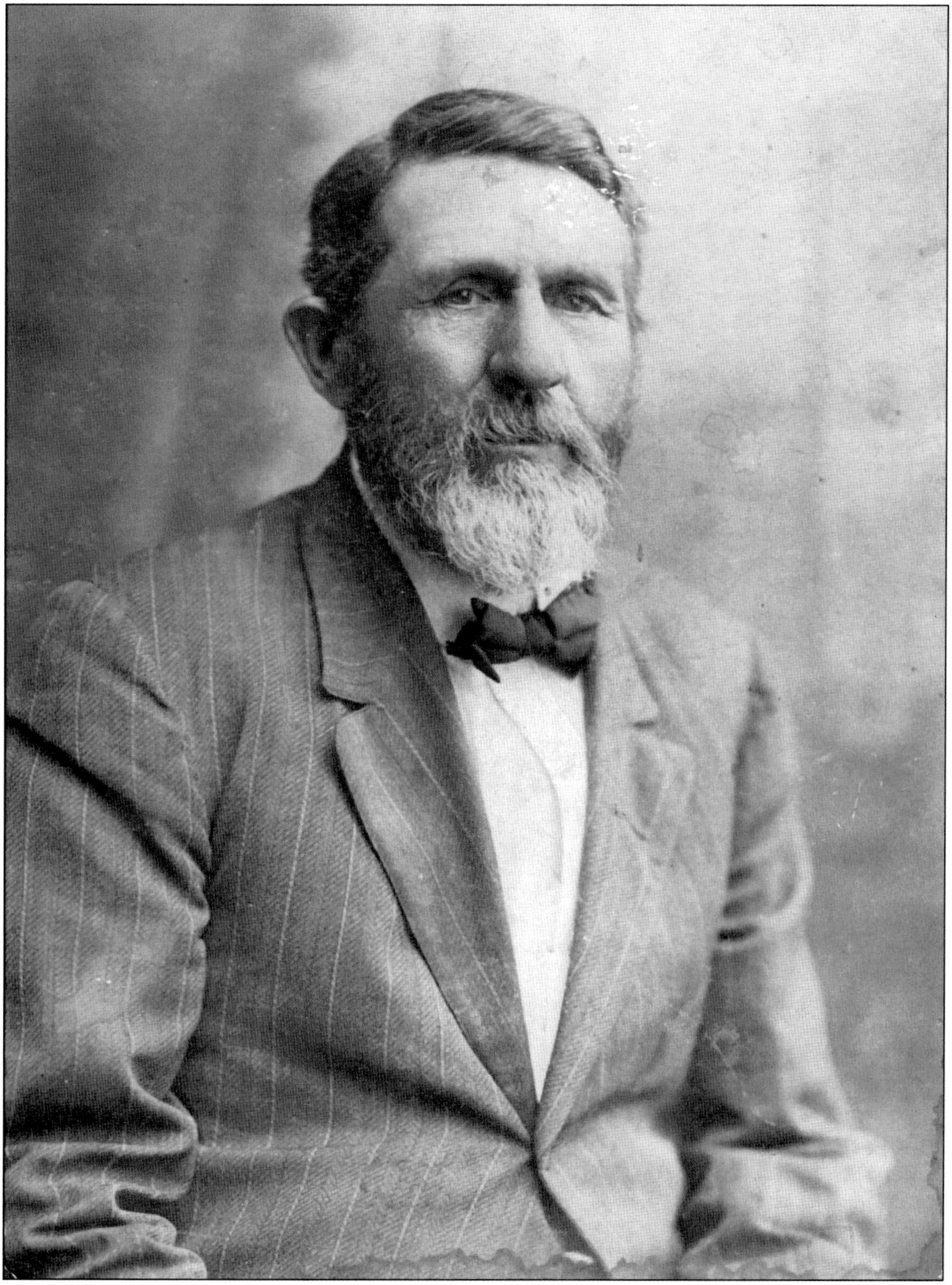

W.G. Sellon came to Bates County from Illinois in 1881. Along with his brother John, Sellon raised shorthorn cattle and Poland China swine on a 240-acre farm in Charlotte Township, west of Butler. A two-term justice of the peace, Sellon was, in the words of William Atkeson, "highly regarded as a substantial and desirable citizen of Bates County." (Courtesy of the Bates County Historical Society.)

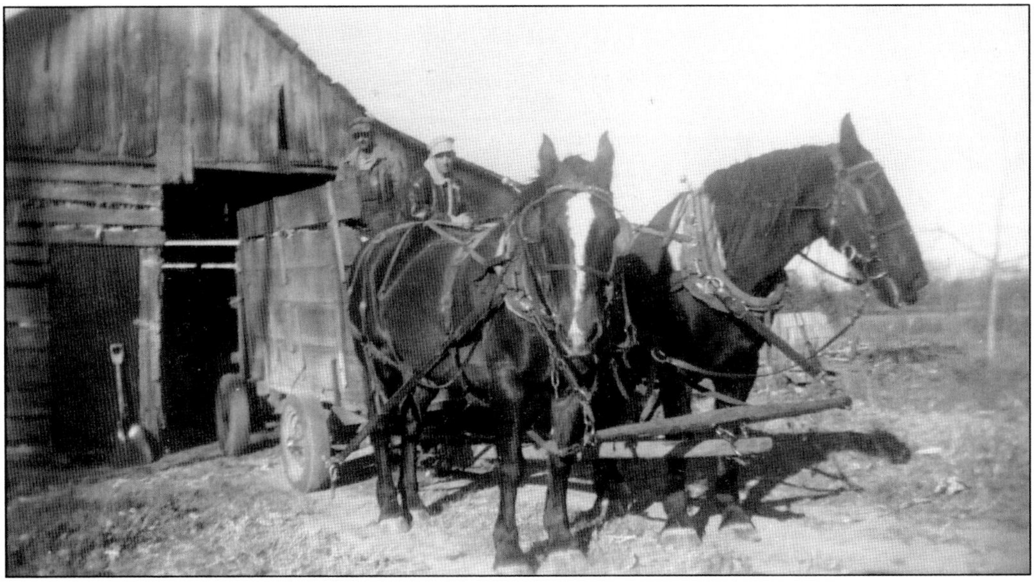

Twins Ernest and Earl Erickson (above) spend a day hauling loads of corn. The Erickson farm, established in 1906 by Swedish immigrant Erick Erickson, was added to the list of Missouri Century Farms (of which there are 83 in Bates County) on February 1, 2006. In 1950, Earl and his wife, Ruby, purchased the land from the senior Erickson and started a dairy business, running a herd of Grade A Guernsey cattle. These included Earl's favorite, Blondie (below), a "real good cow." Earl decided to make the switch to beef cattle in 1976. He retired at the ripe old age of 84, leaving the management of the farm to his daughter Lucille. (Both, courtesy of Lucille Lindsay.)

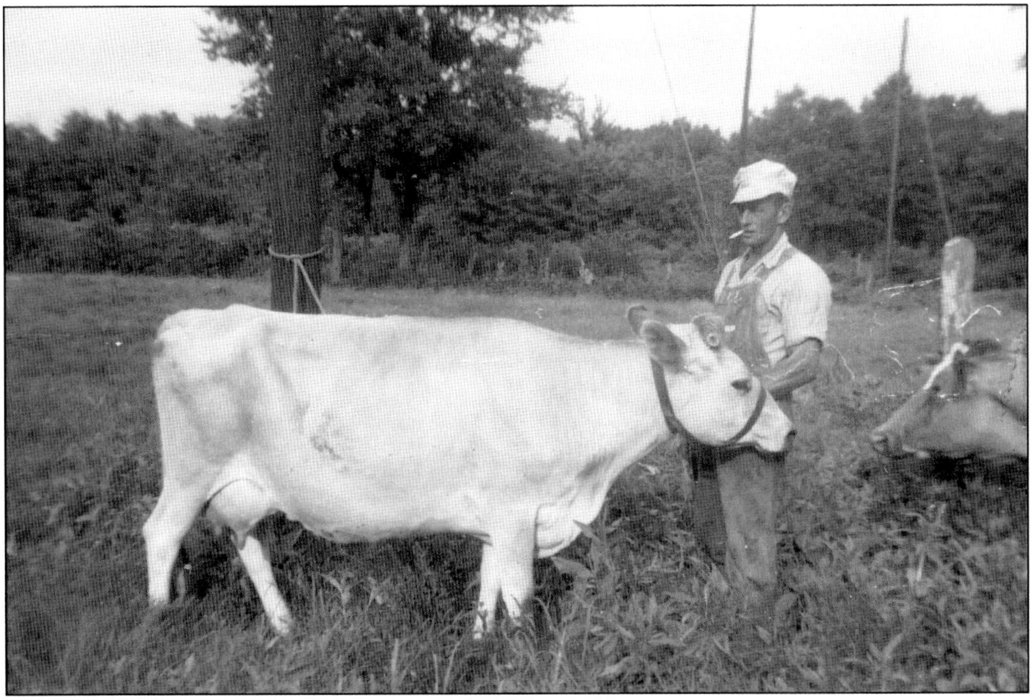

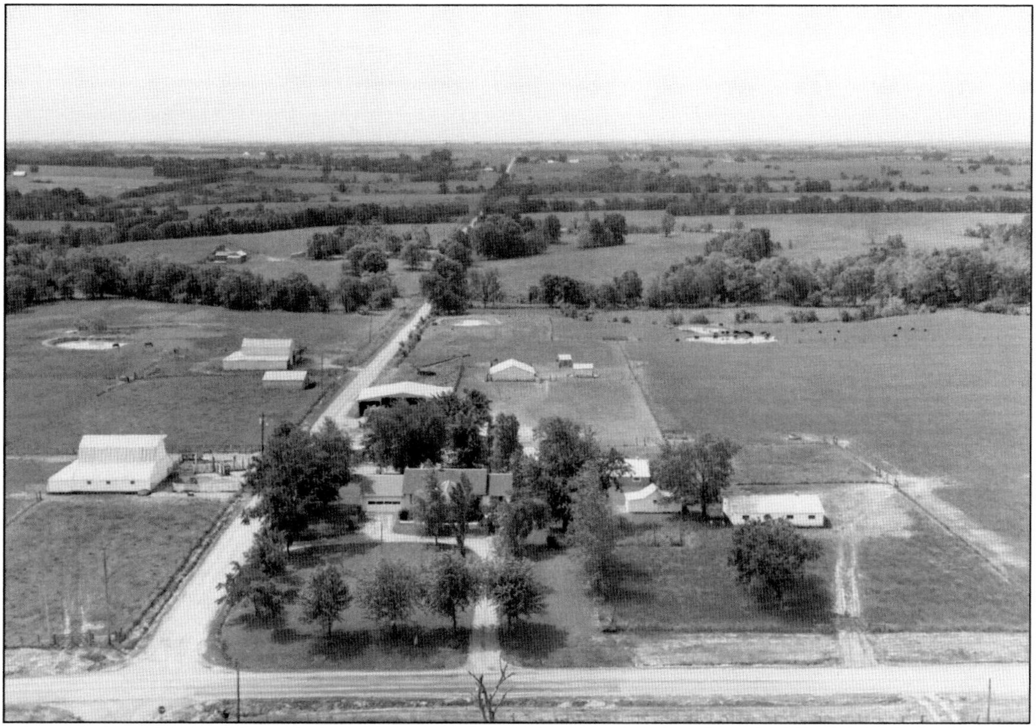

Durst Brothers' Farm was founded west of Butler by Aubrey and Marvin Durst in 1935 and remained in business until Aubrey's death in 1994. This aerial picture was taken in 1982. Today, the only original structures still standing are the white barn in the left foreground and the family residence in the center. (Courtesy of the Durst family.)

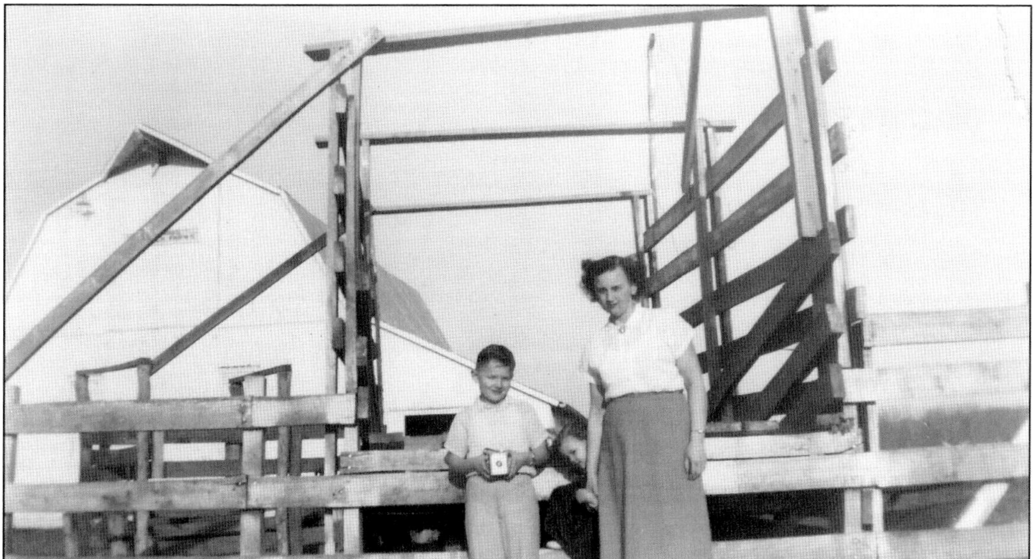

Fern Durst (Aubrey's wife), son Dean, and daughter Pam stand in front of the cattle loading ramp at the Durst Brothers' Farm around 1955. Apart from its intended use, the cattle ramp was a favorite play area for the Dursts' grandchildren. It also promised midnight adventures riding to the stockyards in Kansas City. (Courtesy of the Durst family.)

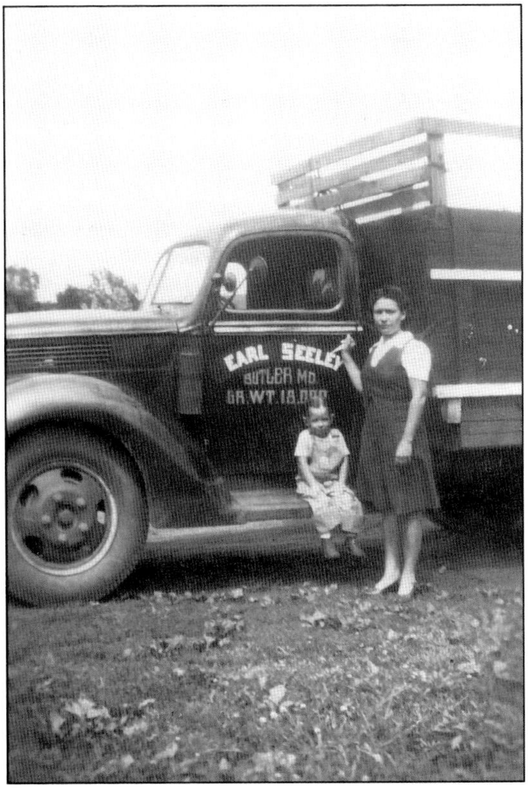

Myrtle Seeley poses with son Roger in front of husband Earl's farm truck around 1950. As a child, her small stature garnered Myrtle the nickname "Tiny." The pet name was humorously coupled with a penchant for beating up boys who made fun of her, resulting in stories she would gleefully recount later in life. (Courtesy of Barbara Herrell.)

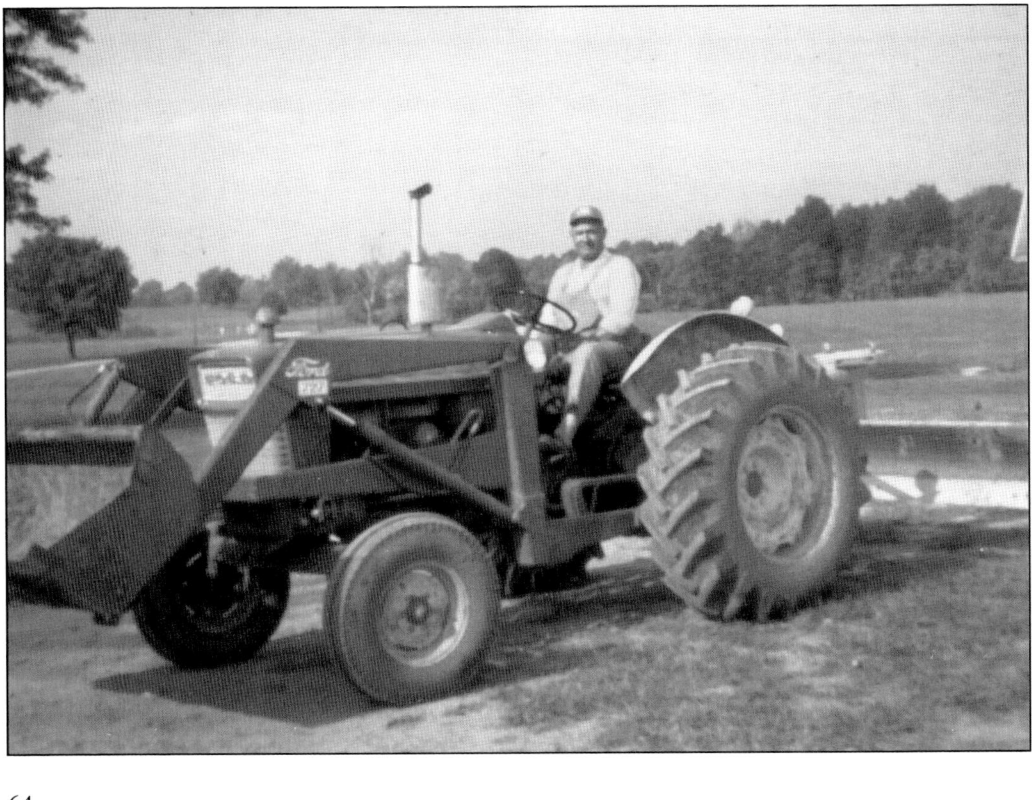

Although Albert Wackerman drove a milk truck for a living, farming was always his first love. He owned, at one time or another, some 500 acres located seven miles west of Butler. Here, he works to clear off his last addition and sow it with grass. Albert died suddenly in 1973, but his widow and children kept the farm running until 2006. (Courtesy of Vickie and Jim Wackerman.)

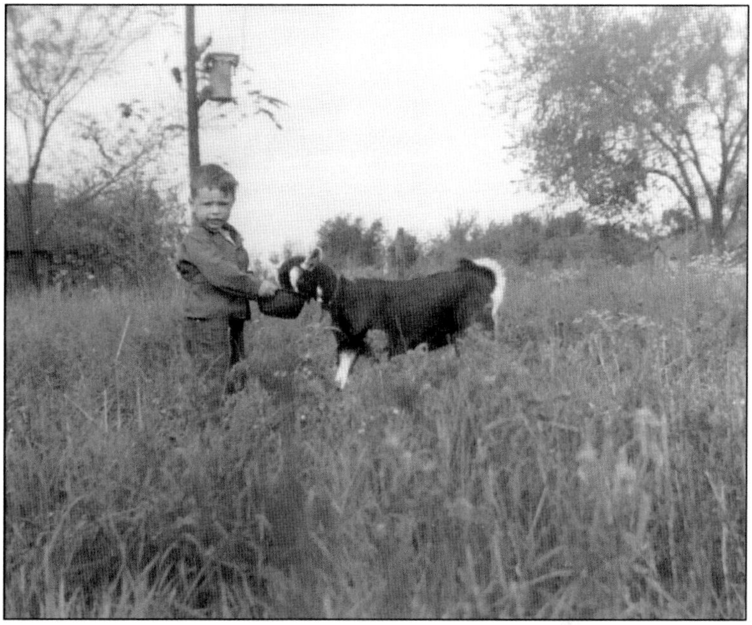

Little Dave tends to his goat at the Alkire home on Prospect Street. The education and encouragement of younger generations have always been a top priority in Bates County. The guiding principles of head, heart, hands, and health are instilled by eleven 4-H clubs spread across the county, and yearly fair activities sponsor youth projects in everything from aeronautics to welding and veterinary science. (Courtesy of Barbara Herrell.)

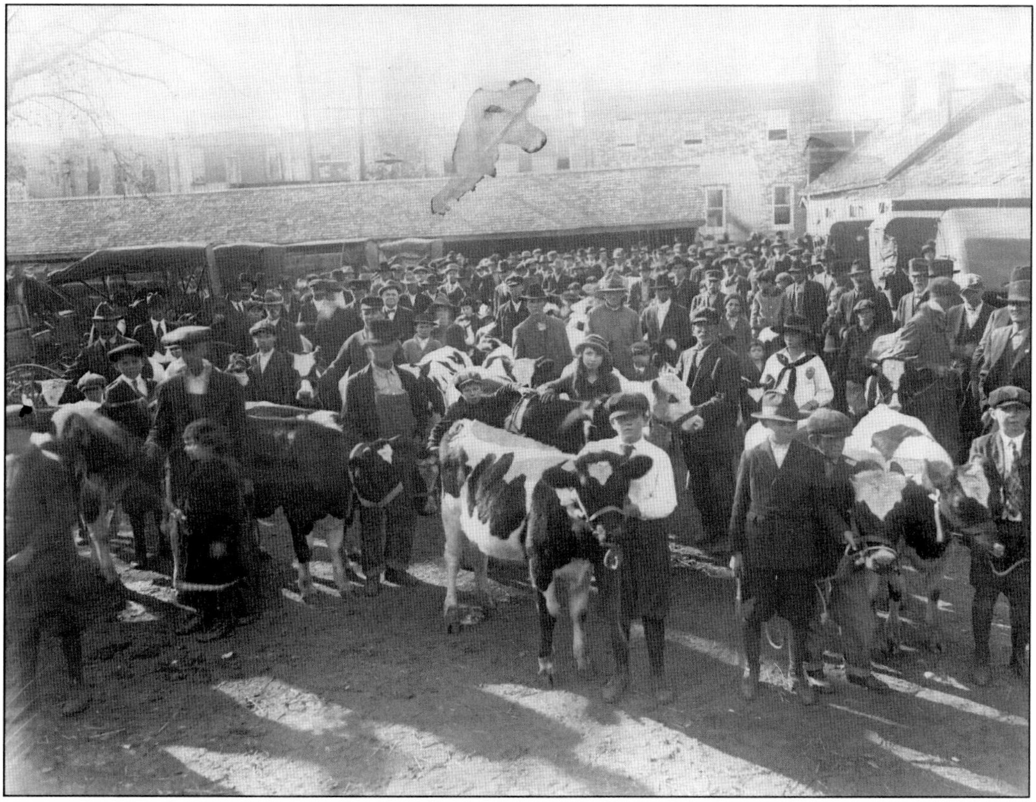

In 1917, People's Bank cashier Wesley Denton and Dr. J.M. Christy formed the Bates County Calf Club. On October 13, the bank purchased 109 Holstein calves and distributed them at cost—and, in some cases, on credit—to the children of the county, to be sold at auction one year later. (Courtesy of the Bates County Historical Society and the Eddie Herrman Collection.)

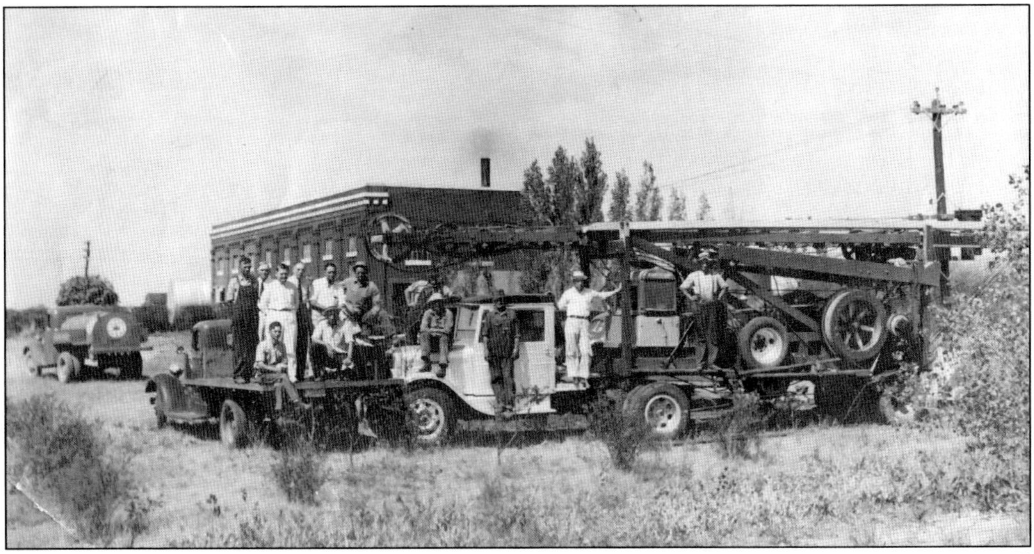

Drill rigs like this one were used all across Bates County to excavate water wells for farms, as well as residences. Posing in Butler with his rig in 1936, Harry Pierce (just below the pulley wheel) is remembered as one of the best well men in the county, always dependable and willing to go the extra mile to help out a client. (Courtesy of the Durst family.)

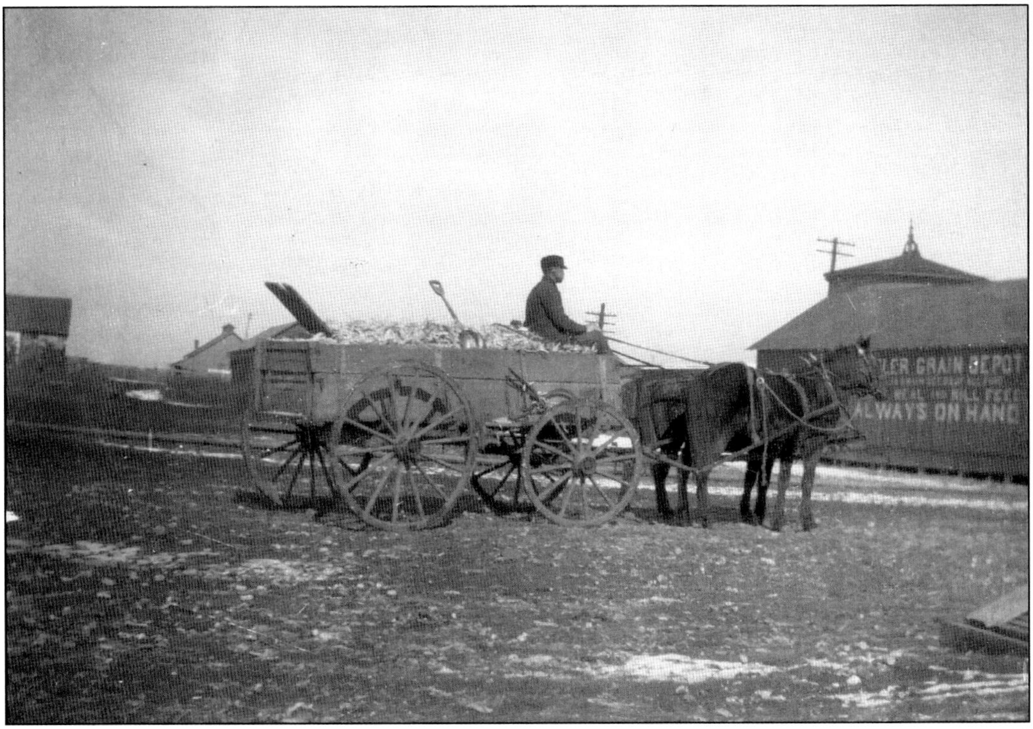

A load of grain makes its way to the depot to hitch a ride on the Missouri Pacific. The Old Settlers remarked on the change that took place in Bates County following the Civil War, from self-sustaining micro-economy to "a great and busy producing and exporting commonwealth." The rails featured prominently in this transformation, bringing markets closer and creating a new demand for surplus. (Courtesy of the Bates County Historical Society.)

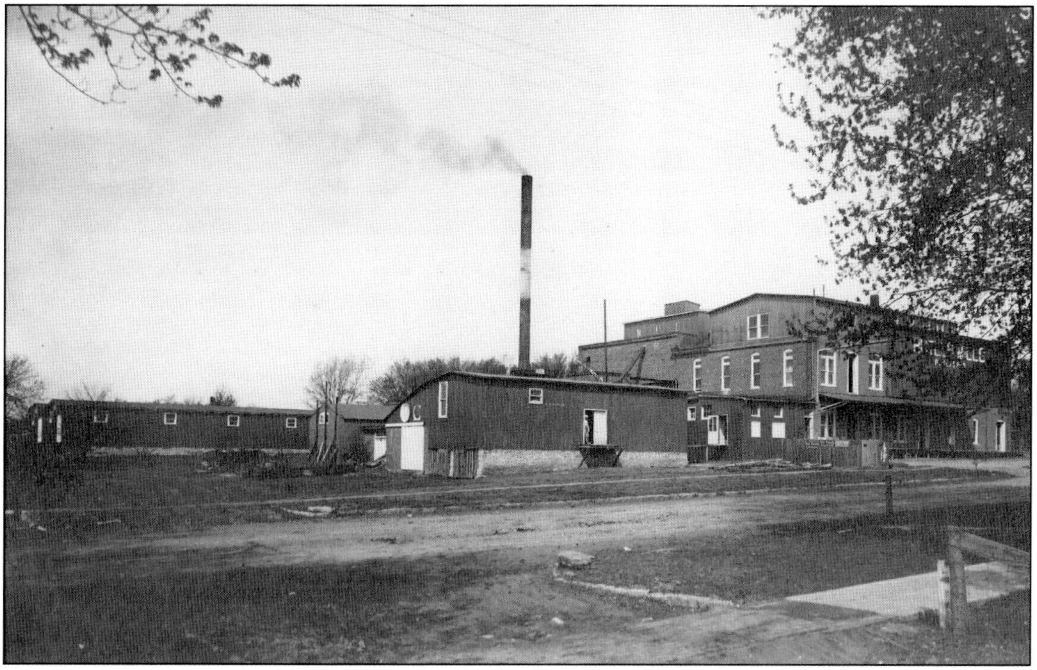

Built by millwright J.C. Garrison, the Butler Mill opened in December 1866. Steam-operated and able to process 40 bushels of corn per hour, it was the first mill built in Bates County after the Civil War. Melvin Power, the original owner, came to Missouri in 1866 from a nine-year stint as a produce and egg dealer in Cuba. (Courtesy of the Bates County Historical Society and the Eddie Herrman Collection.)

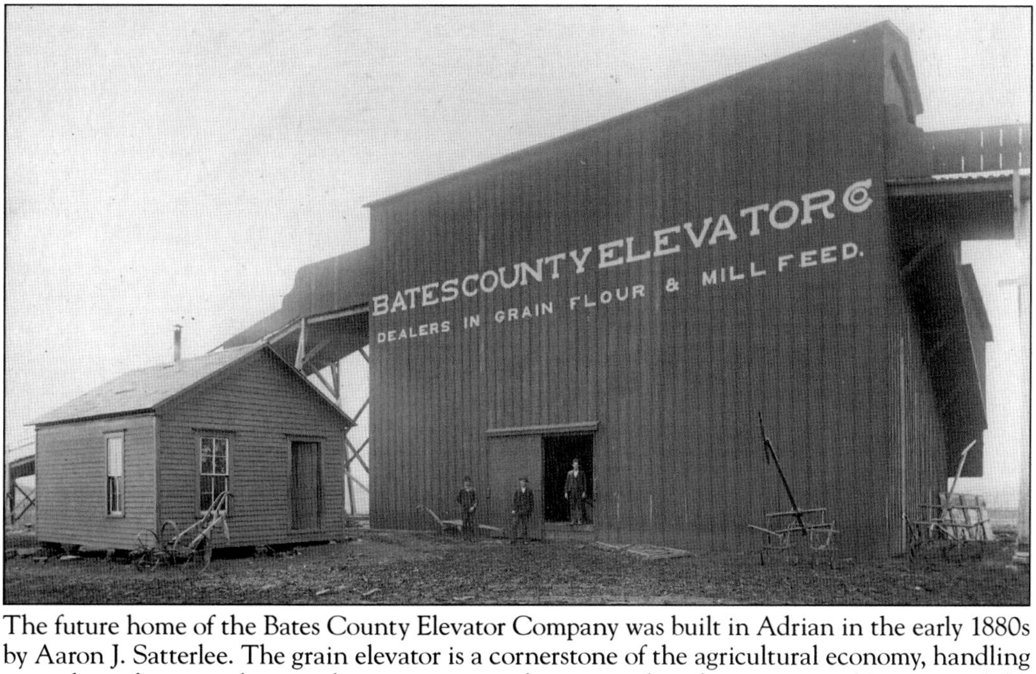

The future home of the Bates County Elevator Company was built in Adrian in the early 1880s by Aaron J. Satterlee. The grain elevator is a cornerstone of the agricultural economy, handling everything from weighing and storage to transferring product for transport. (Courtesy of the Bates County Historical Society.)

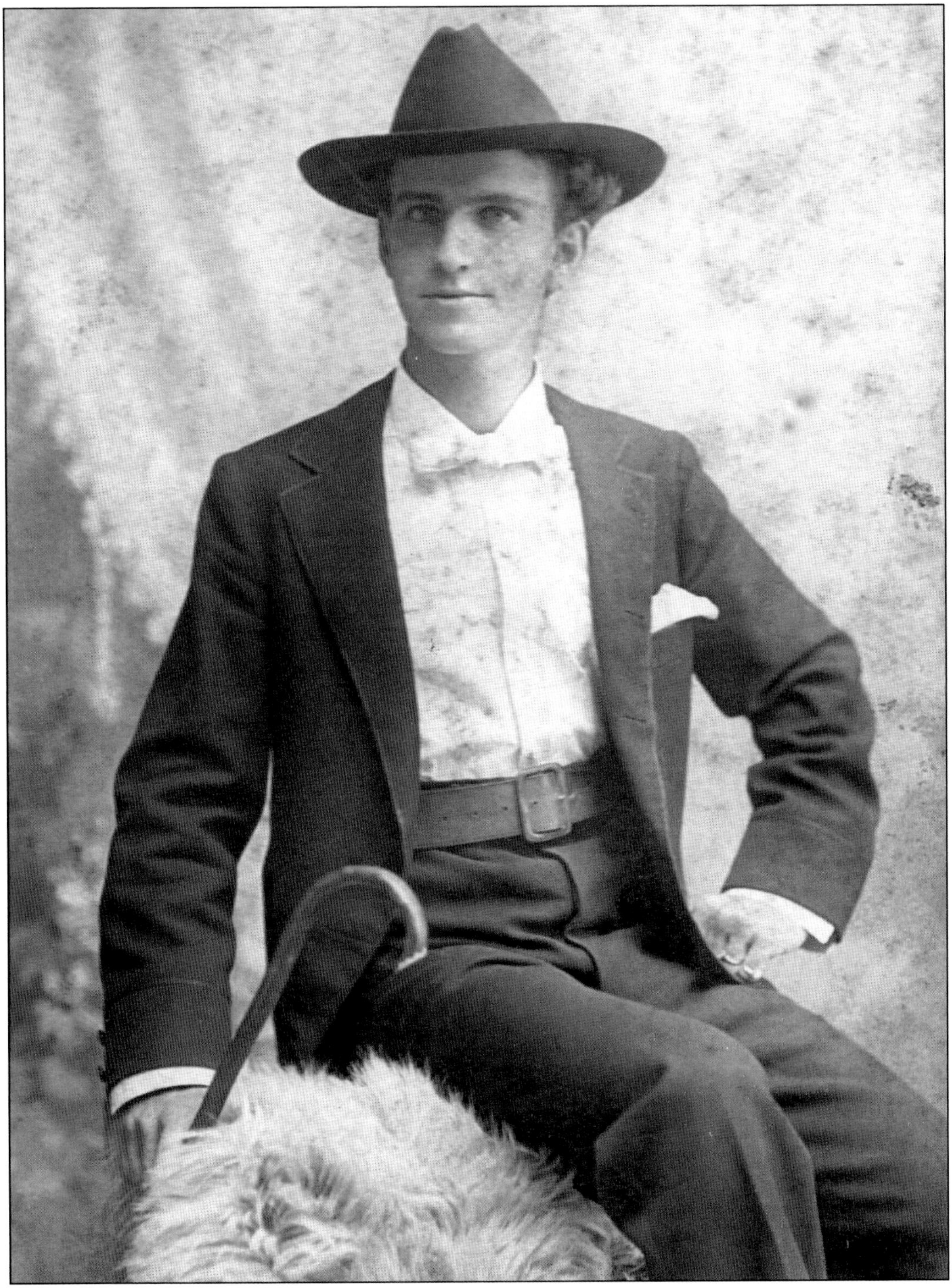

This portrait features "young blade" William Walker Cannon. After two years of military service during the Spanish American War, Cannon returned to Butler and went into the grain trade. His first elevator went up alongside the train depot in 1899 and 1900, and in 1901, Walker and his brother Henry joined forces with Max and Emma Weiner to create the Cannon-Weiner Elevator Company. (Courtesy of the Bates County Historical Society.)

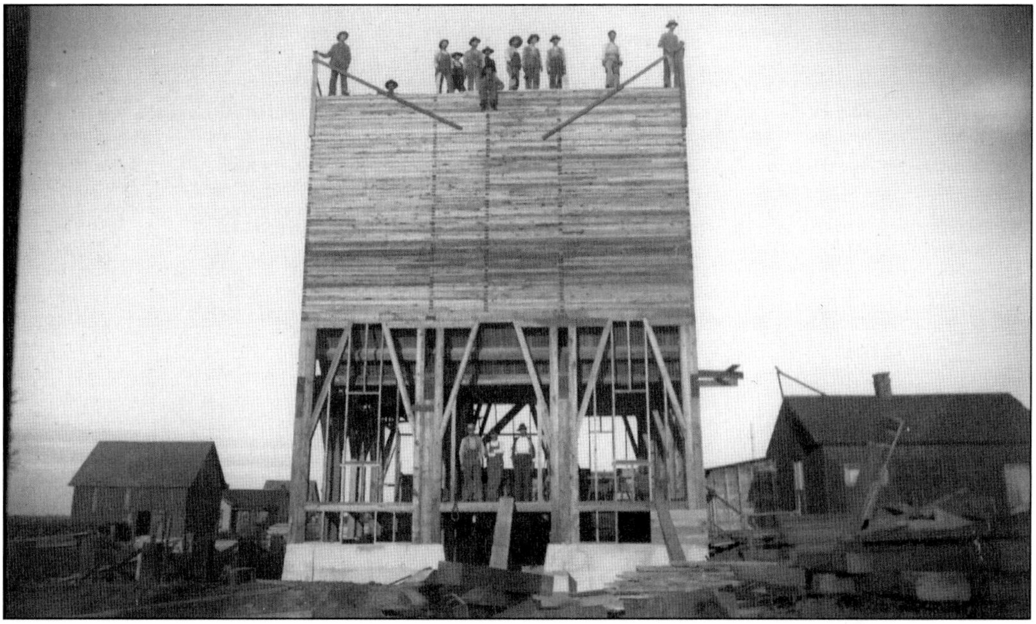

Work moves forward on the Walker Cannon grain elevator, built in 1899 and 1900. According to the inscription on the reverse of the photograph, during the course of this job, Cleve Stotts fell 75 feet from the top of the structure and survived, although he was crippled for life. (Courtesy of the Bates County Historical Society.)

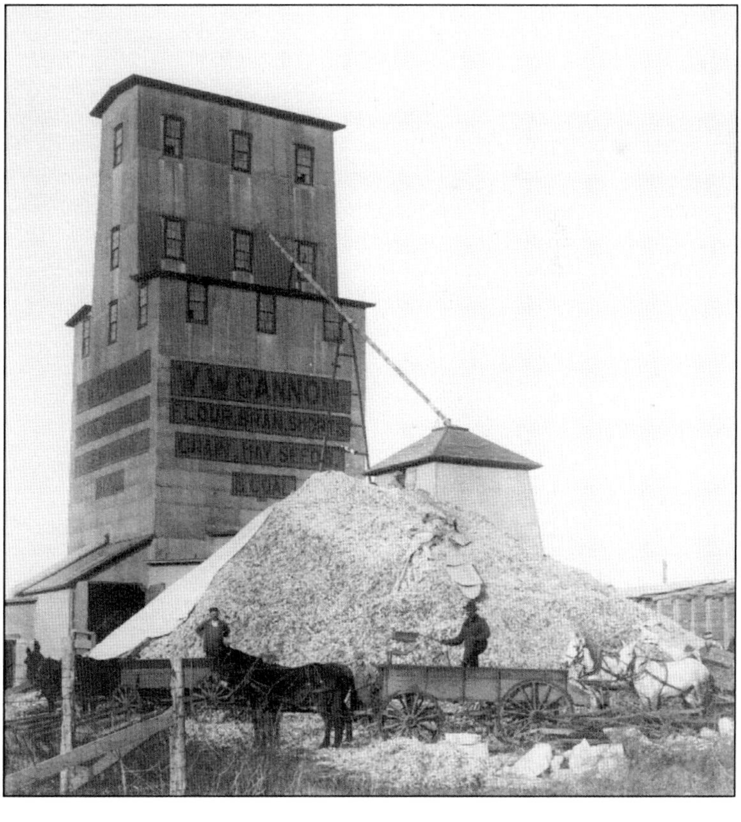

In an agricultural economy, he who owns the grain elevator is king. He is also, apparently, liable. The Cannons and Weiners discovered this in 1906 when a dispute with Edward Boswell over a timothy seed contract (in which Boswell claimed he had been paid $68.15 less than originally stipulated) took them all the way to the Kansas City Court of Appeals. (Courtesy of the Bates County Historical Society.)

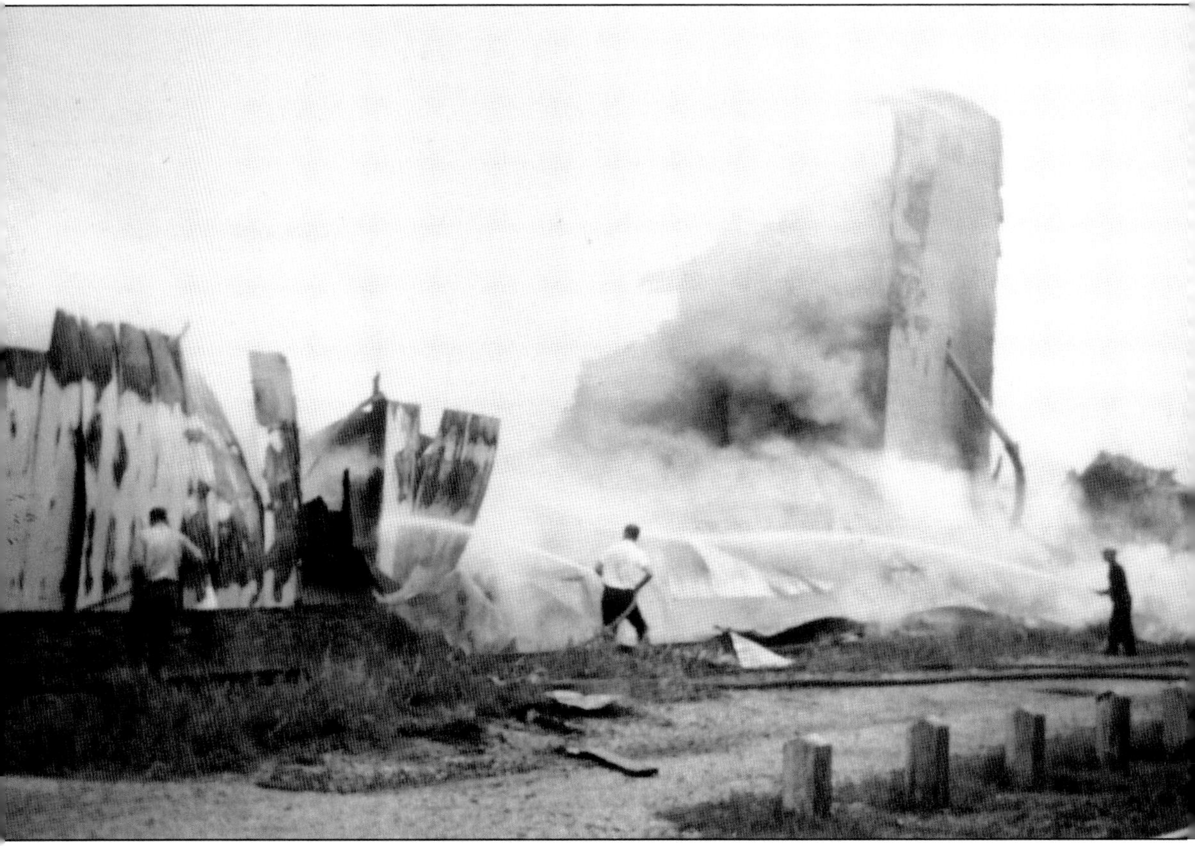

Elevators are also prone to explosions due to the high combustibility of flour and grain dust. In 1958, fire broke out at Arnold Elevator Mills, and the Butler Fire Department rushed to the rescue, but to no avail. There was no stopping the flames, and the business was completely destroyed. (Courtesy of the Bates County Historical Society and the Eddie Herrman Collection.)

Four

FOR GOD AND COUNTRY

Two statues stand on the lawn of the courthouse in Butler. On the northeast corner is the Doughboy, the county's World War I memorial, which celebrates the sacrifices made by the area's sons across the sea in Europe. In the center of the north side of the square, the 1st Kansas Colored Volunteer waits, poised eternally for battle, a timeless reminder of courage shown in the face of overwhelming odds. Together, these monuments are an apt symbol of the county's place in the history of national conflict: from the Civil War to the Spanish American War to the War on Terror, Bates County men and women have shown themselves willing, time and again, to go into harm's way in the interests of their fellow citizens and the greater good. Patriotism has never been just a word here. It has been a way of life.

Along with an abiding love of country, the people of Butler and of Bates County have shared a love of learning. Although photographs are difficult to locate, it must be noted that Butler was once a college town. From 1874 to 1900, the Butler Academy, supported entirely by public patronage, offered a local opportunity to pursue higher education. Public education also abounded, and after the Civil War, new schoolhouses sprang up like weeds out of the prairies of Bates County. Butler itself at one time had four—the three cardinal schools (West, East, and North) and Douglass School, which, prior to desegregation, offered a primary education to the community's black students.

Once upon a time, a newspaper article remarked on the number of high-quality schools in Butler and on its profusion of houses of worship, all of which combined to showcase "the high moral and intellectual character of the place." Affiliation with and participation in local congregations has been historically of great importance to the people of Butler and of Bates County as a whole. Perhaps this is to be expected of the seat of a county whose first settlers were missionaries.

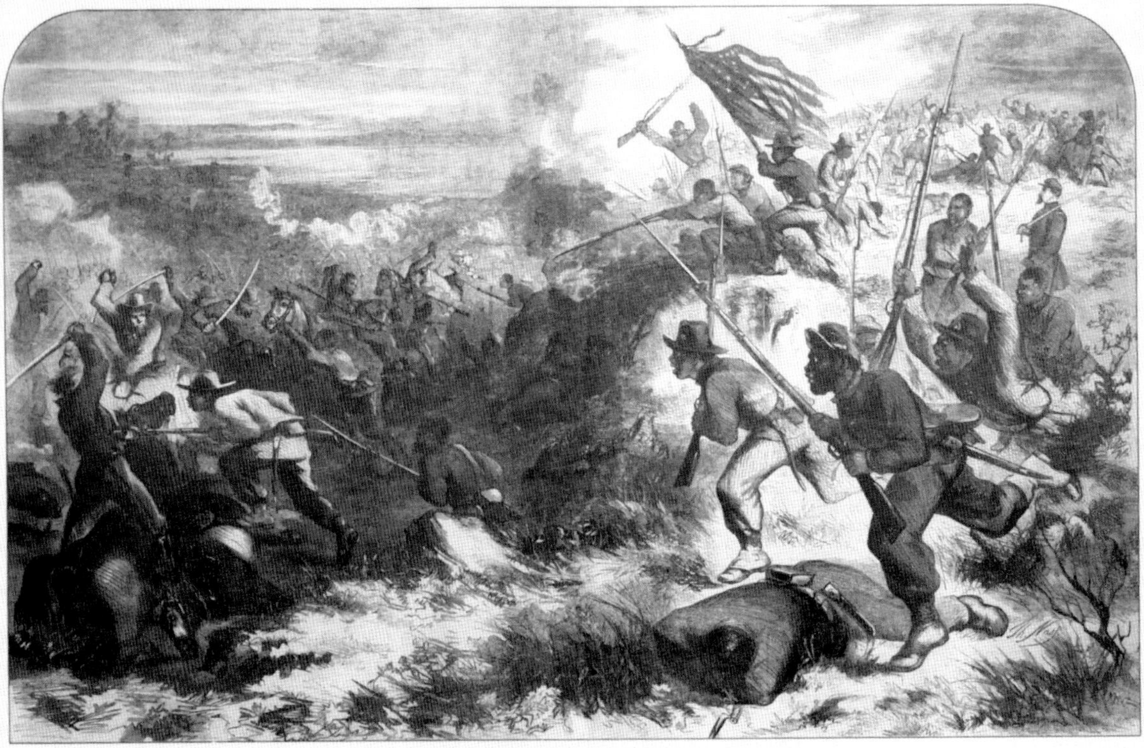

On October 29, 1862, on a hill several miles southwest of Butler called Island Mound, 25 soldiers of the 1st Kansas Colored Volunteer Infantry turned to face a much larger force of Confederate cavalrymen, exploding into history as the first battle-tested African American regiment in the United States. Commanded by Col. Henry Seaman and positioned behind ad hoc fortifications on the John Toothman farm—also known as Fort Africa—the 1st Kansas looked out at noon to see grass fires set by the advancing troops of Jeremiah Cockrell sweeping toward their base. The first unit dispatched disappeared into the smoke; the second, under Joseph Gardner, pursued the enemy against orders and was stranded far from the main Union force. Gardner retreated, setting fires as he went, but was cornered on the south slope of Island Mound. He fell wounded, but his men held fast, allowing reinforcements to arrive and disperse the enemy and inflicting on the Confederates three times the damage that they themselves sustained. They fought like tigers, and they won. (Courtesy of the Bates County Historical Society.)

Sculpted by Joel Randall, the 1st Kansas Colored Volunteer Infantry statue, honoring the soldiers who fought in the Battle of Island Mound, was dedicated by Butler's Amen Society in 2008. Mildred and Walter Wright, members of the society, recall a decade's struggle planning and raising funds, but they are proud of the end result. It has, they believe, helped put Butler back on the map. (Photograph by Vance Woods.)

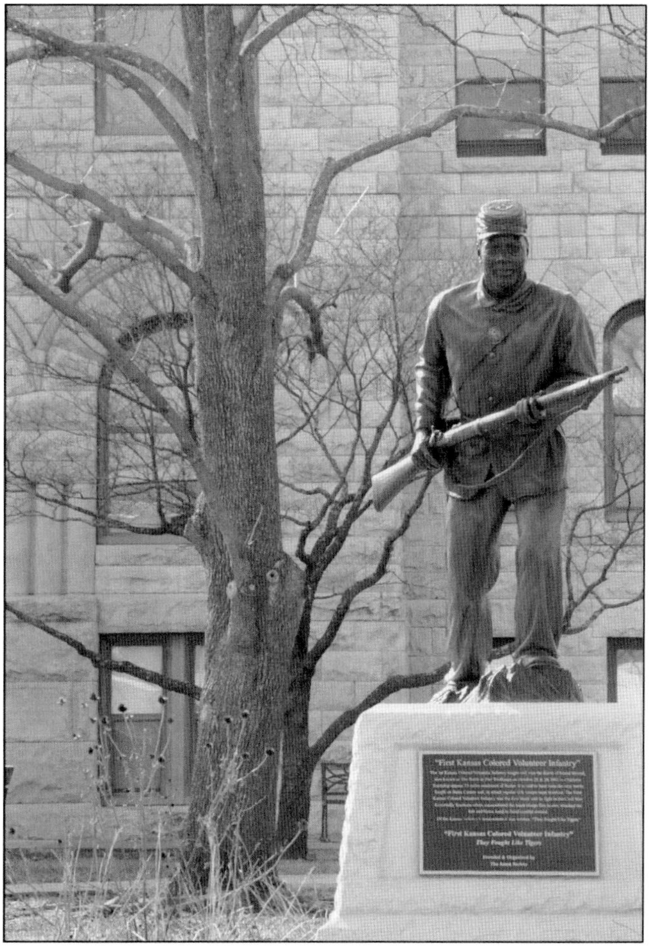

"To hell with Spain, and remember the Maine!" This 1931 parade float memorializes the 33rd anniversary of the explosion of the USS *Maine* in Cuba, reminding spectators of the Bates County boys who heeded the call of duty during the Spanish American War. The estimated number of locals who enlisted is 109. (Courtesy of the Bates County Historical Society and the Eddie Herrman Collection.)

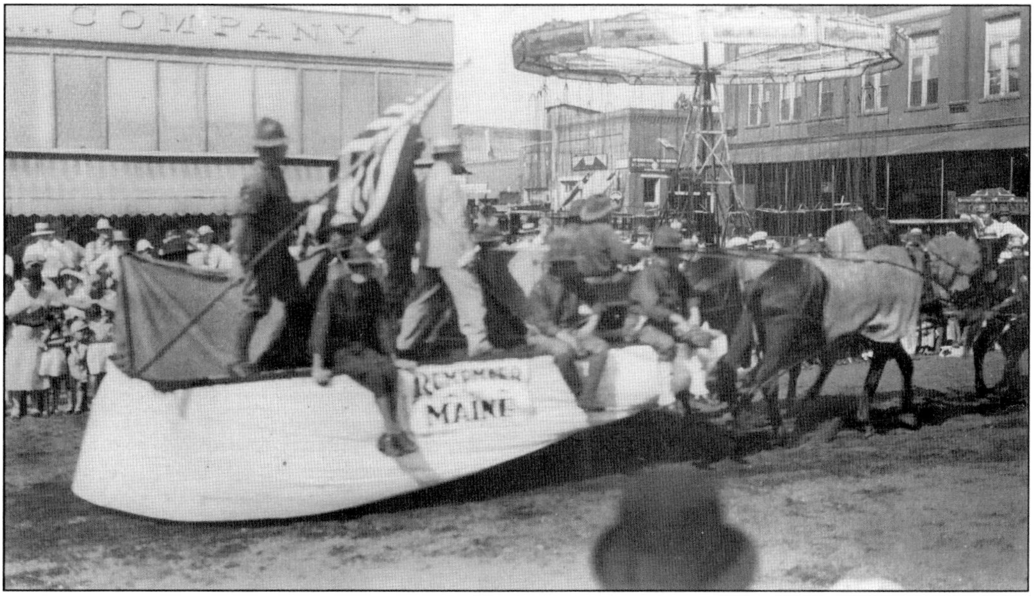

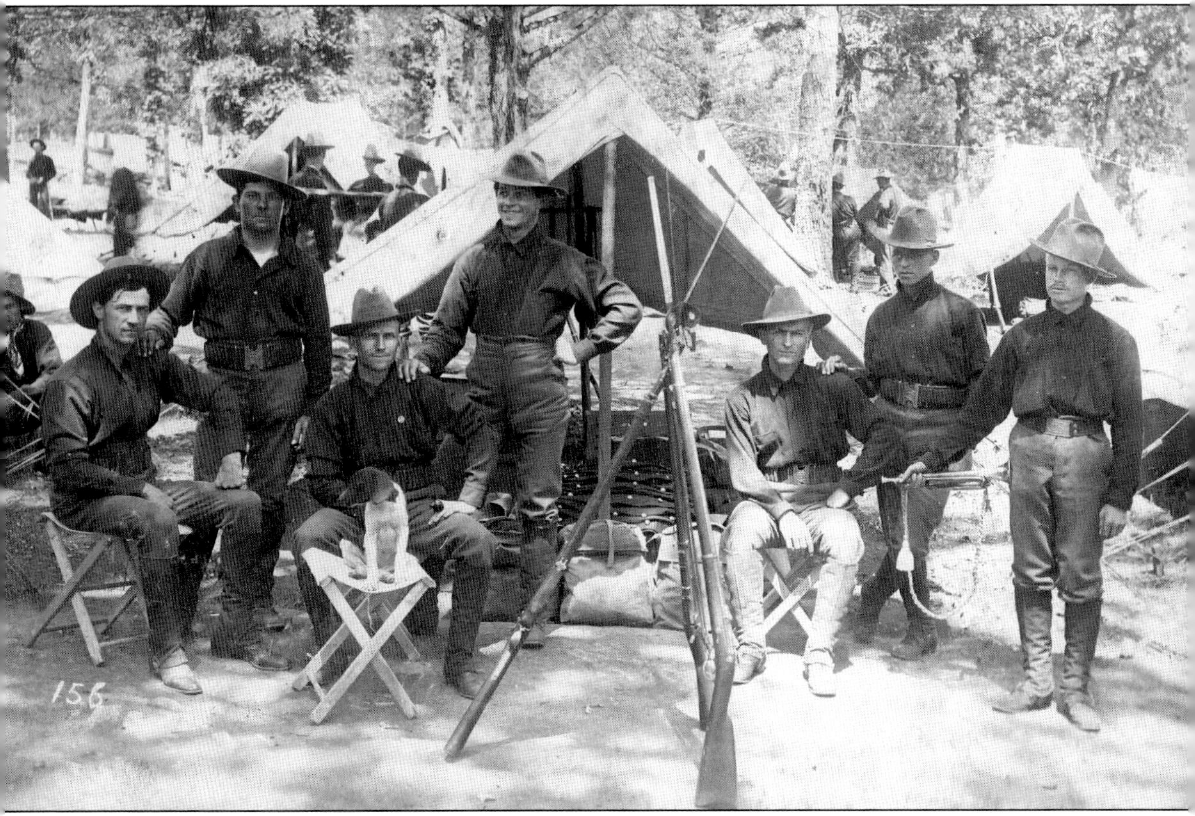

Relaxing at Camp Thomas in Georgia in 1898 (with the camp mascot), these Bates County boys are, from left to right, Mark Graves, Charles Clardy, John Tuttle, Walker Cannon, George Caruthers, Frank White, Fred Hartwell, and Billy Cobb. Members—except for Tuttle—of Company B, 2nd Missouri Volunteer Infantry, they fought mosquitoes and boredom rather than Spaniards during the Spanish American War, though they were willing. (Courtesy of the Bates County Historical Society.)

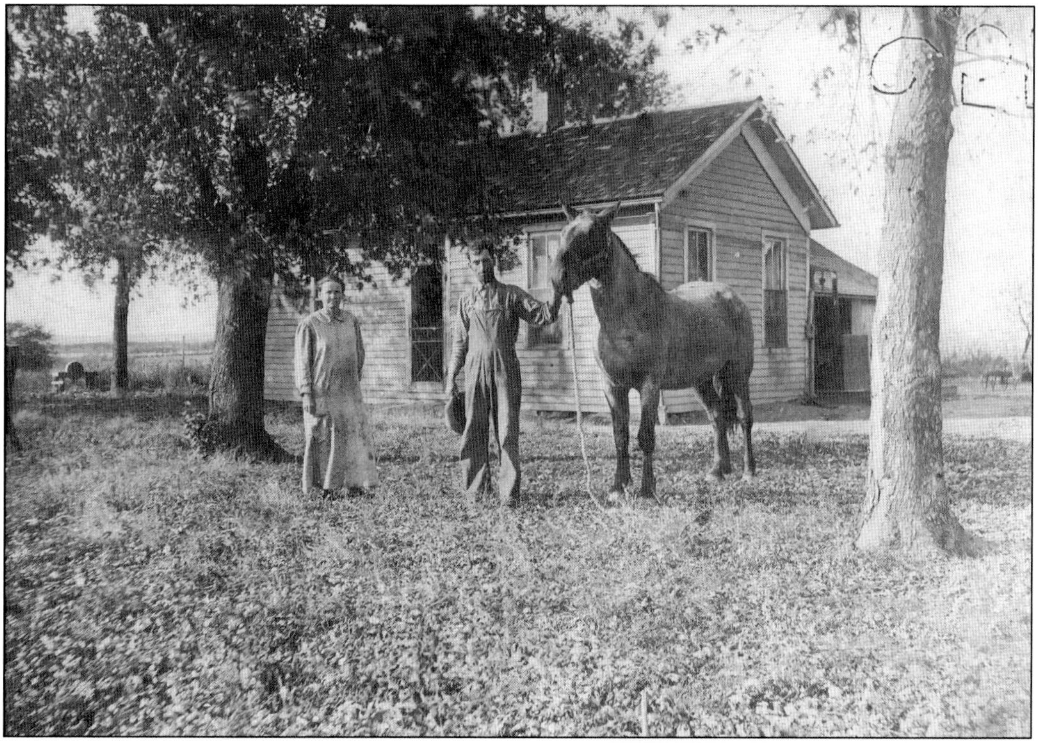

An army photographer captured this image of Mr. and Mrs. Zwahlen of Passaic with their horse Rex, who was sold by his owners for $200 for service in France during World War I. Knowing the horrors the animal likely faced in battle, Mr. Zwahlen always regretted the decision. For her part, Mrs. Zwahlen always regretted not donning a fancier dress for the camera. (Courtesy of the Bates County Historical Society.)

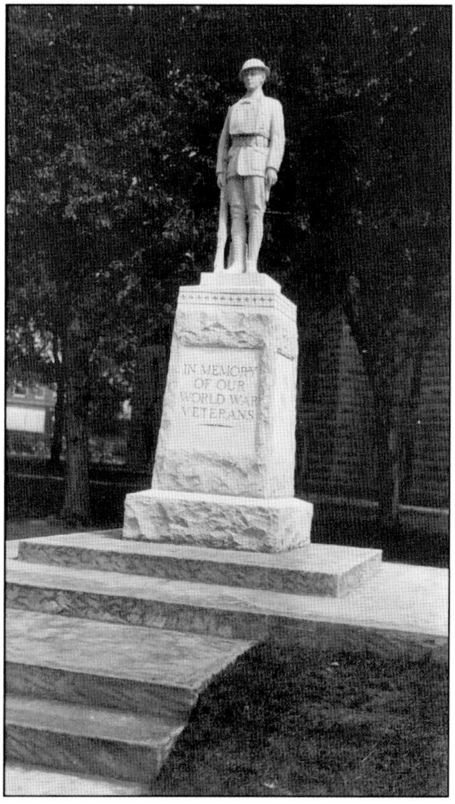

The Doughboy, Bates County's World War I memorial, stands at the northwest corner of the Butler square. Dedicated on Memorial Day 1927 before one of the largest crowds the town had ever hosted, the Doughboy resulted from a 1919 Missouri state grant encouraging counties to undertake commemorative projects. Veteran W.O. Jackson posed for the statue; Kling Monuments created it. (Courtesy of the Bates County Historical Society.)

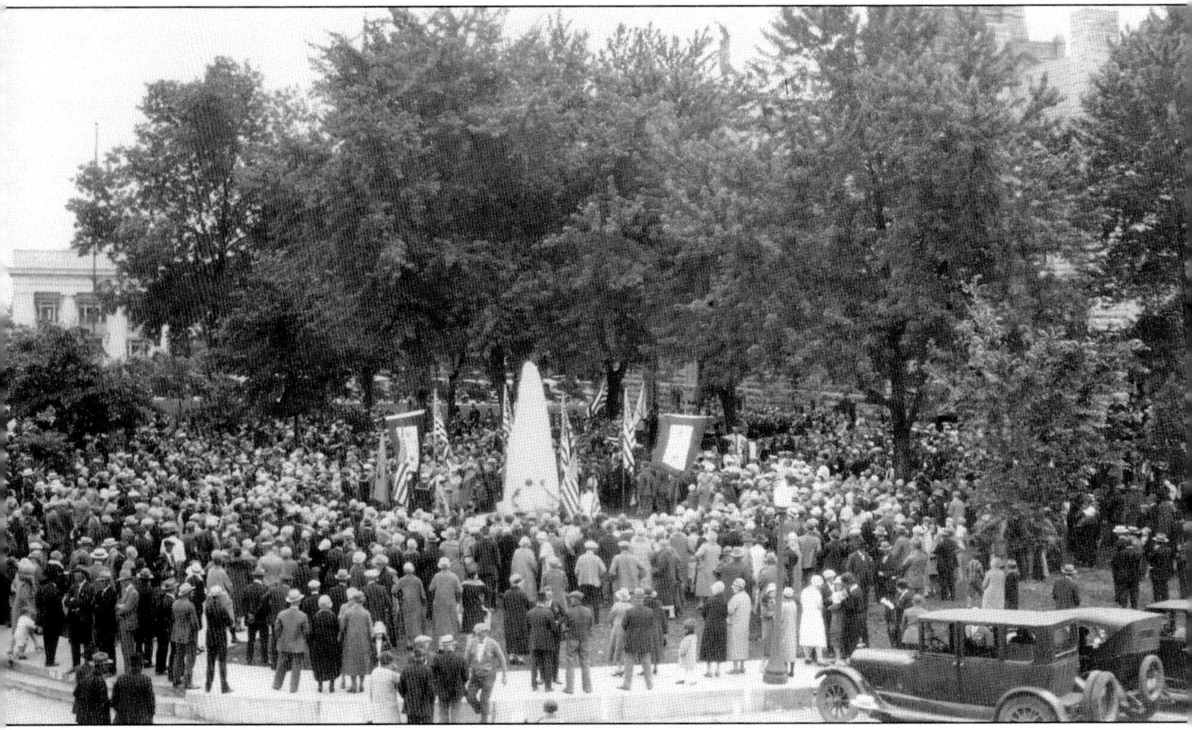

The Doughboy's dedication ceremony was grand, featuring a color guard parade and a speech by Maj. Harry Castlen, state commander of the American Legion. Seven-year-old Peggy Armstrong pulled the cord, unveiling the memorial. Fisk's Theatre even screened a film of the proceedings free of charge the following weekend. (Courtesy of the Bates County Historical Society and the Eddie Herrman Collection.)

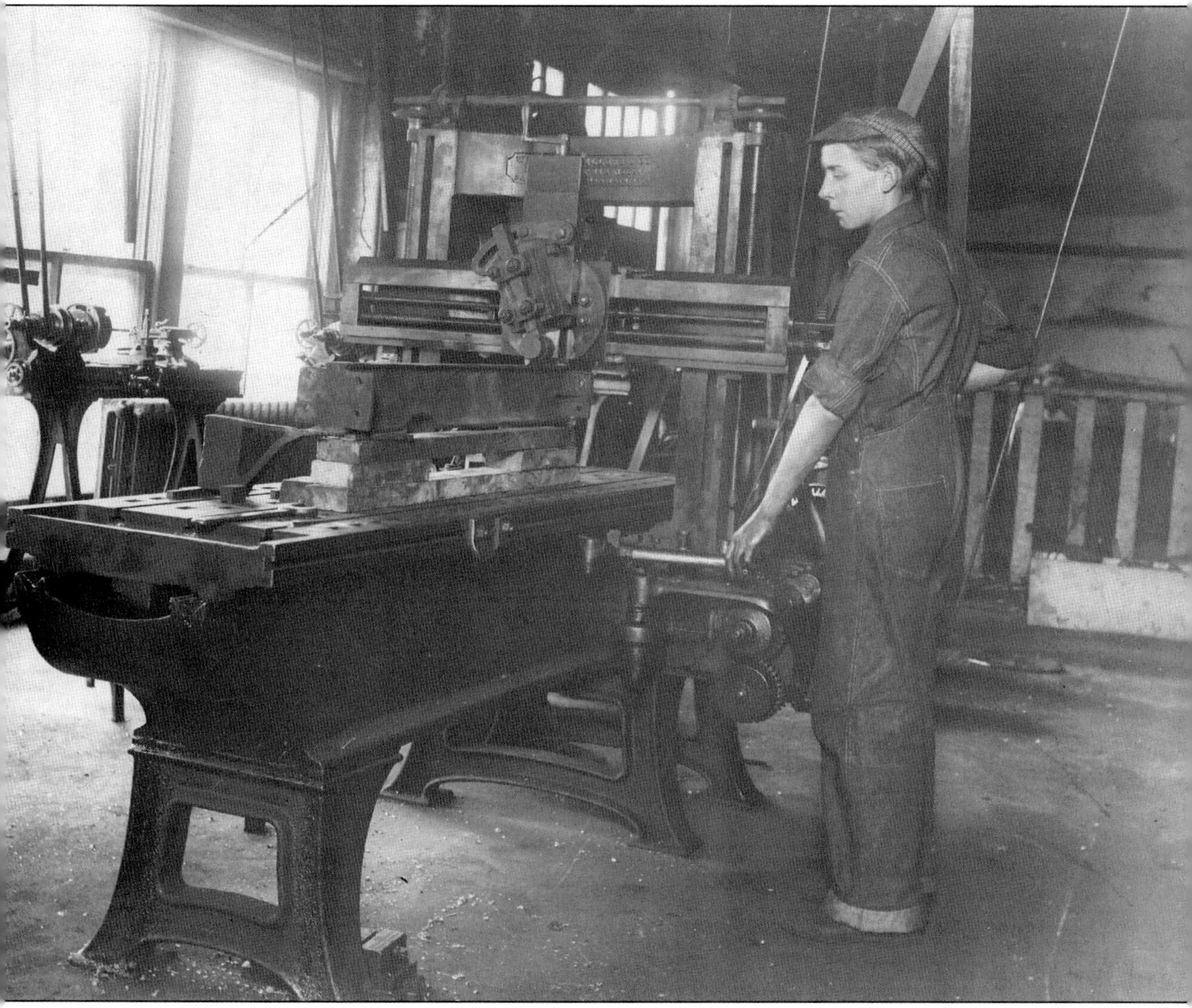

Cloyde Dixon concentrates on his work at Dixon's Furniture and Stoves. Dixon, with a number of other Butler men, served in Company B, 1st and 2nd Infantry Brigades, Missouri National Guard. Inducted into federal service in 1917, his division shipped out to France in May 1918. One year later, Dixon came home. Many of his fellow servicemen did not. (Courtesy of the Bates County Historical Society and the Eddie Herrman Collection.)

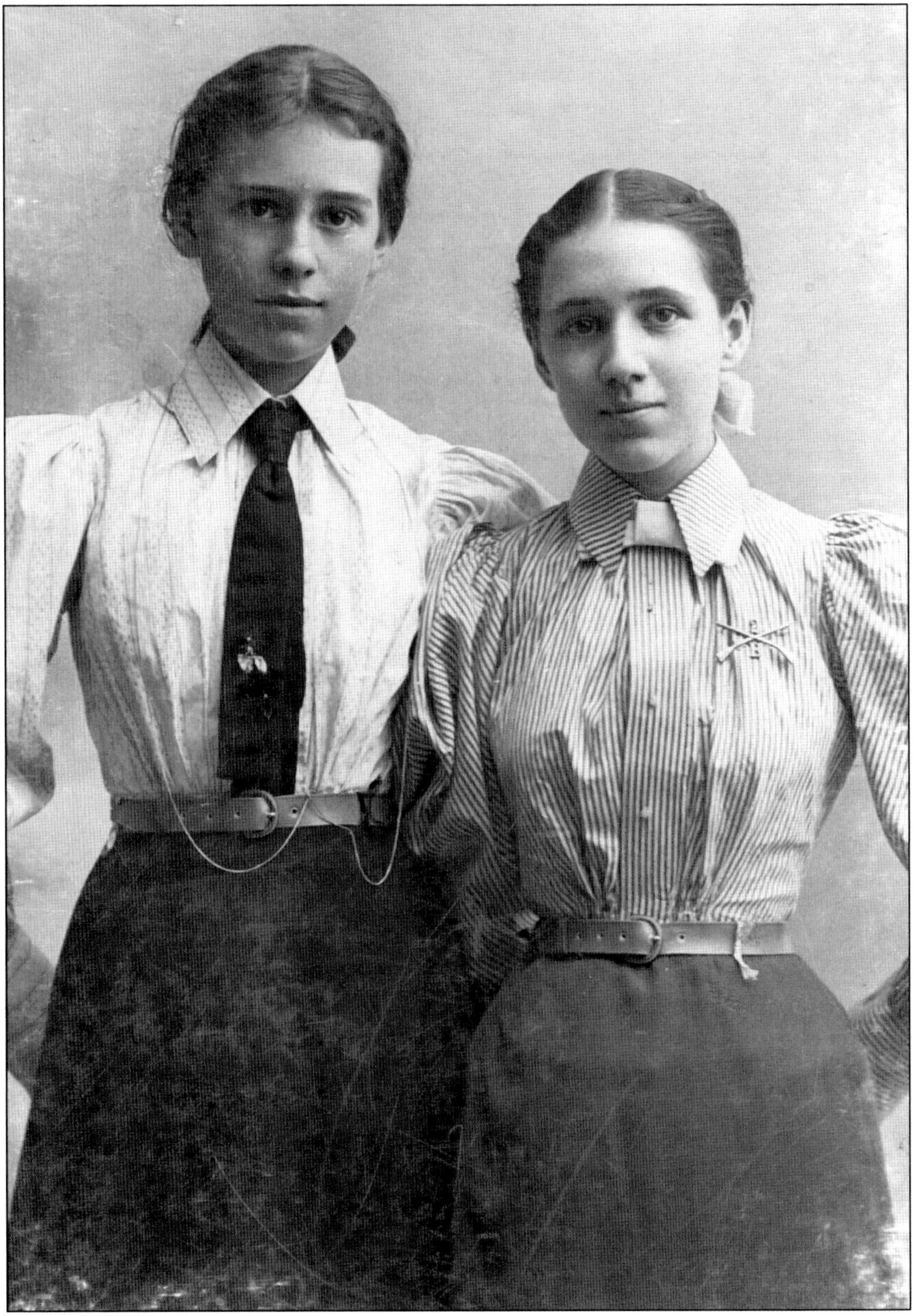

Toots Hannah (left) married a war hero. Her husband, Edward DeArmond, was stationed in France during World War I. He became chief of staff to the 32nd Division of the US Army in 1917 and was promoted to brigadier general at age 40. In 1922, he was awarded the Army Distinguished Service Medal for his outstanding contributions to field artillery training. (Courtesy of the Bates County Historical Society.)

In 1942, Earl Erickson (right) was sent to the Army Air Service Technical Training Command, Chanute Field, Illinois. Erickson was drafted at 32 and spent World War II hopping from one base in the United States to another, family in tow. Daughter Lucille remembers the confusion of last-minute assignment changes, unforeseen moves, and instructions to meet up at the next stop if anything went sideways. (Courtesy of Lucille Lindsay.)

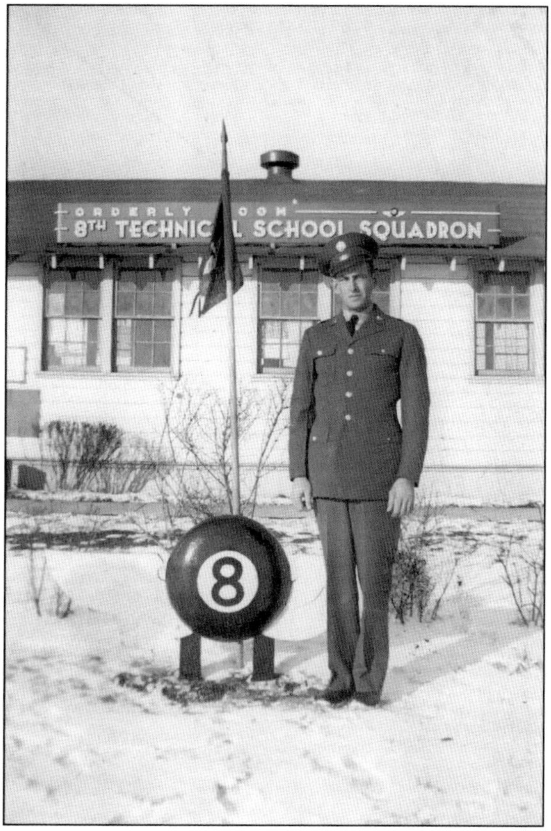

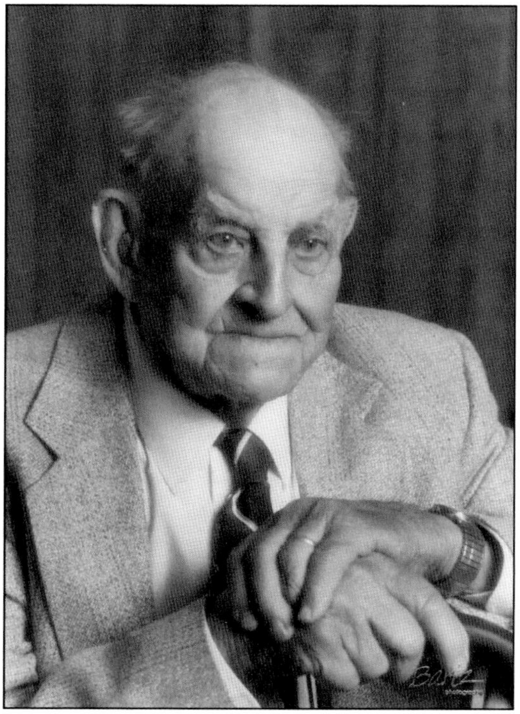

A radio technician, Erickson (pictured here at age 93) spent his days crouched inside aircraft cockpits. He always liked to say he had been in hundreds of planes and had never once left the ground. (Photograph by Bartz Photography, courtesy of Lucille Lindsay.)

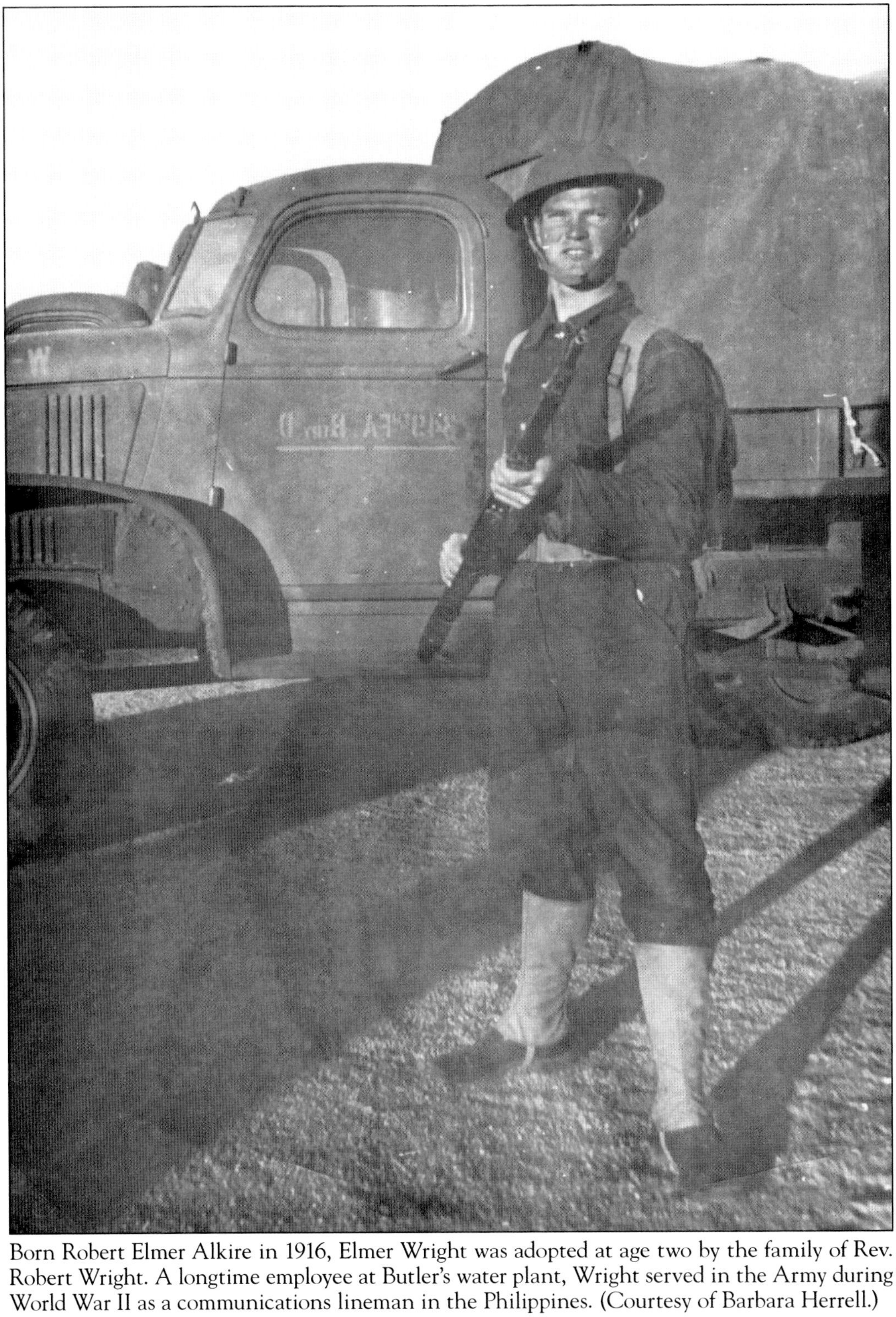

Born Robert Elmer Alkire in 1916, Elmer Wright was adopted at age two by the family of Rev. Robert Wright. A longtime employee at Butler's water plant, Wright served in the Army during World War II as a communications lineman in the Philippines. (Courtesy of Barbara Herrell.)

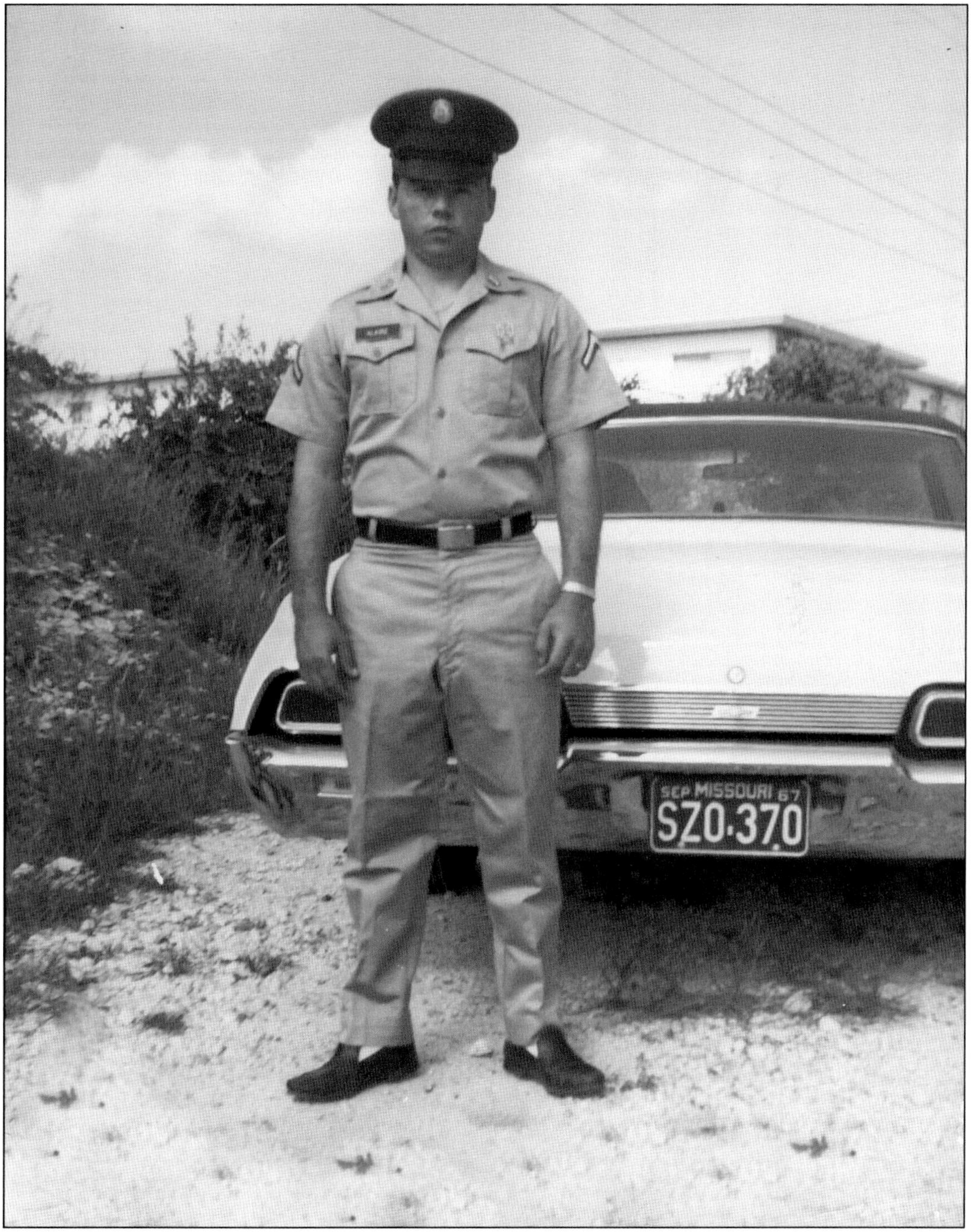

Dave Alkire spent a short time in the Army during the Vietnam War. He did his basic training at Fort Leonard Wood in southern Missouri and was stationed briefly at Fort Hood in Killeen, Texas. Being the only son of a fully disabled veteran—his father's leg was severely damaged by a grenade during World War II—he was required by law to forgo further service. (Courtesy of Barbara Herrell.)

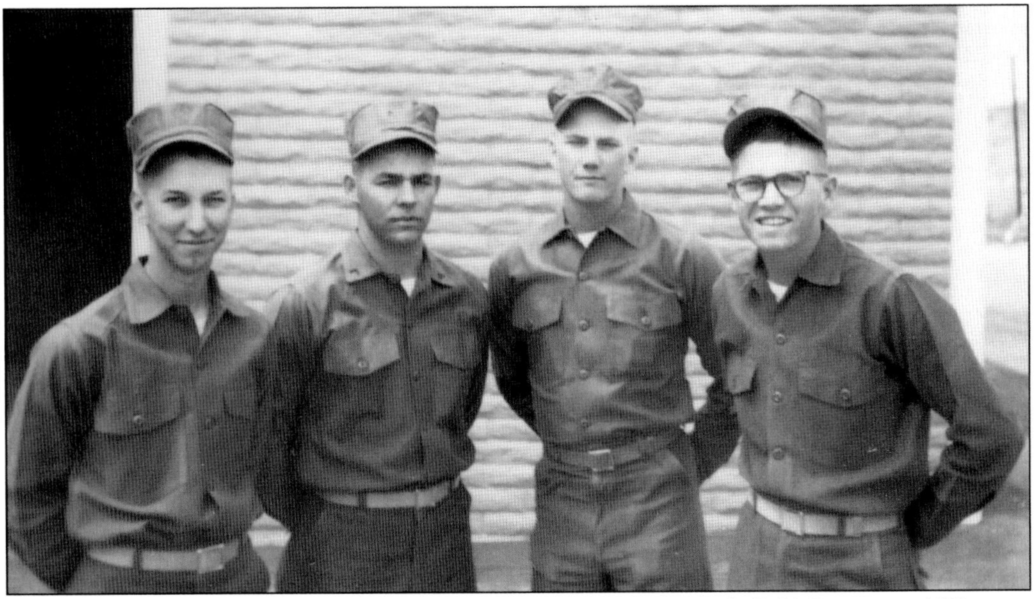

Jim Wackerman (second from left) poses with fellow marines Kapowich (left), Rector, and Wagoner (right) during a six-week stint with the Infantry Training Division at Camp Pendleton. A nine-month tour in Vietnam soon followed. Below, Corporal Wackerman (left), a driver in the 11th Motor Transport Battalion, Bravo Company, enjoys a few brews with pal Cpl. Randy Samples at the Enlisted Men's Club outside Da Nang. Once, while transporting a group of military engineers to the post exchange at Freedom Hill, Wackerman found himself in a sticky situation. While parking his vehicle, he accidentally ran over and crushed one of his passengers' feet. Wackerman was convinced he was headed for the stockade, until the soldier admitted he had stuck his foot under the wheel intentionally, having just been told he was not going home. (Both, courtesy of Vickie and Jim Wackerman.)

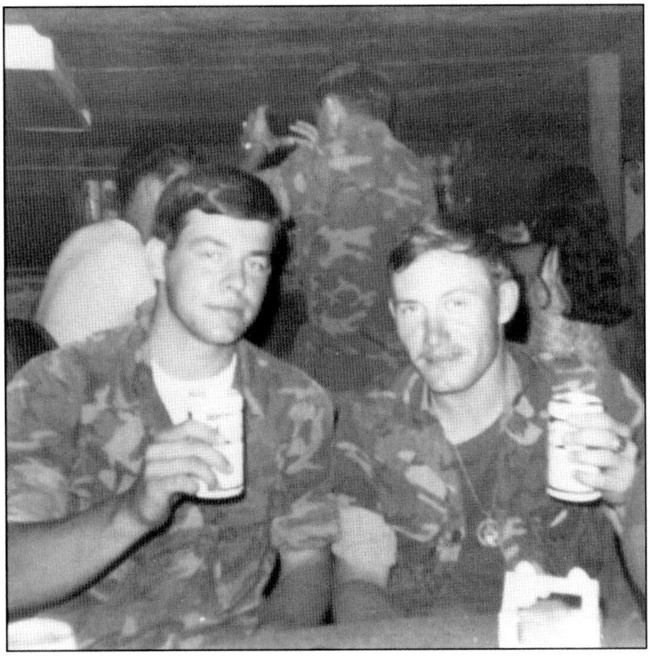

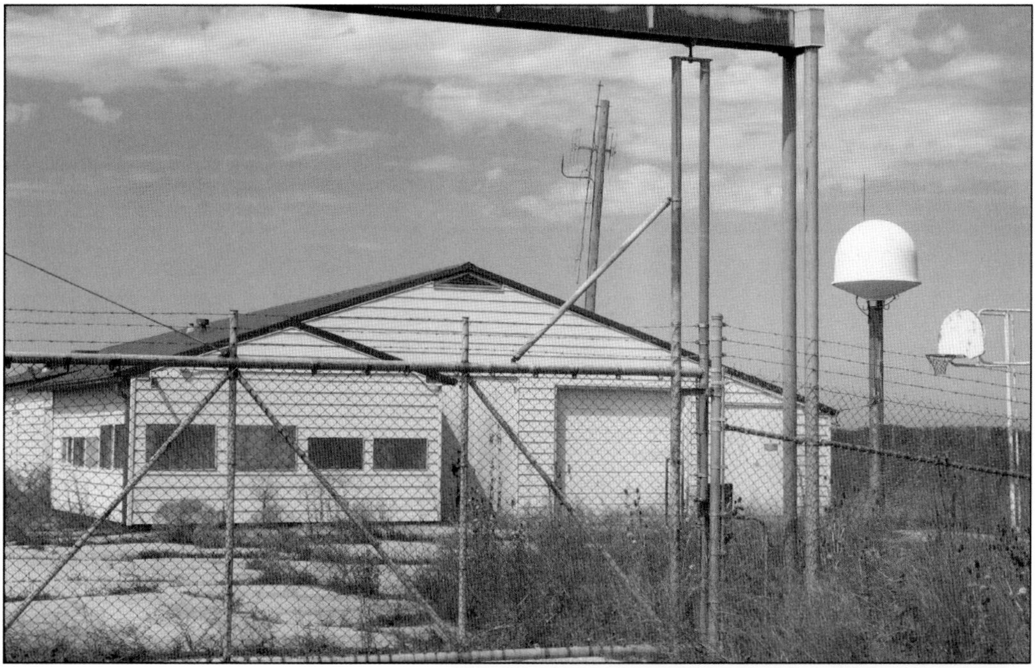

The dilapidated exterior of this small structure belies the role it once played in the history of Bates County and of the world. Now the property of Terry VanSandt, these are the remains of Launch Control Facility K-1. One of two in the county, K-1—or "George's," as personnel called it—sat at the heart of a flight of 10 Minuteman nuclear missiles scattered across the countryside in 90-foot underground silos. An arm of the 351st Strategic Missile Wing out of Whiteman Air Force Base, K-1 was active from the early 1960s to the mid-1990s. With these powerful weapons, plus seven more in eastern Bates County, aimed directly at the Soviet Union, locals were torn between pride at serving their country and uneasiness at the knowledge that any number of enemy rockets were likely pointed right back at them. (Photographs by Vance Woods.)

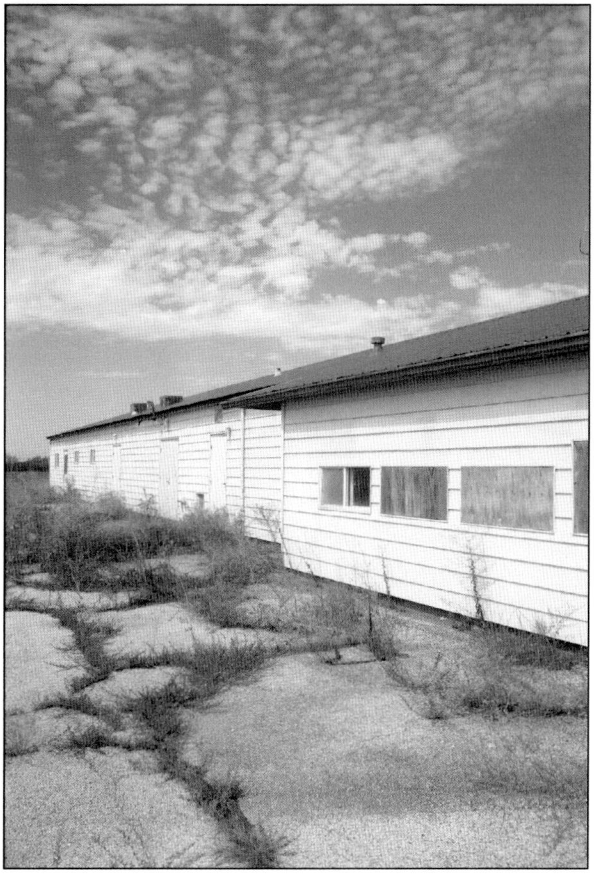

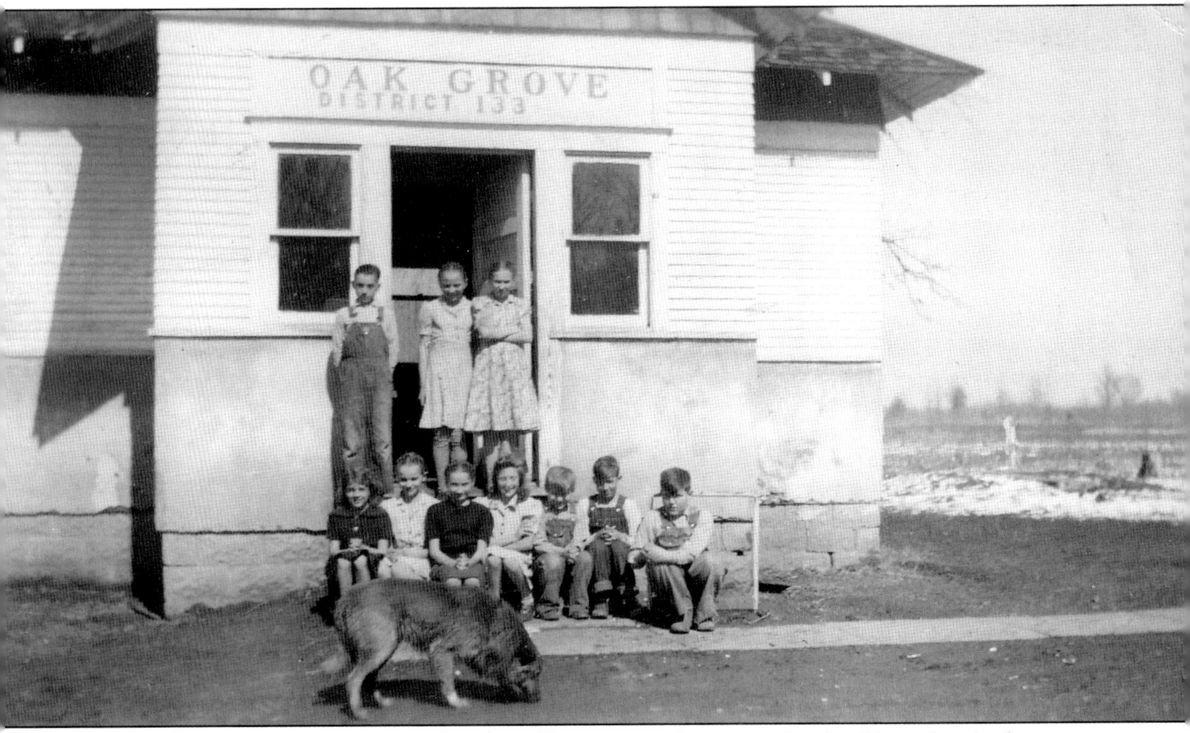

Oak Grove School, northeast of Rich Hill, was one of a network of public schools that sprang up throughout Bates County in the late 1860s. The county's school fund, supported by loans on real estate securities, survived the Civil War almost intact. This, plus rising postwar land values, provided for the construction of 40 to 50 new schoolhouses in 1867 and 1868. (Courtesy of the Durst family.)

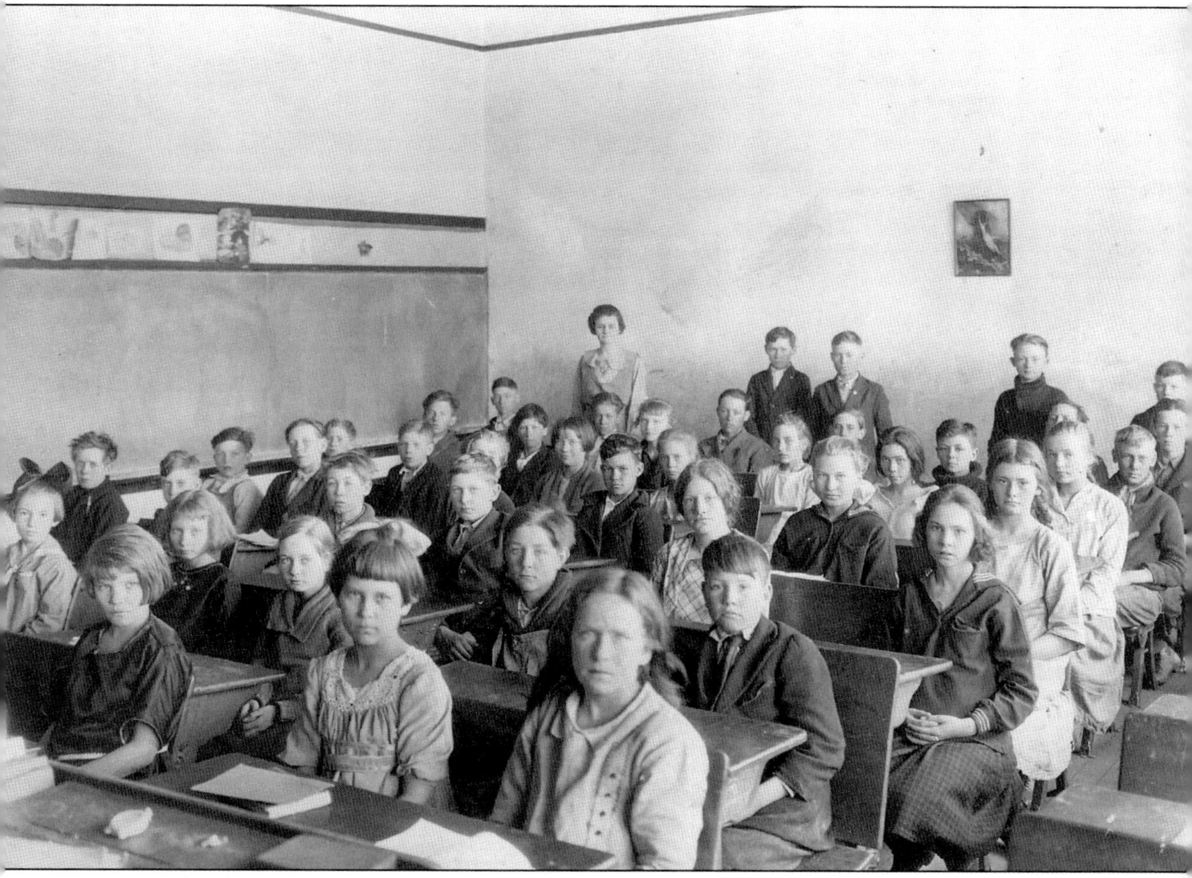

Bessie Taylor (standing at the back of the room) teaches her students in one of the numerous public schoolhouses that popped up in Bates County after the Civil War. In May 1869, a series of regular teachers' institutes began with a session at Butler's First Presbyterian, attended by 50 public schoolteachers. These, plus careful superintendency, ensured the excellence of Bates County's school system. (Courtesy of the Durst family.)

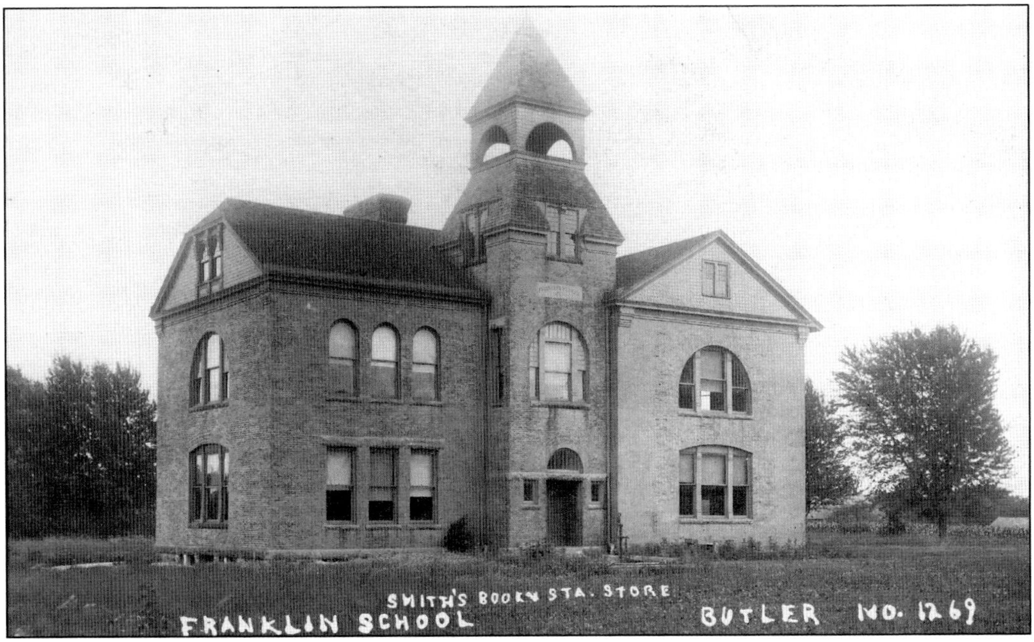

In the 1880s, the Franklin, or East, School and its students (below) were organized into four departments presided over by Prof. J.W. Reisner, Miss A. Walker, Ida Crume, and Miss E.A. Wade. A similar system was instituted at the West, or Washington, School, while Douglass School (the school for black students) was under the care of G.W. Lowry, who was by all reports an excellent teacher. Over them all reigned Principal J.F. Starr, who appears to have been a great fan of legible handwriting. Each student was required to submit three penmanship samples per year, which were then pasted together and posted for public perusal, a sort of trial by ink. (Both, courtesy of the Bates County Historical Society and the Eddie Herrman Collection.)

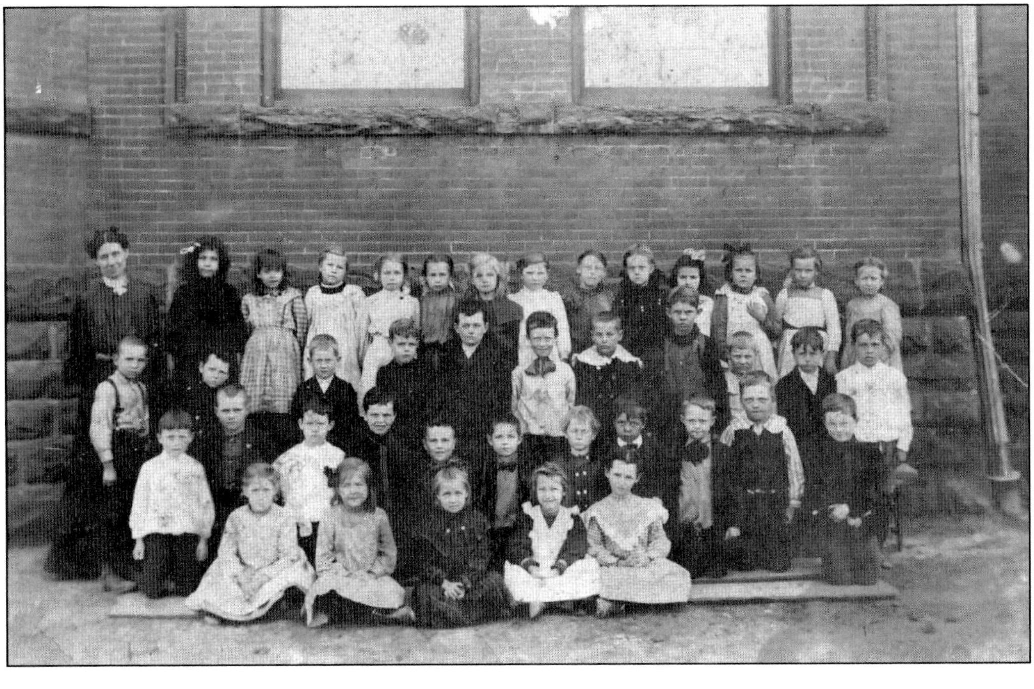

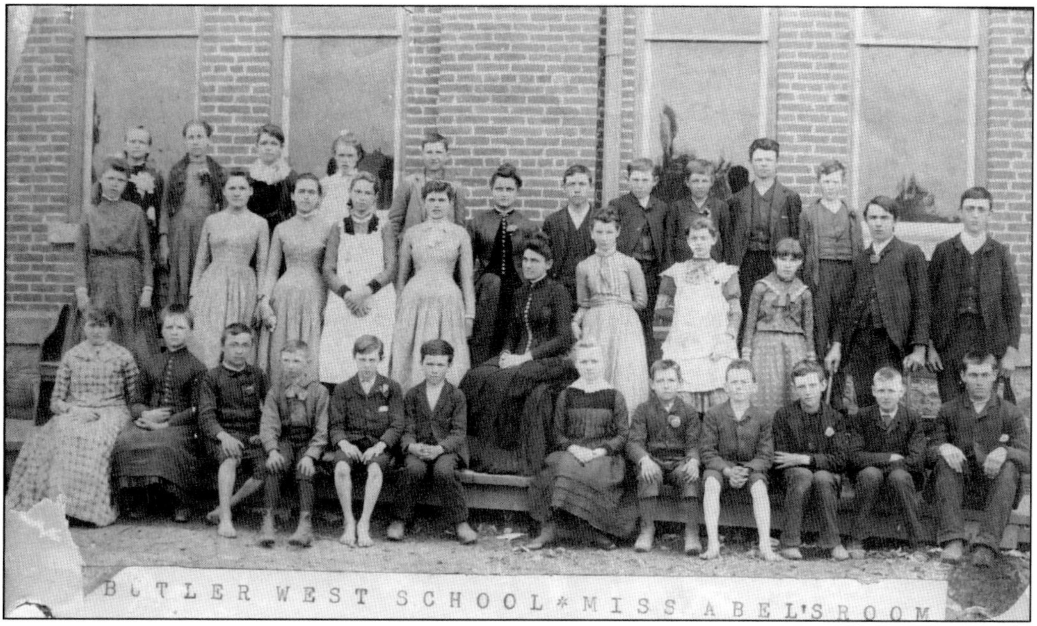

All American schoolchildren are familiar with the class portrait, and in 1889, Miss Abel's class lined up outside Washington School for theirs. Washington School stood at the head of Ohio Street on the spot formerly occupied by the first brick schoolhouse ever built in Bates County. It was erected in 1869 at a soaring cost of $8,000. (Courtesy of the Bates County Historical Society and the Eddie Herrman Collection.)

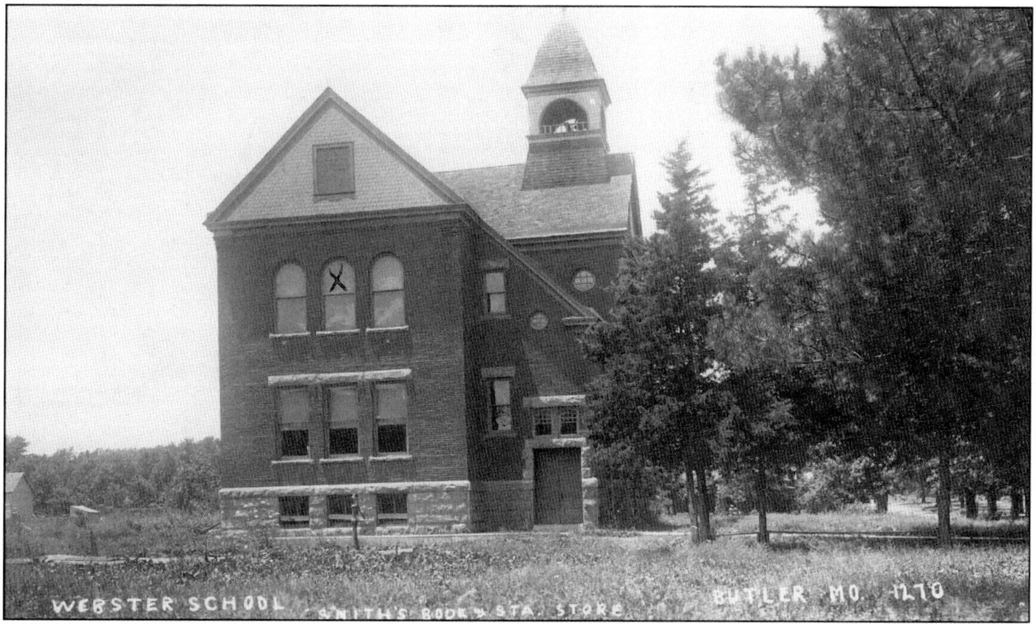

Dating from 1900, Webster School, also known as the North School, was the last of Butler's cardinal schools—West, East, and North—to be built. Now gone, it is memorialized by a stone marker at the intersection of Mill and Havanah Streets. Additionally, its former cornerstone has been incorporated into the sidewalk. (Courtesy of the Bates County Historical Society and the Eddie Herrman Collection.)

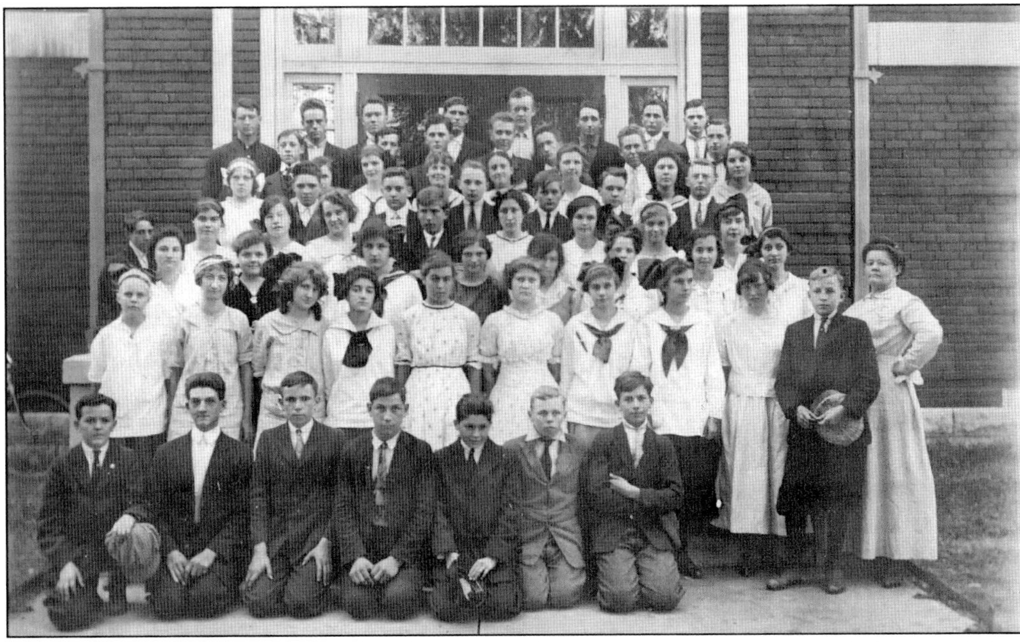

For many years, Butler's high school students shared a campus with one of the town's four elementary schools at the West, or Washington, School. In 1912, however, they were given their own space when a new high school opened at the corner of Pine and Havanah Streets. In 1915, the freshman class posed for this photograph. (Courtesy of the Bates County Historical Society and the Eddie Herrman Collection.)

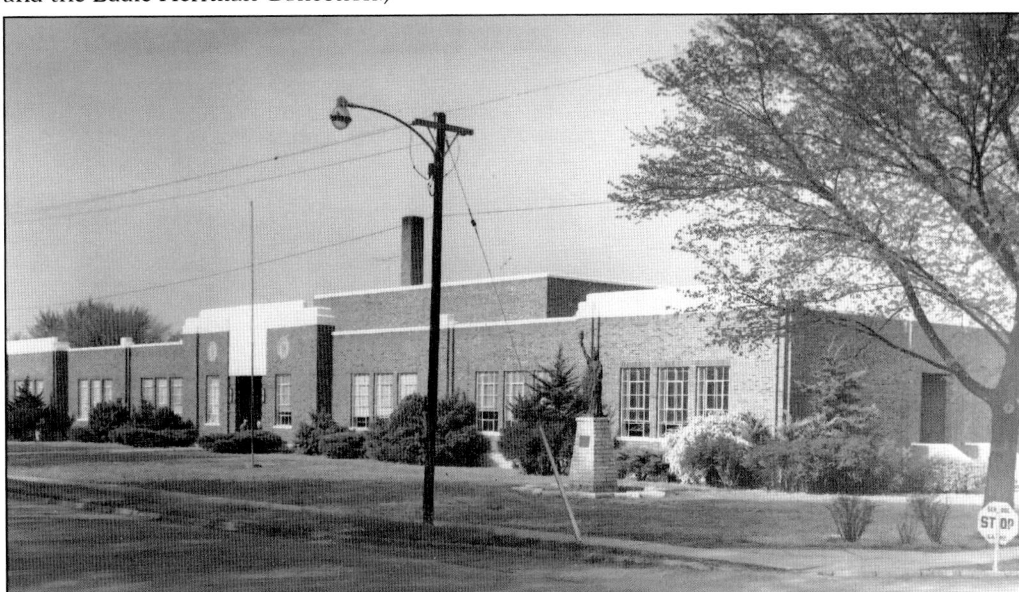

Butler's elementary school was completed in 1939. In front of the building stands a replica of the Statue of Liberty. Dedicated in 1951, it is one of 200 such facsimiles donated in the 1950s to communities throughout the United States and its territories as part of a Boy Scout initiative to remind America of the freedoms it enjoys. (Courtesy of the Bates County Historical Society and the Eddie Herrman Collection.)

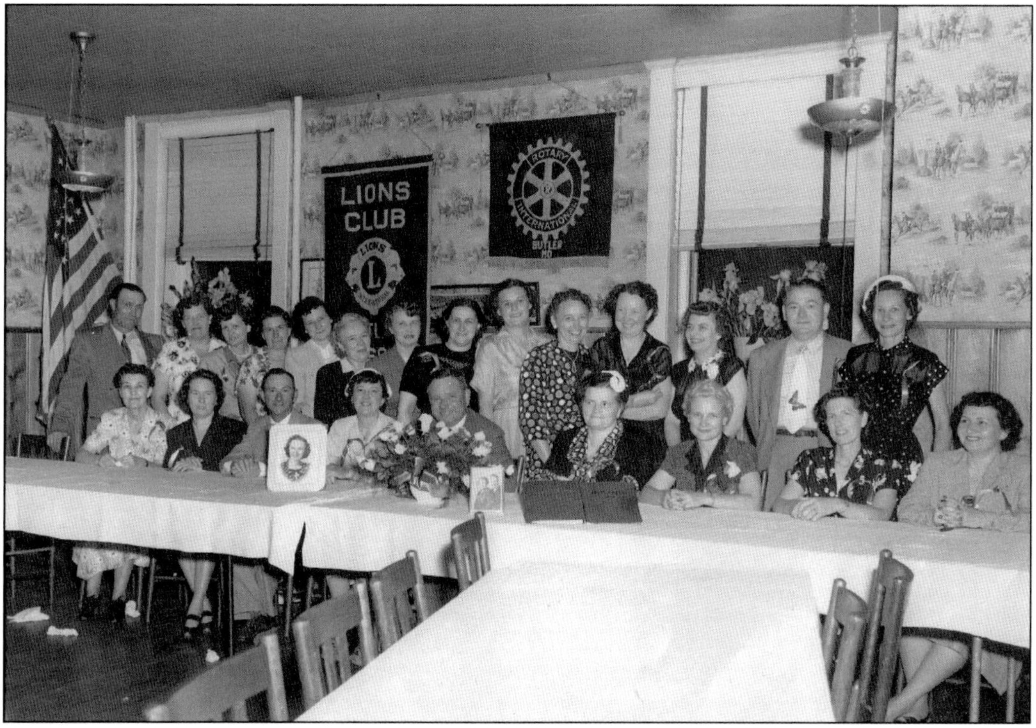

In 1951, the Butler High School class of 1926 gathered for their 25th reunion. The event was hosted by the alumni association, which was organized by the graduating class of 1888 at the home of the superintendent of schools J.F. Starr. (Courtesy of the Bates County Historical Society and the Eddie Herrman Collection.)

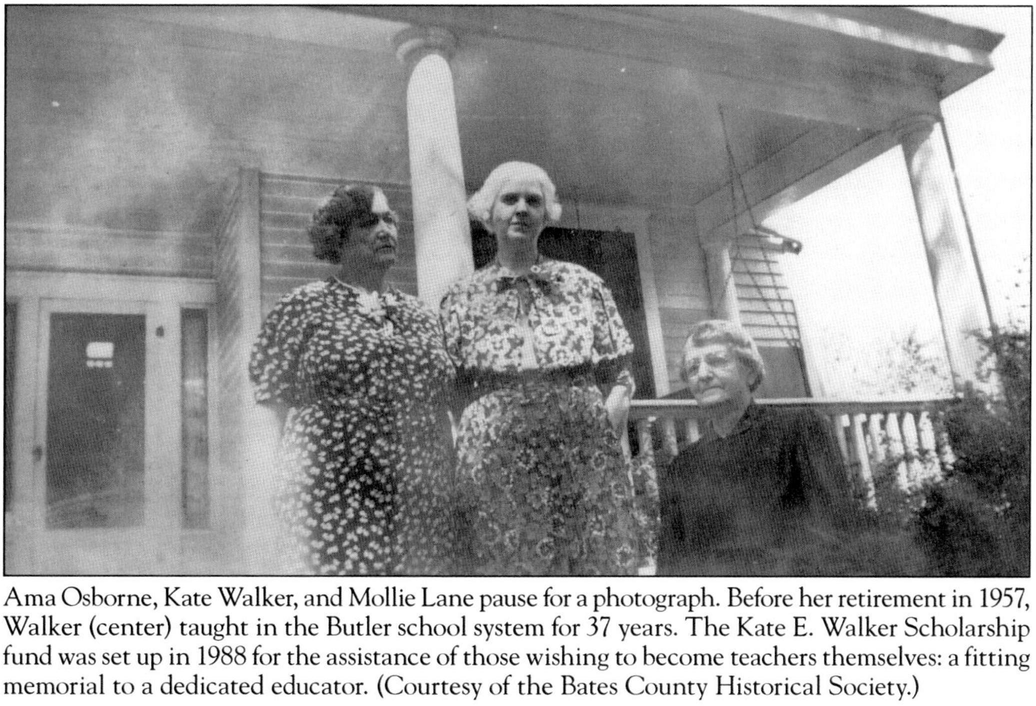

Ama Osborne, Kate Walker, and Mollie Lane pause for a photograph. Before her retirement in 1957, Walker (center) taught in the Butler school system for 37 years. The Kate E. Walker Scholarship fund was set up in 1988 for the assistance of those wishing to become teachers themselves: a fitting memorial to a dedicated educator. (Courtesy of the Bates County Historical Society.)

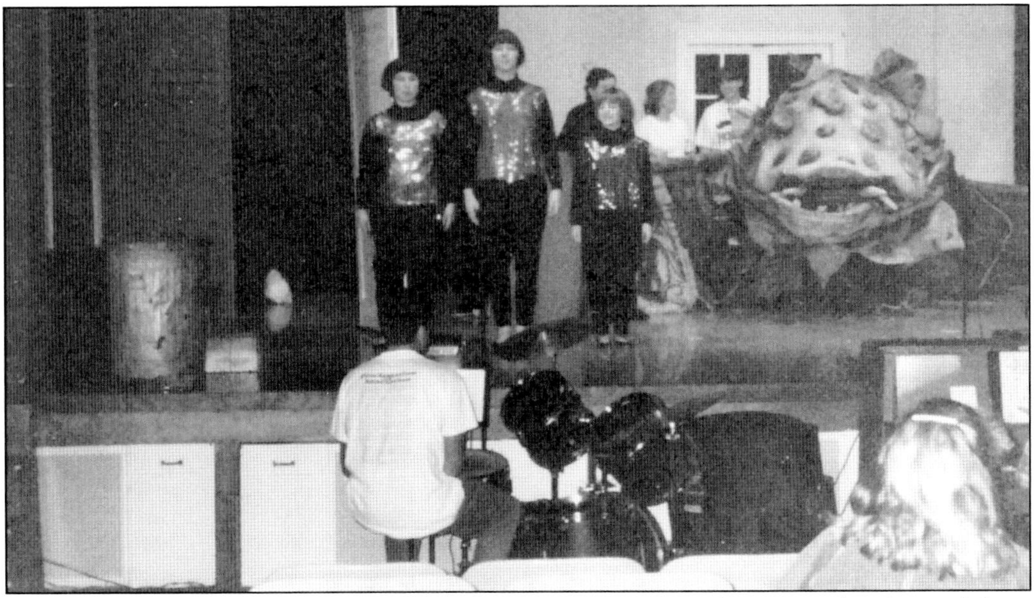

Butler High School stages two plays a year. From 1976 to 1998, Alan J. Mundey directed these shows. In this photograph from a November 1995 dress rehearsal of *Little Shop of Horrors*, the street urchin Greek chorus includes, from left to right, Heather Rogers, Jammie Sanders, and Tammy Herrell; also visible are Jesse Schowengerdt (on the drums) and a hungry-looking flytrap. (Courtesy of Barbara Herrell.)

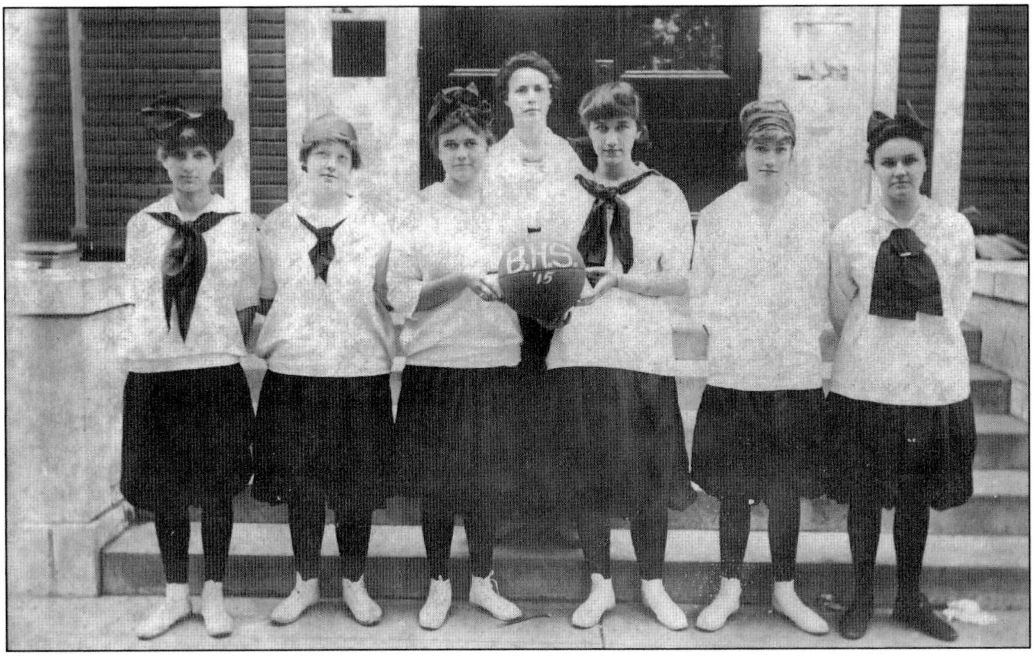

The 1915 Butler High ladies' basketball team shows off the game ball outside the new high school. At that time, the high school did not have a gymnasium, so the girls played in the basement of the Southern Methodist Church. This is just one of many examples of ways in which local congregations have integrated themselves into Butler's community life. (Courtesy of the Bates County Historical Society and the Eddie Herrman Collection.)

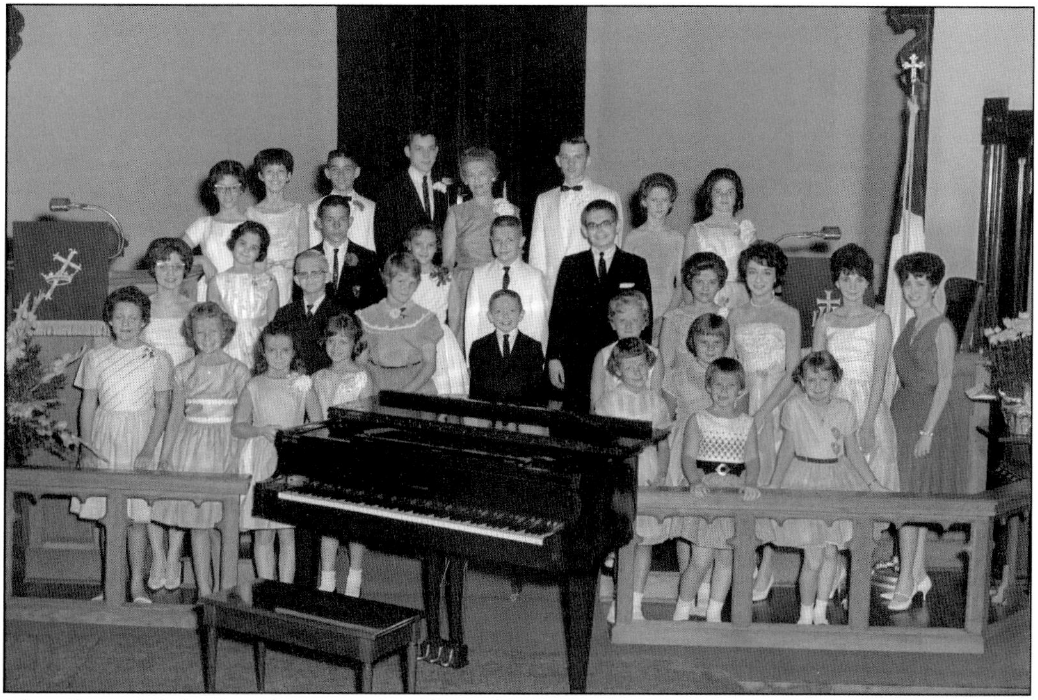

Ohio Street Methodist also opened its doors for use by the Butler community. In the 1950s and 1960s, local piano teacher Agnes Cox (center, rear) held her students' annual recital in Ohio Street's sanctuary. In more recent years, another local teacher, Ruth Weil, has continued this tradition. (Courtesy of the Durst family.)

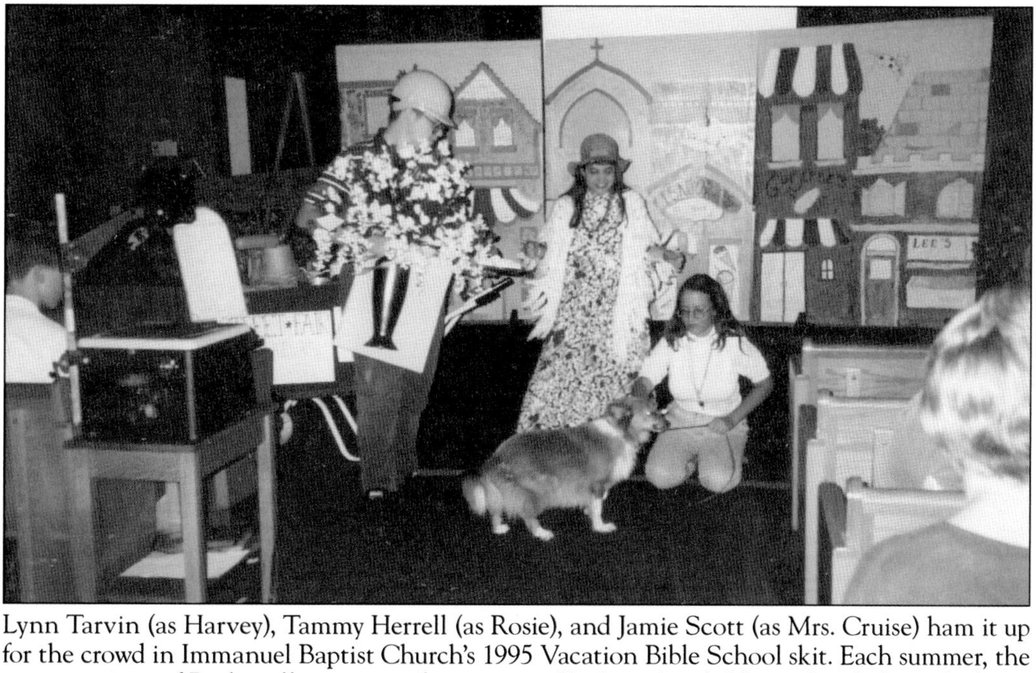

Lynn Tarvin (as Harvey), Tammy Herrell (as Rosie), and Jamie Scott (as Mrs. Cruise) ham it up for the crowd in Immanuel Baptist Church's 1995 Vacation Bible School skit. Each summer, the congregations of Butler offer a series of activities, affording the children a break from the heat, and the parents a break from the children. (Courtesy of Barbara Herrell.)

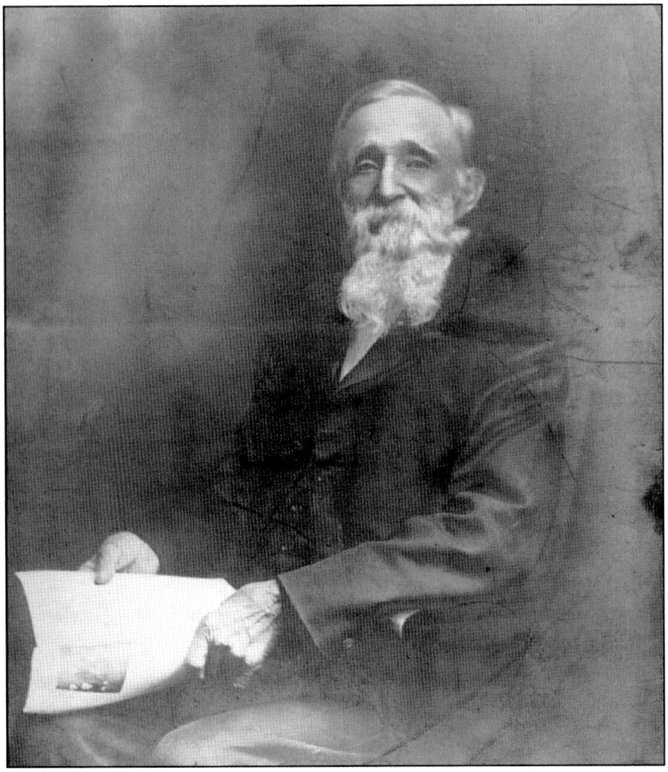

Rev. Abram H. Lewis is fondly remembered in Bates County and deservedly so. In 1872, accompanied by his wife Geraldine, Lewis came to Bates County and took up the cloth, earning a very high reputation as missionary and minister. The existence of the county's Baptist churches owes much to Lewis, whose circuit encompassed much of Bates and Cass Counties. By the time he celebrated his 79th birthday in 1905 (pictured below), his name had become synonymous in the region with "earnest endeavor and right living." (Both, courtesy of Missie Good.)

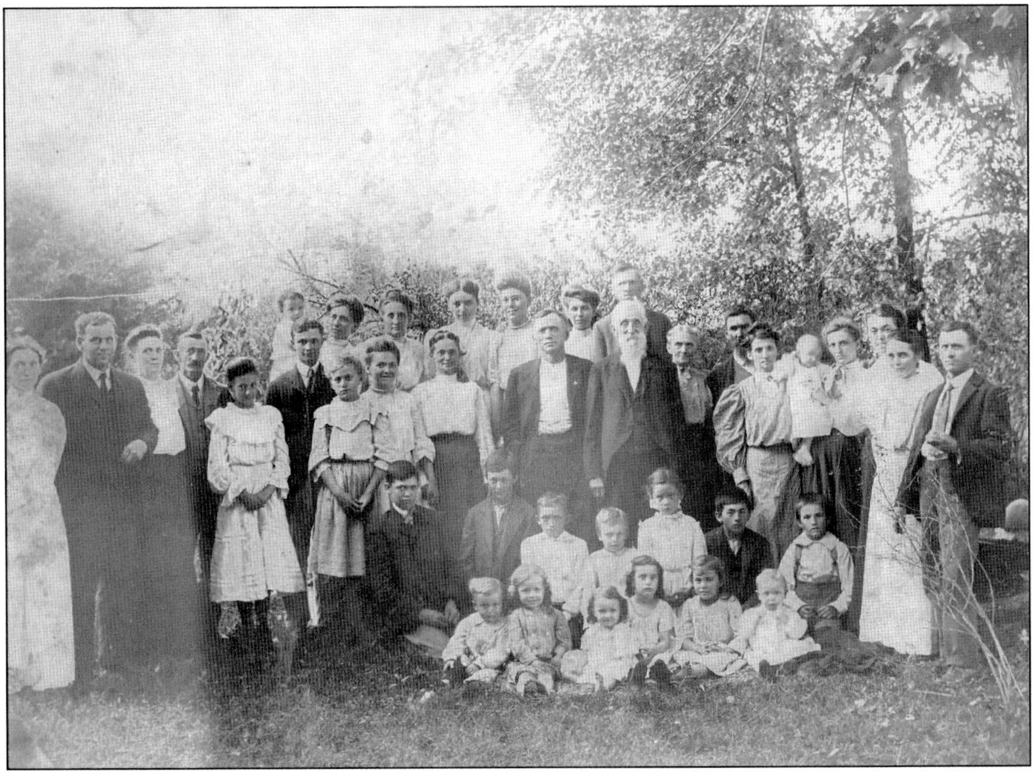

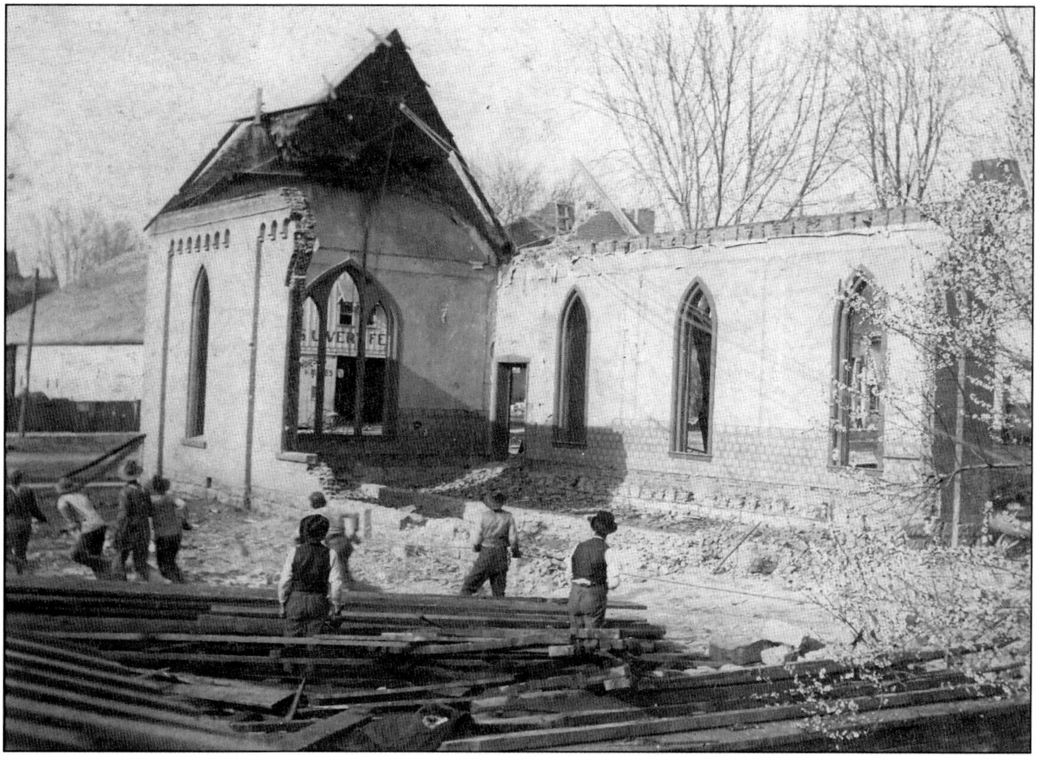

History holds that the Pyles, the first new settlers to arrive in Butler after the Civil War, were Methodists. The year following their arrival, in the spring of 1866, a circuit preacher by the name of Callaway was assigned to their small congregation. His were the first sermons preached in Butler after the war. Callaway initially met with a group of 17 in the frame building then serving as county courthouse, but attendance increased rapidly, and the original Ohio Street Methodist Church went up in 1870. It was demolished (above) in 1901 and replaced by the present structure (below). In 1919, Ohio Street merged with Butler Methodist, South, and together, they became Ohio Street Methodist-Episcopal Church of Butler. (Both, courtesy of the Bates County Historical Society.)

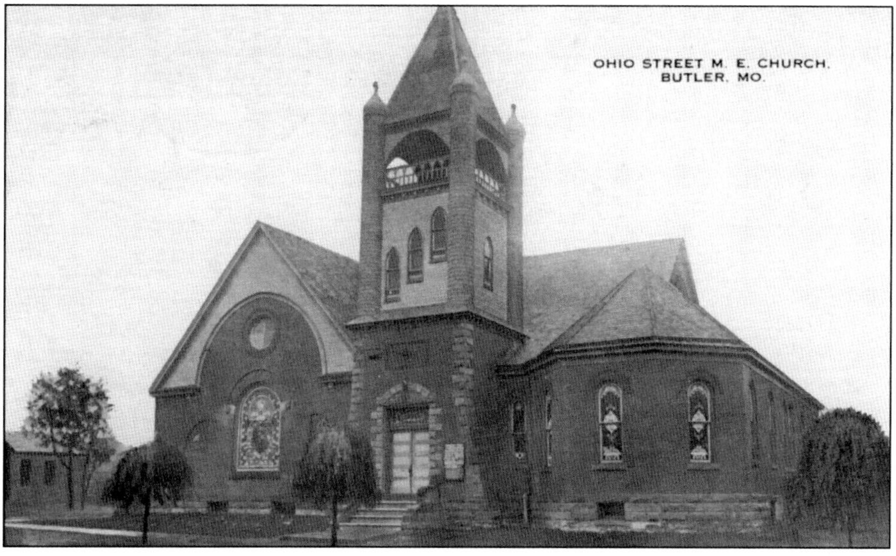

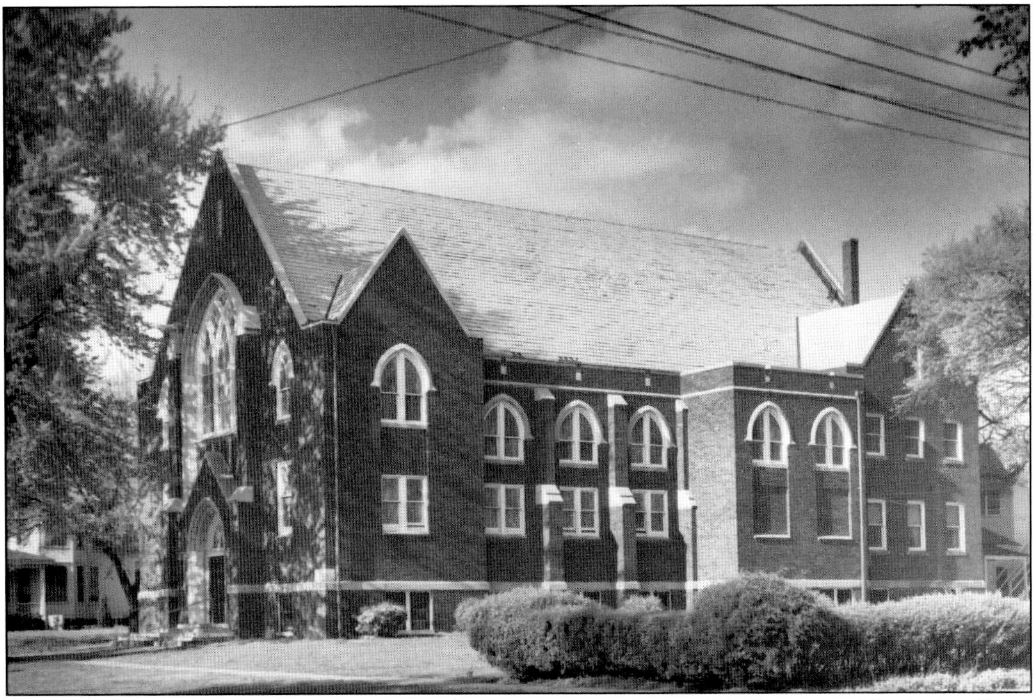

First Christian's first building went up with the town itself. In 1856, the year of Butler's official founding, an all-purpose facility was built to double as a schoolhouse during the week and a chapel on weekends. For four years, the Christian congregation of Butler shared this meeting hall with other local denominations, eventually constructing their own church in 1860. Like so many others, this structure was destroyed by fire during the Civil War. After the war, the Christian congregation once again shared a building, this time with the Cumberland Presbyterians. In 1929, they moved to their present location. The congregation's 100th birthday (pictured below) corresponded with that of the town. (Both, courtesy of the Bates County Historical Society and the Eddie Herrman Collection.)

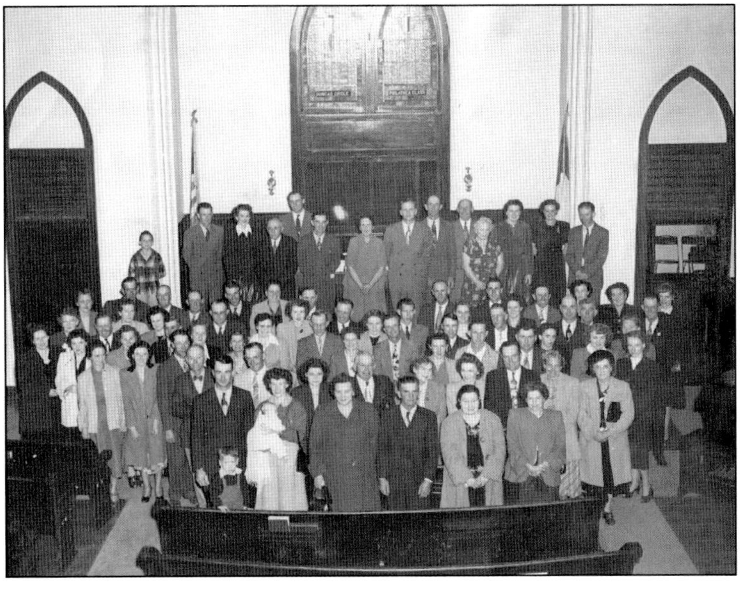

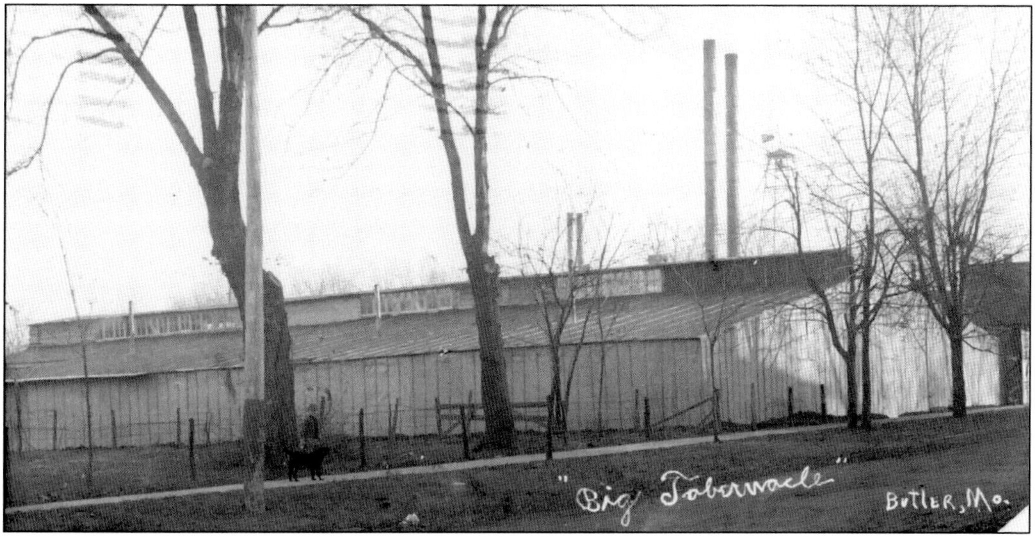

This postcard features the "Big Tabernacle" on North Main Street. In 1908, several Butler churches came together and raised the temporary structure for use during a revival led by Lincoln McConnell, a circuit lecturer and evangelist known for his dashing physique and his witty banter. There were 80 people who joined the Christian Church during this event. (Courtesy of the Bates County Historical Society.)

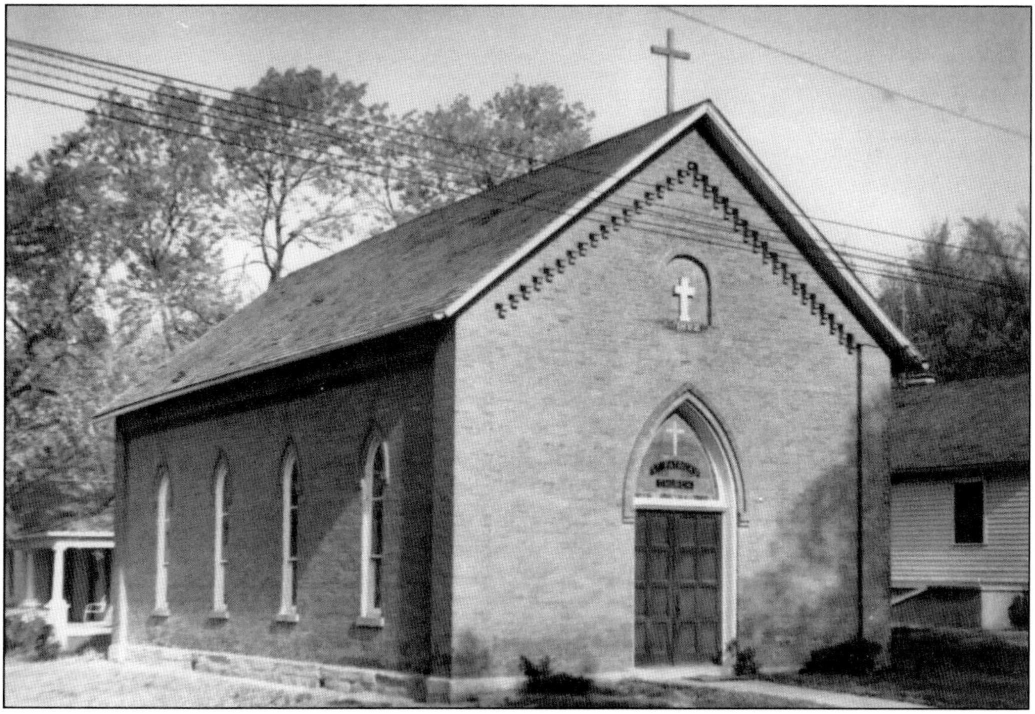

Catholicism came to Butler in 1882 through a mission of the Rich Hill parish, St. Bridget's, led by Rev. J. Fogarty. Two years later, this small brick church, dedicated to St. Patrick, was erected in Butler at the corner of High and Ohio Streets. In 1941, these two communities' roles were reversed: parish headquarters moved to Butler, and Rich Hill was given mission status. (Courtesy of the Bates County Historical Society.)

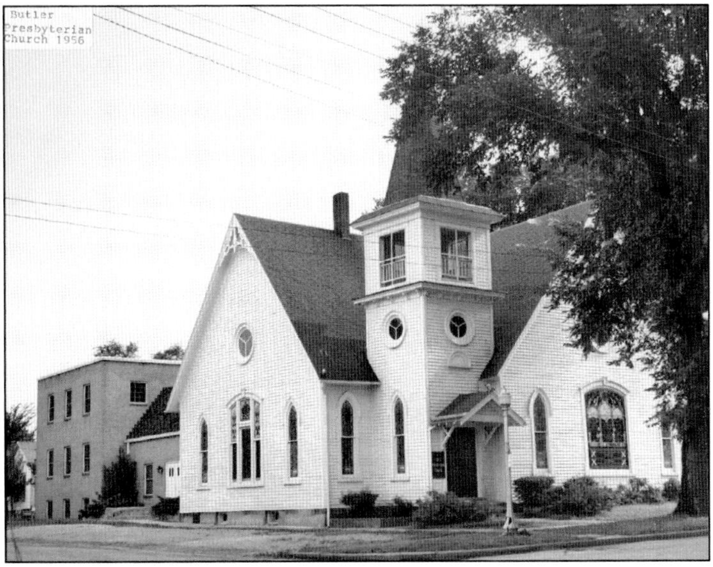

Although Butler Presbyterian Church (at the intersection of Fulton and Pine Streets) was not built until 1884, the history of Presbyterianism in Butler predates the Civil War. The Cumberland denomination arrived first, in 1857; they were followed in 1867 by the USA denomination under the guidance of Rev. Seth Clark. The two united in 1906. (Courtesy of the Bates County Historical Society and the Eddie Herrman Collection.)

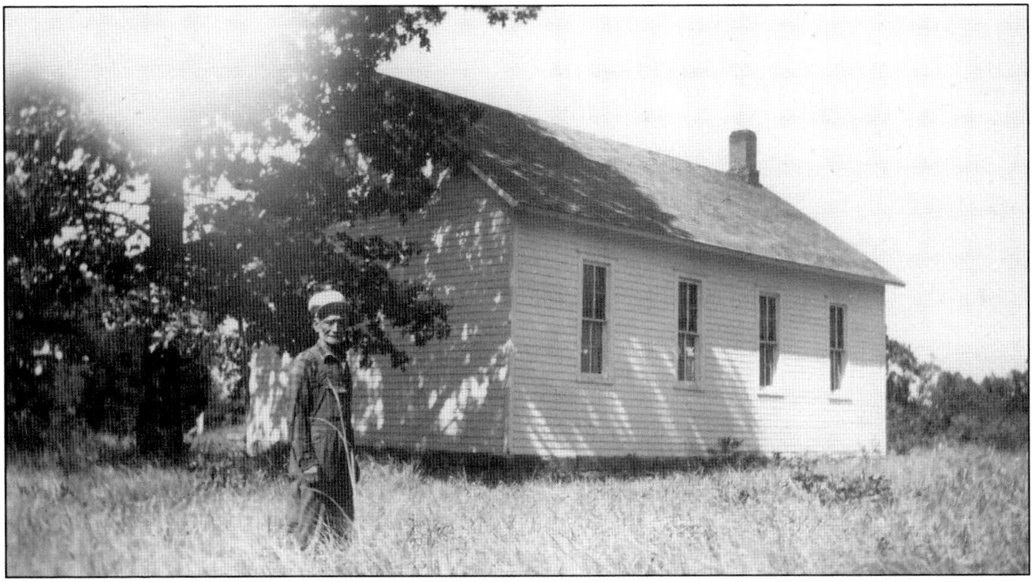

The old Star Schoolhouse south of town provided Butler's Reorganized Church of Jesus Christ of Latter Day Saints (RLDS) congregation with its first home, and its first service was held on November 17, 1912, under the leadership of pastor James A. Marstellar. When that venue was closed to it, the congregation moved first to the Miller schoolhouse southeast of Butler, and then, in 1928, into Butler itself. (Courtesy of Barbara Herrell.)

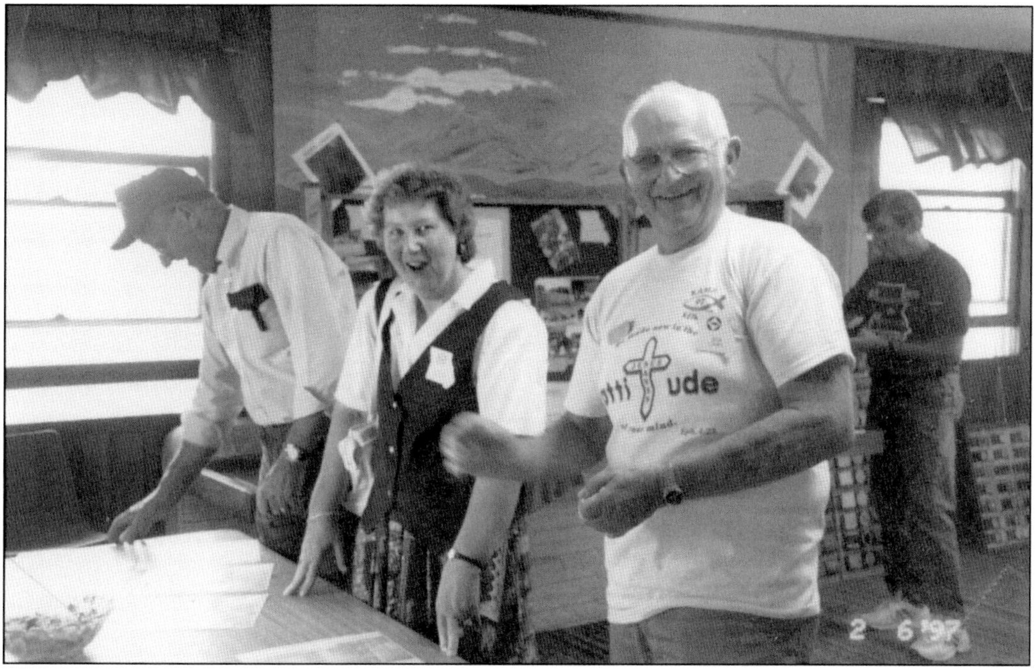

Pictured from left to right, Bill Hayes, Leta Hayes, and Bob Laws enjoy themselves at the 1997 Osage River Baptist Association annual picnic. In 1867, five churches—three from Bates County and two from Cass—came together to form the Western Missouri Baptist Association. The name has since changed, and membership has expanded over the years to now include congregations in three counties: Cass, Bates, and to the south, Vernon. (Courtesy of Wendell Teagarden.)

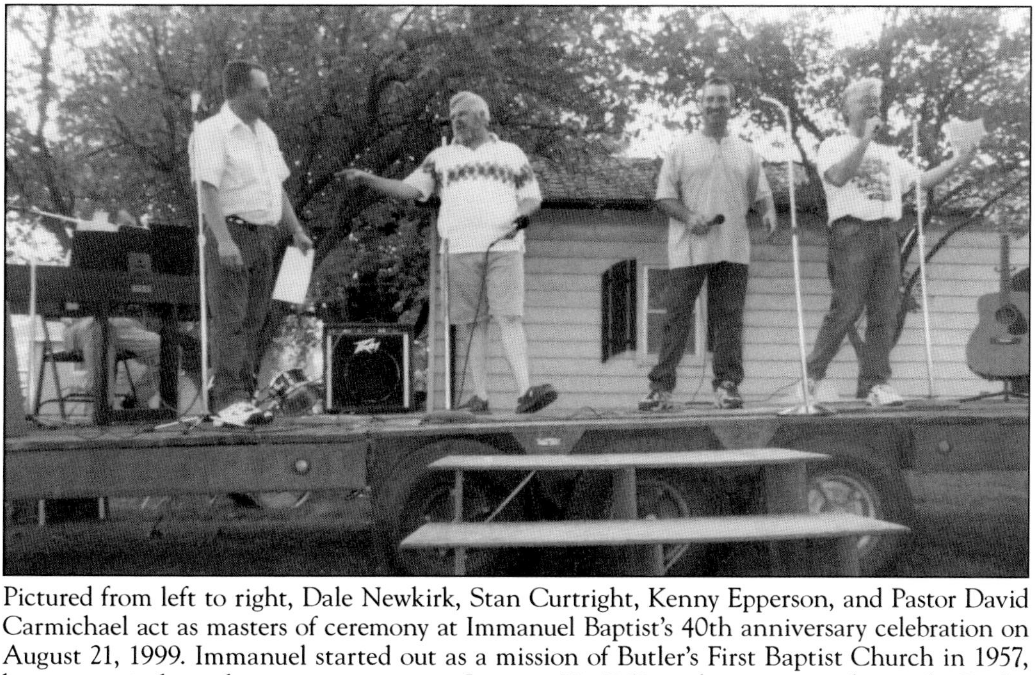

Pictured from left to right, Dale Newkirk, Stan Curtright, Kenny Epperson, and Pastor David Carmichael act as masters of ceremony at Immanuel Baptist's 40th anniversary celebration on August 21, 1999. Immanuel started out as a mission of Butler's First Baptist Church in 1957, became an independent congregation on January 28, 1959, and was accepted into the Butler Baptist Association on August 11 of that year. (Courtesy of Barbara Herrell.)

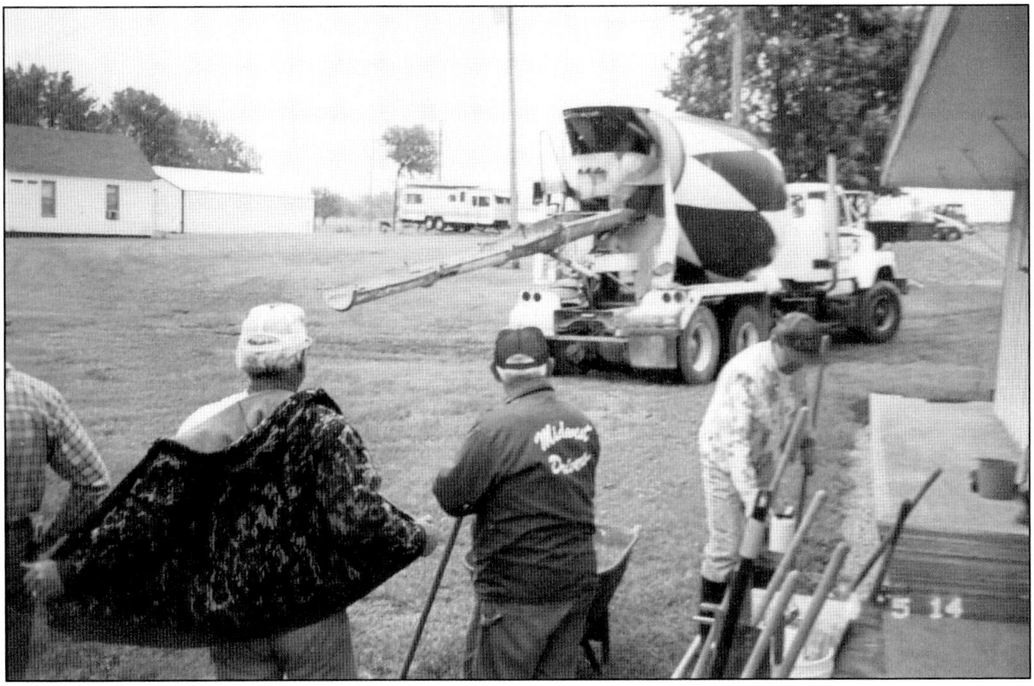

Wendell Teagarden (above, wearing the white cap) doffs his jacket in preparation for an arduous day of cement pouring. Elsewhere, pictured below, Terry Hubbard (in the white shirt) and Bob Laws install a colorful new sign. In recent years, it seems some kind of construction is always going on at Kamp Keirsey. Every summer, children and youth of the Osage River Baptist Association flock to the camp, rarely failing to find something new awaiting their arrival. Situated on land donated in 1967 by John and Darlene Ephland, Keirsey began as a dining hall, a shower facility, and a gaggle of tents. It now includes two swimming pools, an air-conditioned chapel, and 11 comfortable cabins. This expansion owes much to the vision of Wendell Teagarden (camp manager since 1995) and the loyal support of Osage River's churches. (Both, courtesy of Wendell Teagarden.)

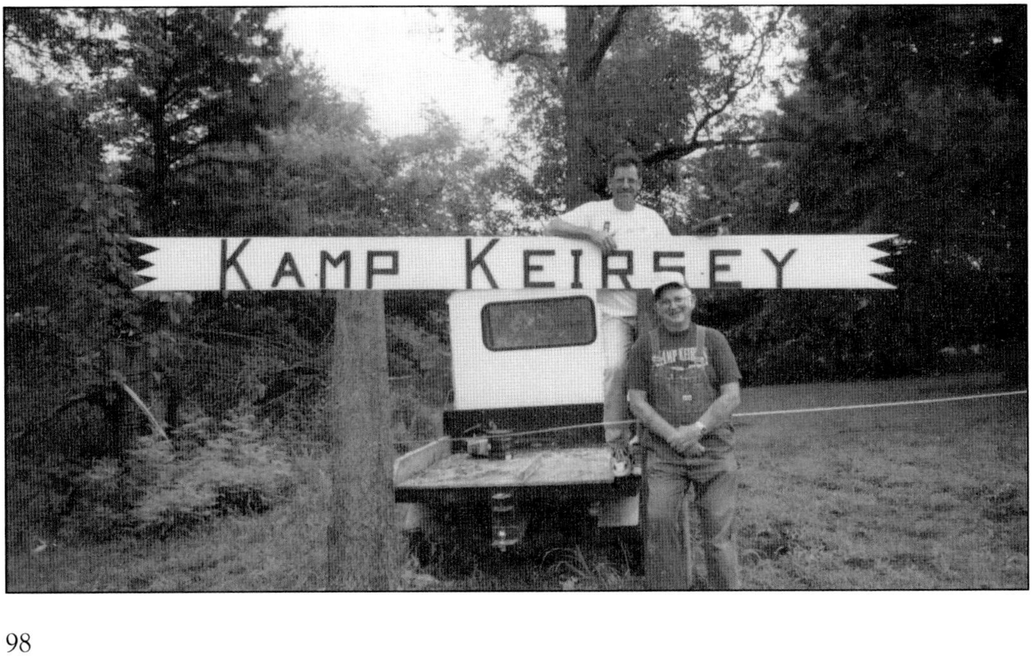

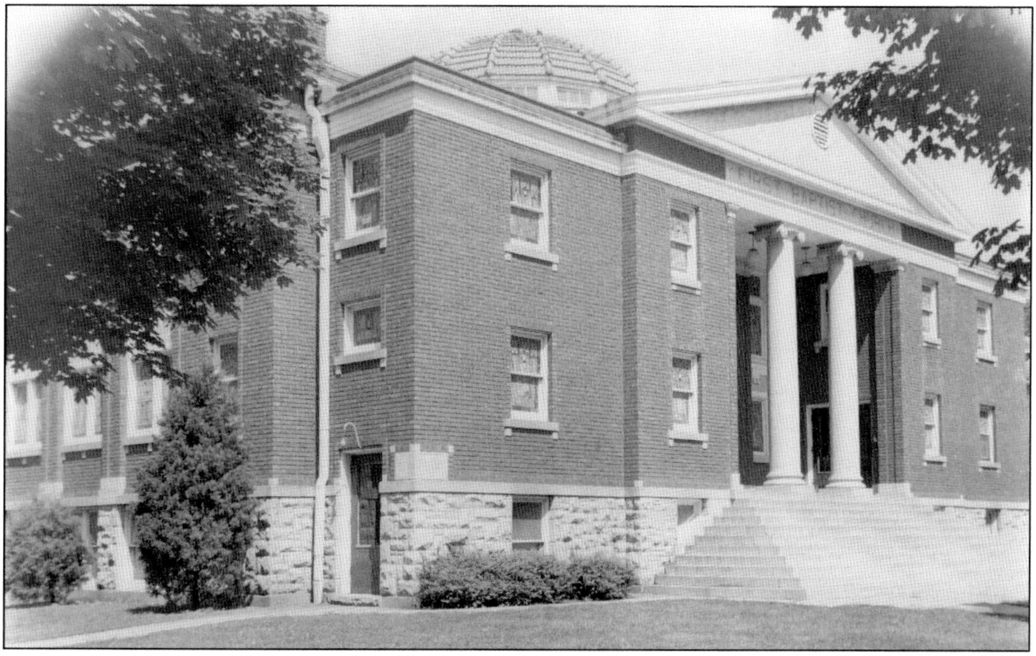

In May 1867, John Smith was called by a fledgling Baptist congregation to come to Butler as their first minister. A decade later, Ohio Street Baptist was born. In 1915, the congregation sold its property to the government (to be used for the new post office), moved to its current location on Delaware Street, and changed its name to First Baptist. (Courtesy of the Bates County Historical Society and the Eddie Herrman Collection.)

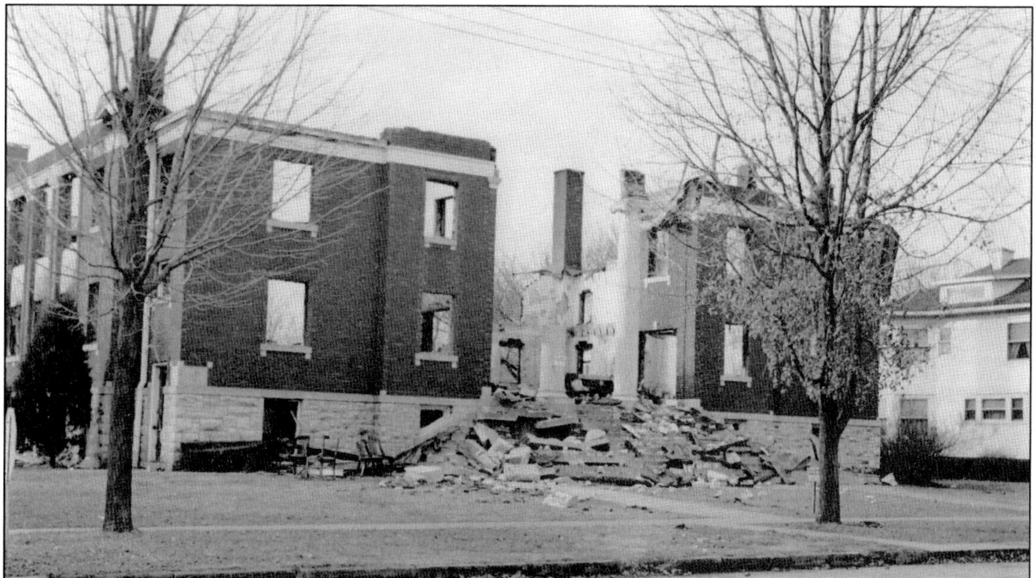

On the night before Thanksgiving 1943, a fire broke out in First Baptist's red brick building. The church's records were saved by the quick action of Pastor David Emery, who ran through the flames to rescue them, but the structure itself was gutted, the fire leaving little more than the outer walls in its wake. (Courtesy of the Bates County Historical Society and the Eddie Herrman Collection.)

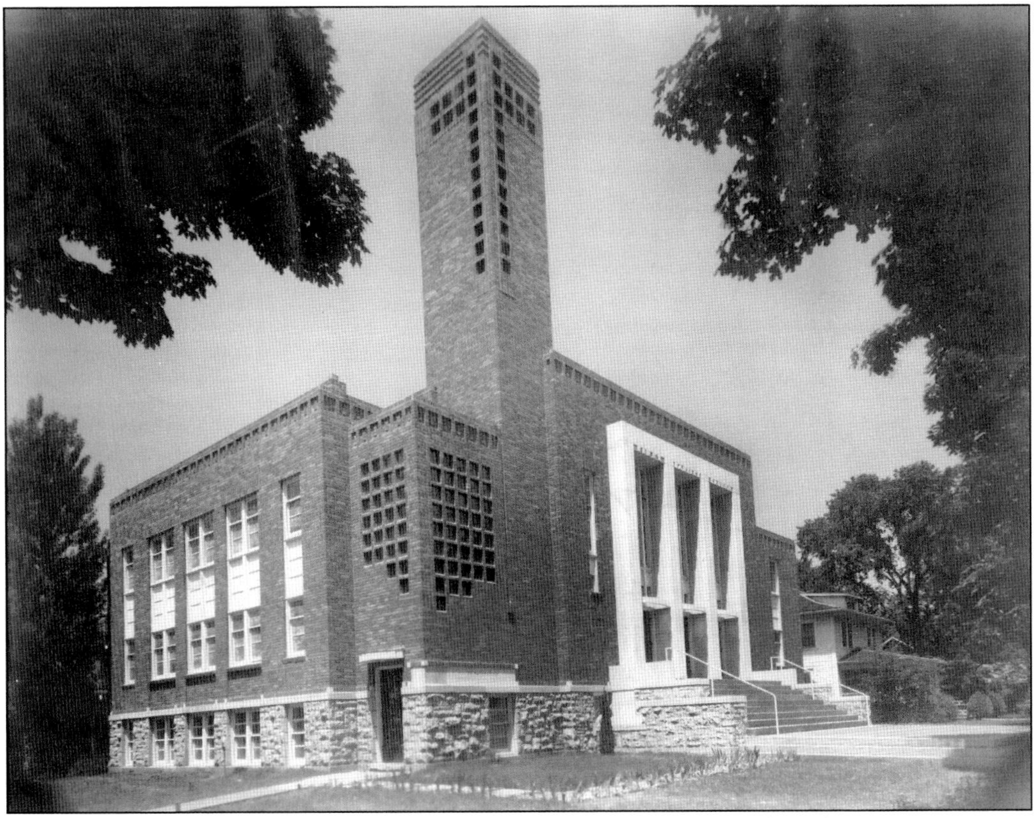

Undaunted, the Baptist congregation went back to the drawing board, and construction on a new church building began 10 months after the fire. The new design featured a tremendous brick tower in place of the original domed roof. The dedication of the restored church, with 300 in attendance, took place on Sunday, June 9, 1946. (Courtesy of the Bates County Historical Society and the Eddie Herrman Collection.)

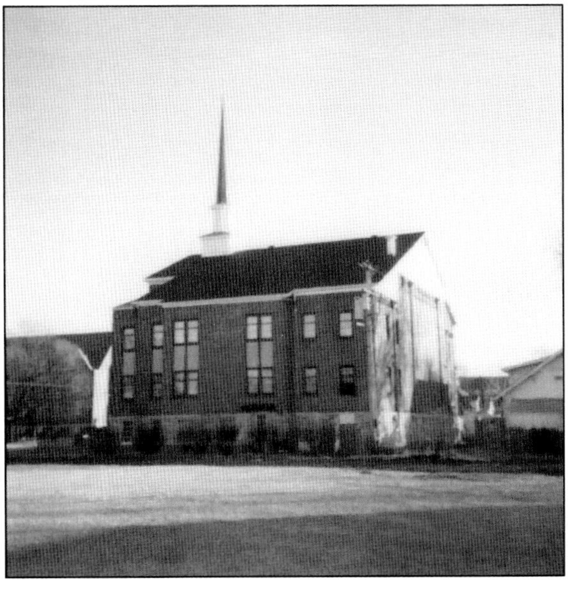

Of all the church buildings in Butler, First Baptist's design has changed the most since its original conception in 1917. Just as a tower replaced the dome following the fire in 1943, a steeple replaced the tower in 1987. The original membership of six has grown to one almost 100 times its initial size. (Courtesy of the Bates County Historical Society and the Eddie Herrman Collection.)

Five

SHINE ON . . .

From July 2010 to May 2011, Butler boasted a world record: the most flashlights lit simultaneously, counted at 1,000. They were surpassed shortly by NASCAR fans at the Charlotte Motor Speedway in North Carolina, but for a brief, shining moment, the world heard the tale of a town's worth of people gathered around a courthouse with a truckload of flashlights, looking for a place in the *Guinness Book of World Records*. They also gathered to have a little fun and be together, in community with one another.

Community is people, and people are makers of history. In the end, it is the people of Butler that make—and have made—their town truly shine. Without getting to know their stories, which are what really define where a community has come from and where it is going, one only ever sees half the picture. After all, it is the stories that everyone wants to hear. They want to hear about the cast of characters that populates their personal pasts, because these so often give greater meaning to the present.

Butler is a town full of characters, and so it is a town full of stories—"his-stories" and "her-stories." It is also a town eager for its story to be told and heard, and in this, it is a reflection of so many small communities around the United States. They are the birthplaces of so much that is unique about and inseparable from the American experience. This, then, is the story of Butler. Let it serve as a reminder of the importance of identity, of origins, and of the great variety of places people call home.

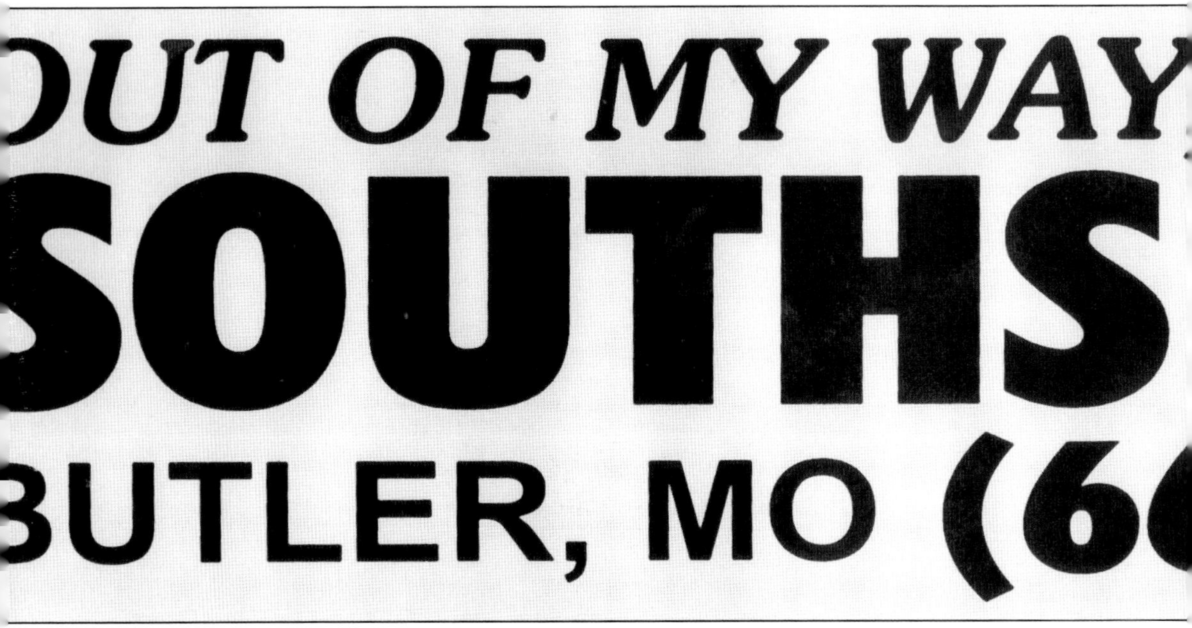

Southside Cafe has been a favorite dining and gathering spot of Butler folks for 18 years—especially those who enjoy going out for breakfast. The space it occupies has housed its share of eateries, beginning with a saloon reportedly frequented by outlaw Jesse James. It has also, according to owner Randy Weiss, housed its share of spirits. Weiss would often arrive at work to find sweetener

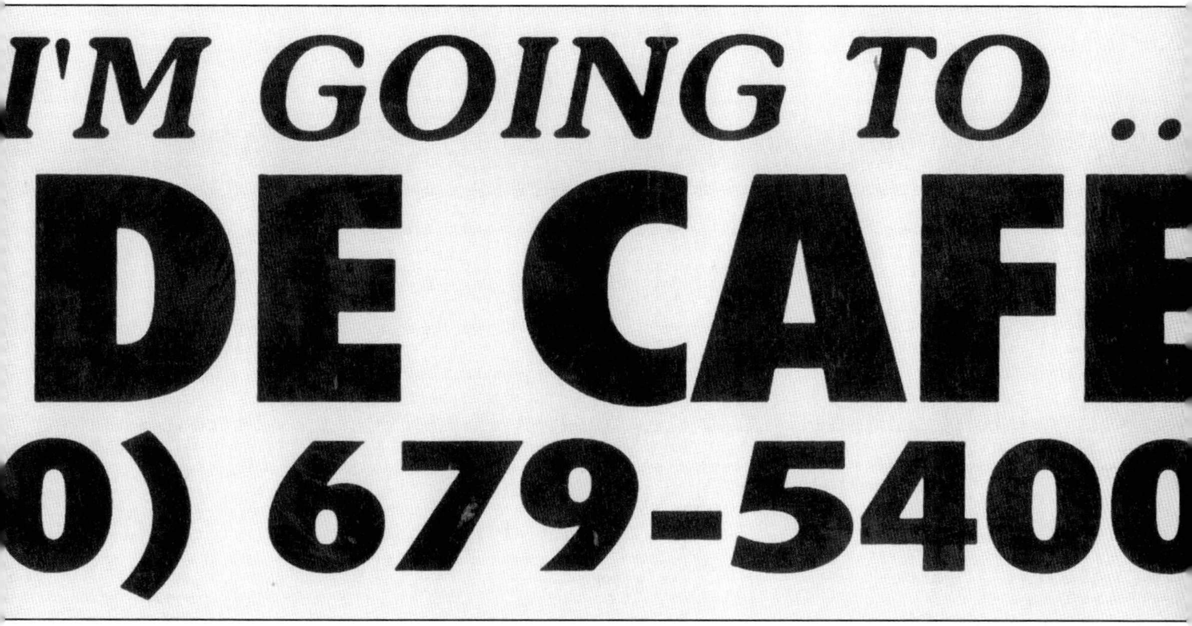

packets strewn across the floor or glasses moved from upper to lower shelves. Convinced that his restaurant was haunted, he called in a minister to pray over the establishment. (Courtesy of Randy Weiss.)

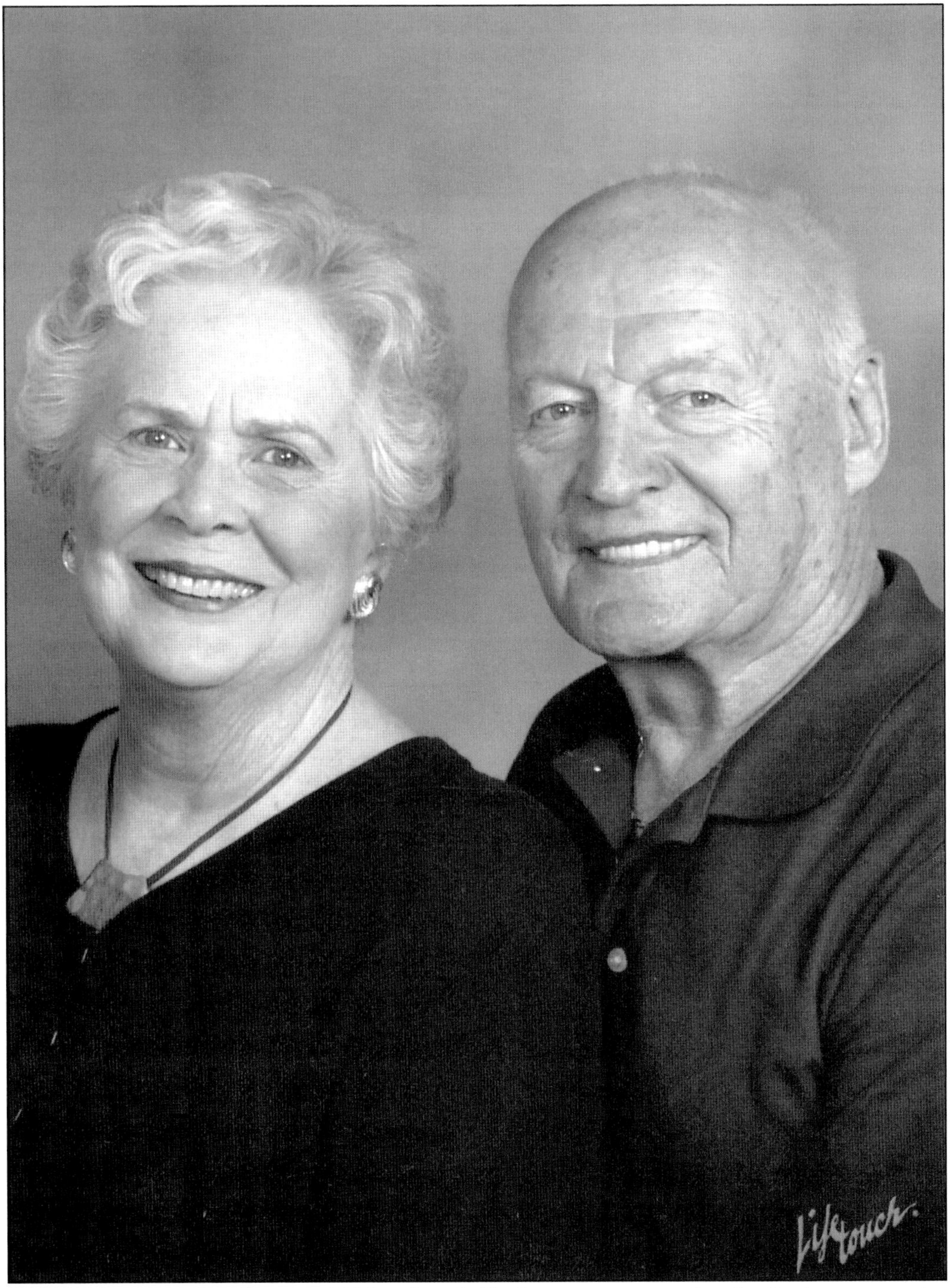

Eddie Herrman, pictured here in 2008 with wife Shirley, was renowned in the Butler community for his "Historical Happenings," a regular column in the *News X-Press* from 1985 to January 13, 2012. Herrman earned his reputation as a serious historian with a serious sense of humor. He is proof that, sometimes, amateurs make the best professionals. (Courtesy of the Bates County Historical Society and the Eddie Herrman Collection.)

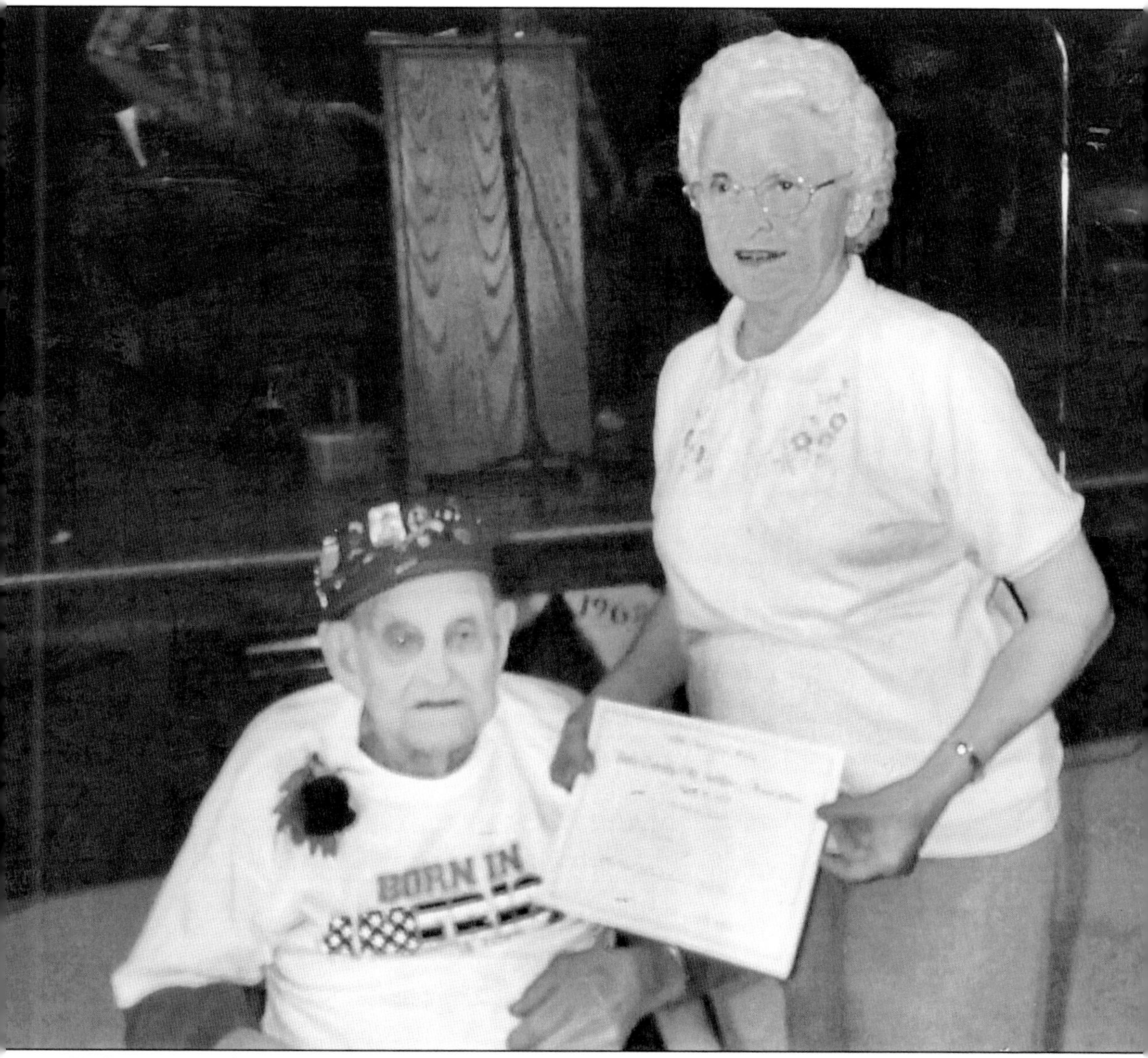

Each year, on Old Settlers' Day, the Old Settlers' Society recognizes Bates County's oldest citizen in attendance. In 2006, the title went to Earl Erickson. Erickson, born February 1, 1907, was 99 years old and, according to his daughter Lucille, thrilled beyond words at the honor conferred upon him. (Courtesy of Lucille Lindsay.)

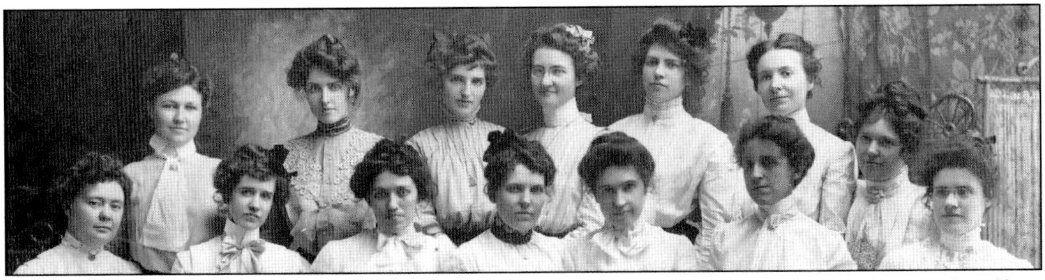

A bevy of Butler belles engage in a bit of playful coquetry. They are, from left to right, (first row) Daisy Stanley, Agnes Arnold, Edith Everingham, Gertrude Silvers, Ella Meek, Mable Bennett, and Mable Haire; (second row) Lucille Sevier, Genevieve Holloway, Nell Austin, Marian Vaughan, Johnnie Shutt, Jess Stanley, and Lou Silvers. (Courtesy of the Bates County Historical Society.)

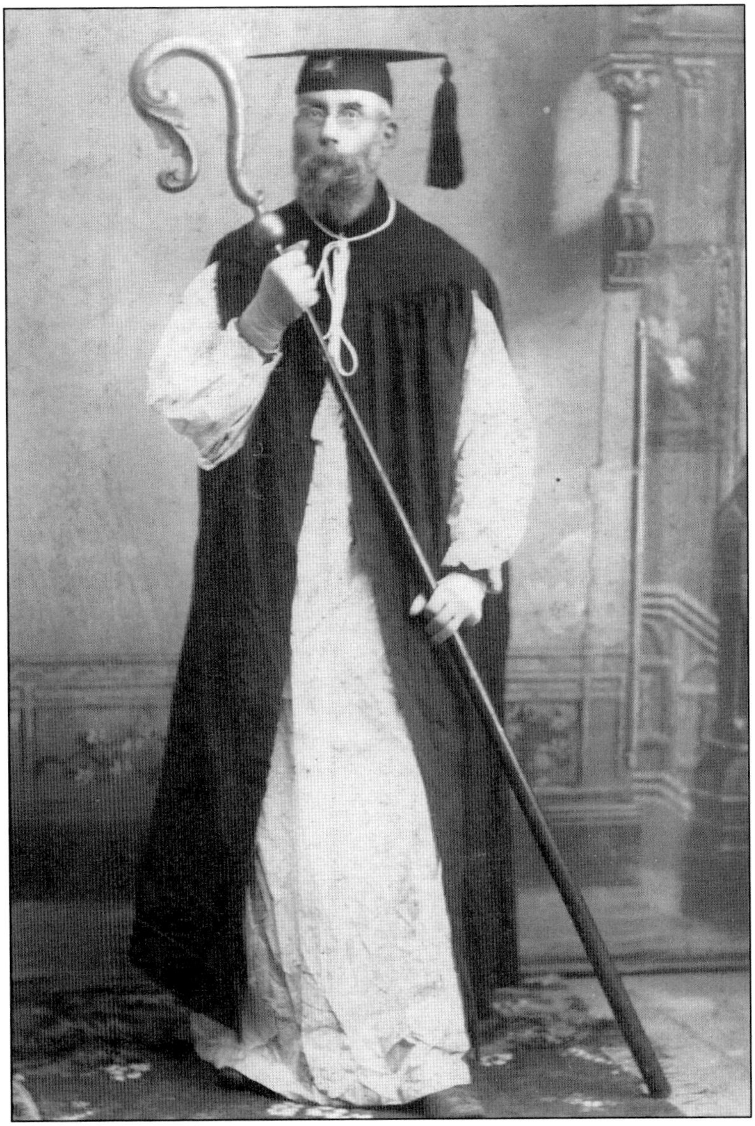

William W. Ross was highly active in the Butler community in the late 1800s. A brick mason by trade, Ross was also a Freemason and one of the founders of Gouley Commandery Knights Templar No. 35 in 1879. He sat on the school board in the 1880s and is listed as a charter member of the Ohio Street Baptist Church in 1877. (Courtesy of the Bates County Historical Society.)

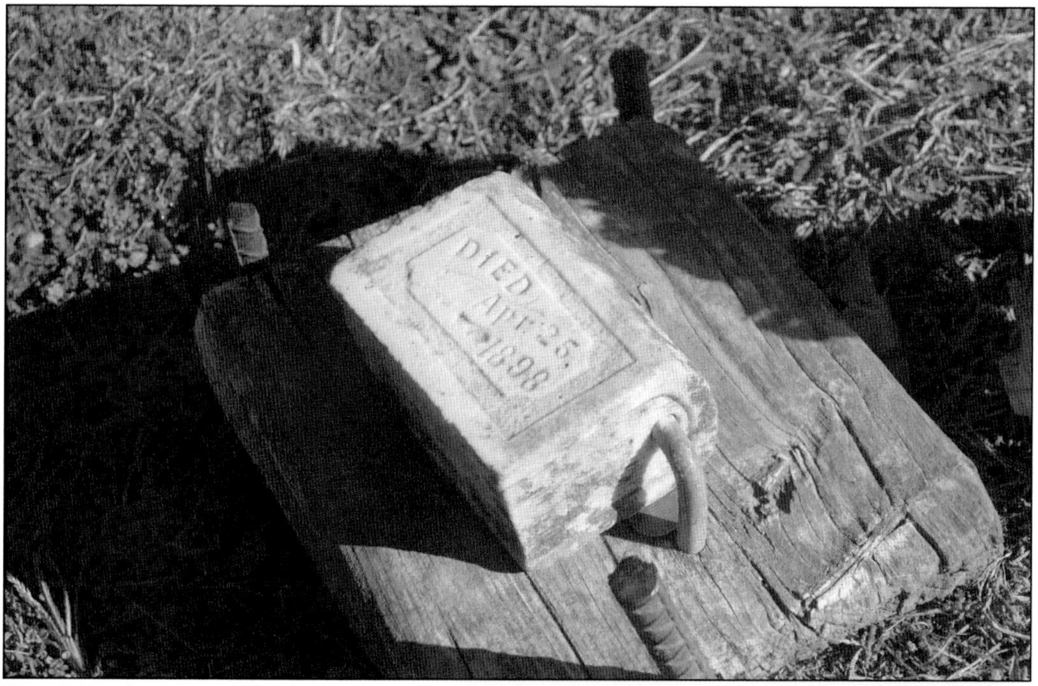

Dated April 25, 1898, the diminutive stone Bible marks the grave of Linnie Crouch. Most assume the headstone marks the resting place of a child, or even a stillborn infant; beyond this, little Linnie remains a mystery. One story tells that the child's father, perhaps a black laborer named Daniel Crouch, carved the memorial by hand and personally set it in place. The gravestone was freestanding until a temporary theft in the 1970s prompted the installation of a metal bar to hold it firmly in place. In 1966, the publication *Ripley's Believe It or Not: Tombstones and Graveyards* designated Linnie's tombstone "the world's smallest," at 4.2 inches long, 2.9 inches wide, and 1.9 inches thick. (Photographs by the Vance Woods.)

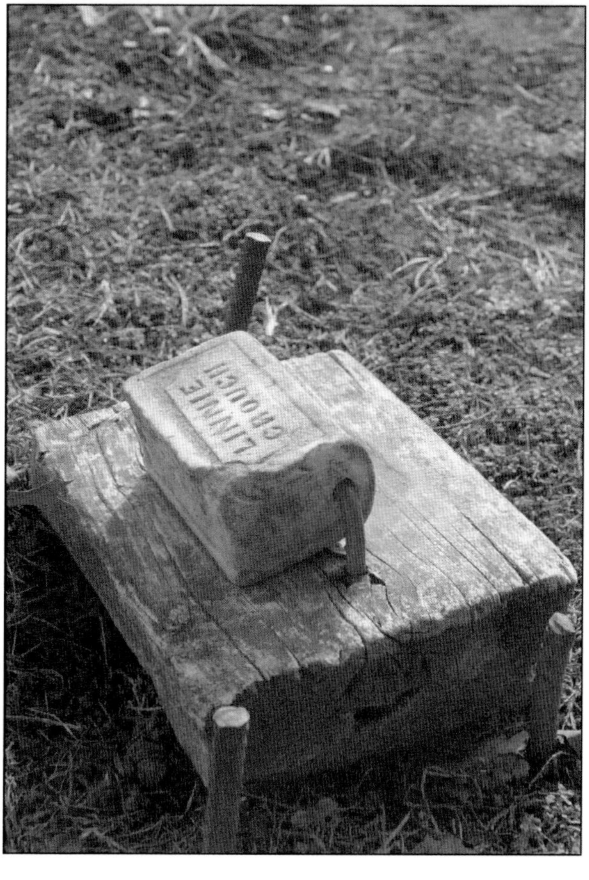

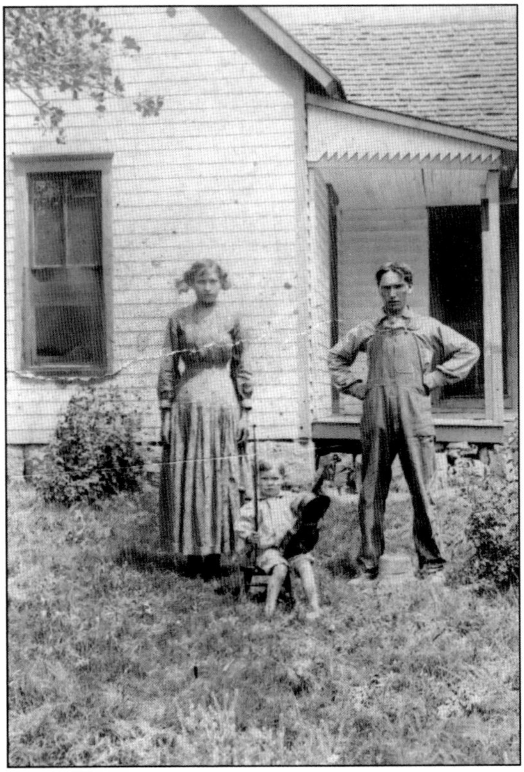

Dove and Maud Alkire stand outside their home (a converted schoolhouse) around 1912, while son Othel brandishes his father's fiddle. Maud was a seamstress, and Dove, who never learned to read or write, could fiddle with the best, often supplementing the family's income playing dances and barn raisings. (Courtesy of Barbara Herrell.)

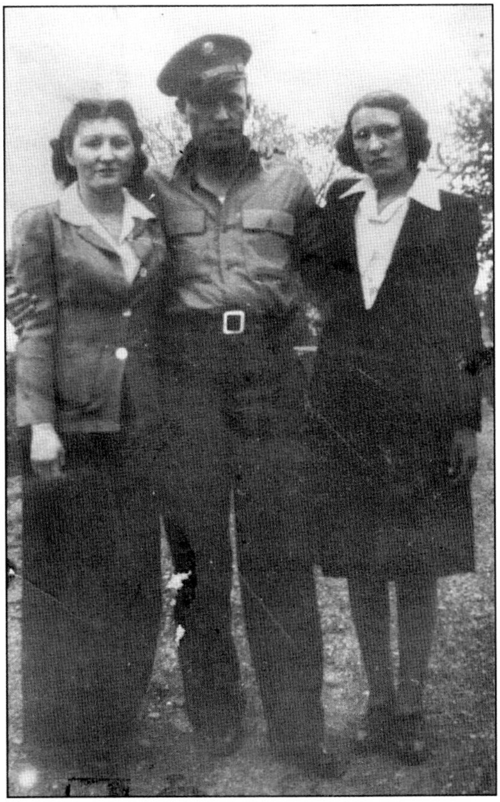

Most knew Iley (center) and Irene (left) Alkire, seen here with Iley's mother, Maud, simply as "Buck" and "Nine," respectively. A veteran of World War II, Buck had such a keen sense of fashion that Nine was more than happy to let him handle her wardrobe. Both were avid antiquers, and on weekends, they would go out "garage-hopping" in search of new treasures. (Courtesy of Barbara Herrell.)

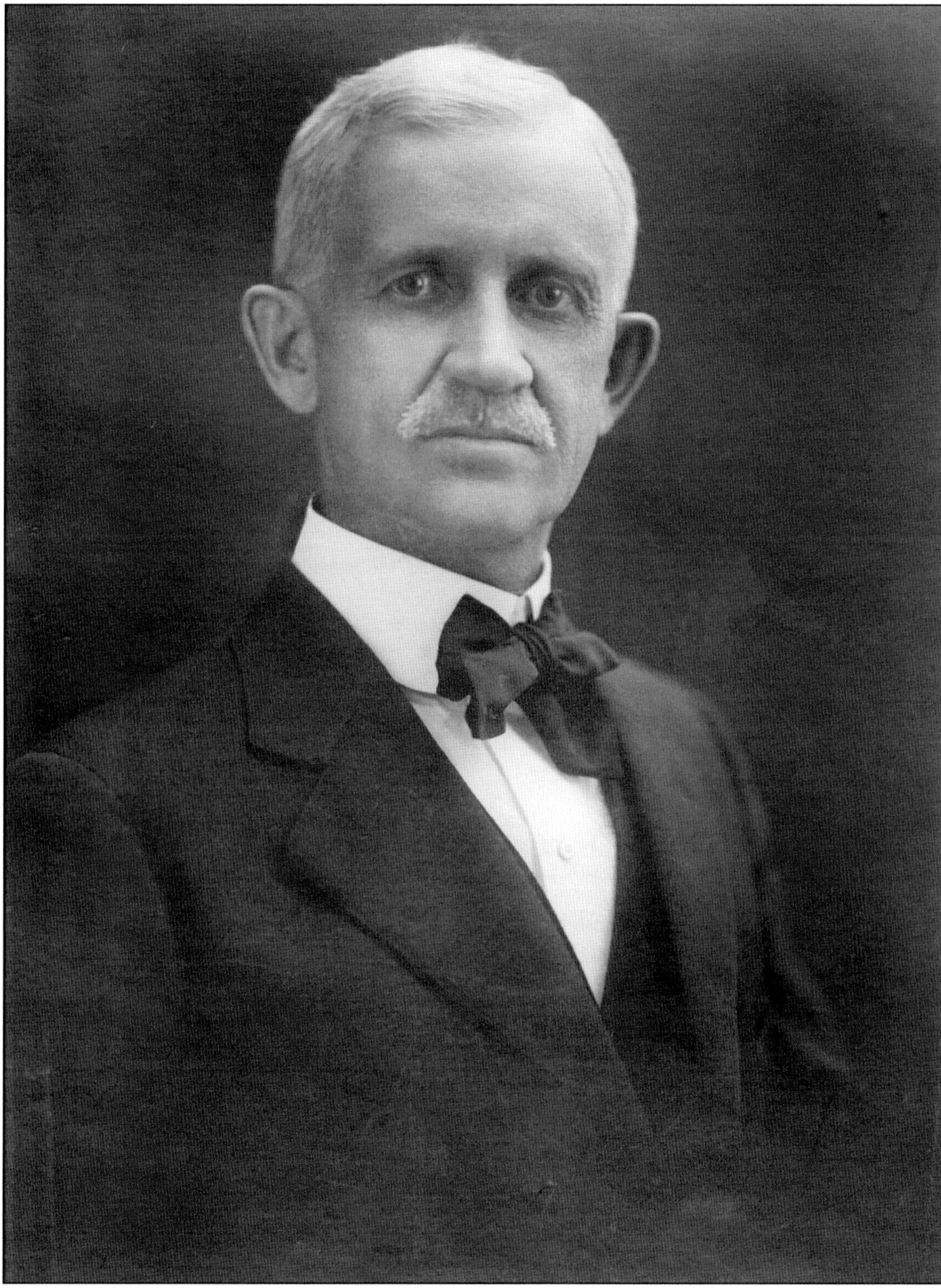

Former Missouri governor Herbert Hadley boasted that the Honorable Charles A. Denton, who acted as the state's pardon attorney under Hadley from 1911 to 1913, was a man whose integrity was "unhesitatingly conceded by all who [knew] him." A Butler attorney for over 30 years, Denton instituted Missouri's first uniform pardon and parole system, under which the problem of recidivism was dramatically reduced. (Courtesy of the Bates County Historical Society.)

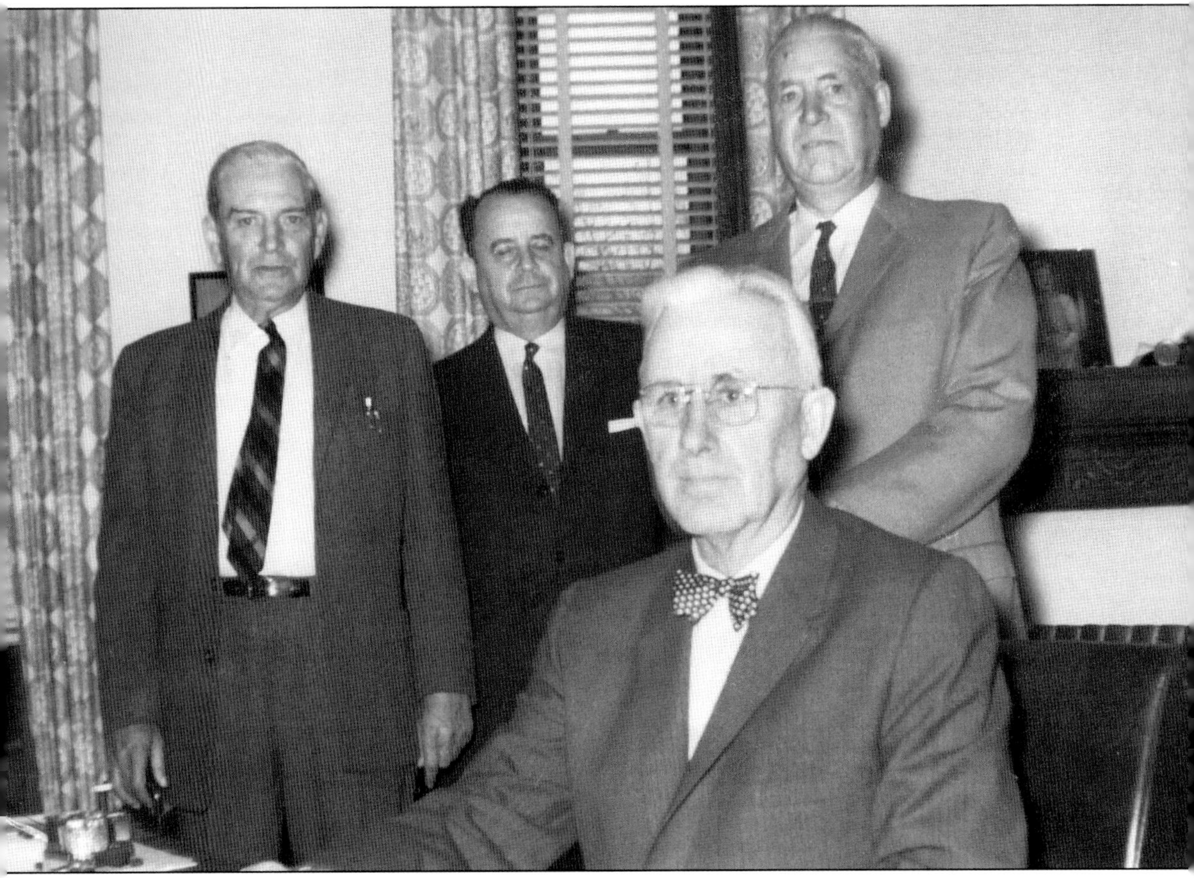

John M. Dalton (center, rear), 45th governor of Missouri, visits the office of Butler mayor H.L. Oberweather (seated) in 1962. To the left of the governor stands local attorney W.O. Jackson, immortalized as the model for Butler's Doughboy monument, and to the right is Andy Cummings, mayor of Butler from 1942 to 1946. (Courtesy of the Bates County Historical Society and the Eddie Herrman Collection.)

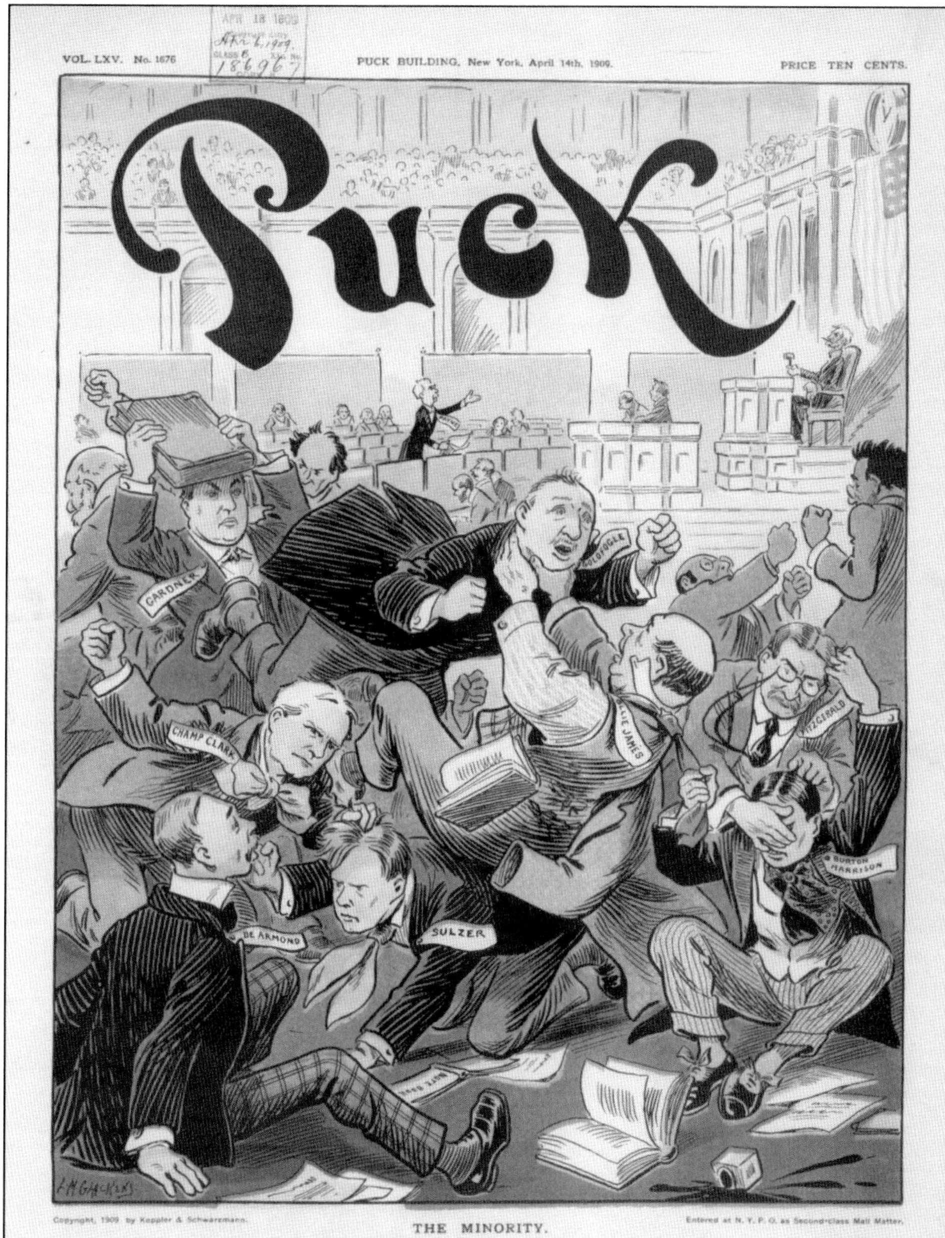

Down on his rump in the lower left corner of this cartoon is a depiction of David DeArmond of Butler, who, in 1890, defeated five other candidates for a Democratic seat in the US House of Representatives. All caricature aside, DeArmond was a man greatly admired by his constituents. They trusted in his complete dedication as an advocate for their well being. In Congress, DeArmond was recognized as a leader of his party and earned the reputation of a great debater, unafraid to cross the aisle. He, along with grandson David, died in a house fire in Butler in 1909, just before he was to return to his duties in Washington, DC. His family reported that, as the flames consumed the porch where he and the boy were sleeping, DeArmond was heard consoling the child with his last breath: "Don't be scared, little son: Granddaddy will get you out." (Courtesy of the Library of Congress.)

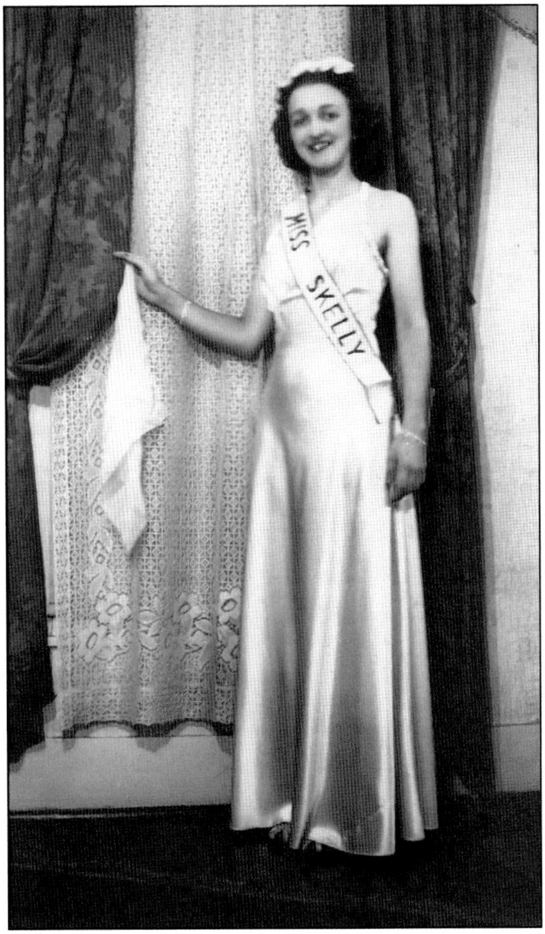

Helen DeArmond, daughter of Butler mayor James DeArmond and granddaughter of US representative David DeArmond, models her Fair Queen finery at the home of Marvin and Opal Durst. Years later, on January 3, 1941, DeArmond became Bates County's version of Amelia Earhart. With a five-minute solo flight and a perfect landing, she earned her wings at the Street Port Flying School in Nevada, Missouri. (Courtesy of the Durst family.)

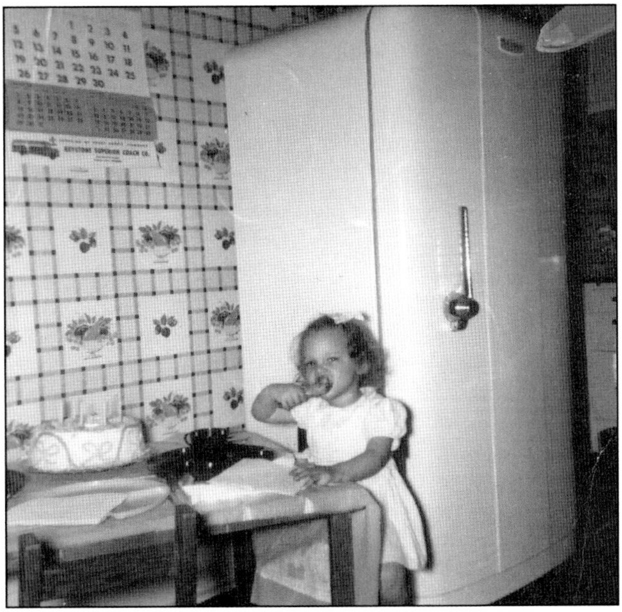

Pam Durst thoroughly enjoys a chicken leg during a birthday party at her aunt Opal and uncle Marvin's house. The Durst women, Opal and Fern, were excellent cooks, their skills honed by years of feeding hungry farmhands. Fern's chocolate pie is still remembered with fondness throughout the county, and Opal's pickled beets rarely outlasted the first opening of the jar. (Courtesy of the Durst family.)

In a tradition as old as photography itself, Debbie and Vickie Ratje shiver in their Easter finery, around 1960, waiting impatiently for the shutter to click. Debbie, who much preferred the summer, has fond memories of the annual Independence Day gatherings at her grandfather's house, except for one year when it was so cold, they had to wear their coats in July. (Courtesy of Barbara Herrell.)

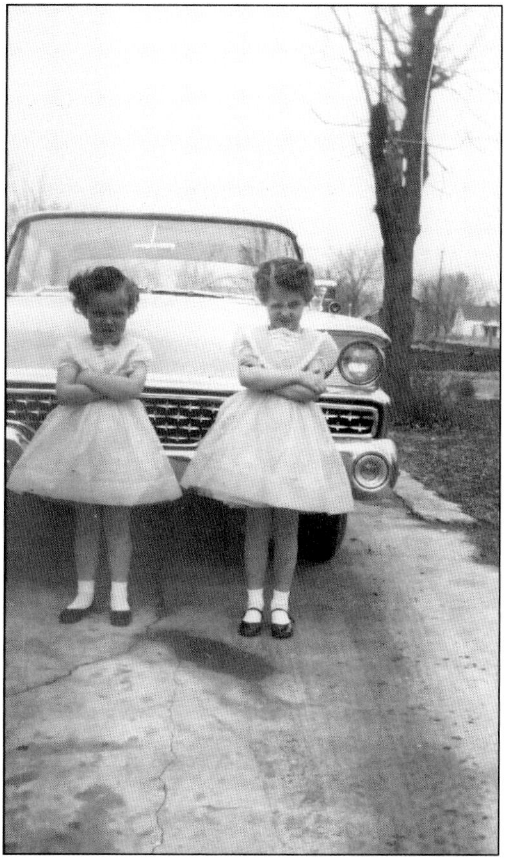

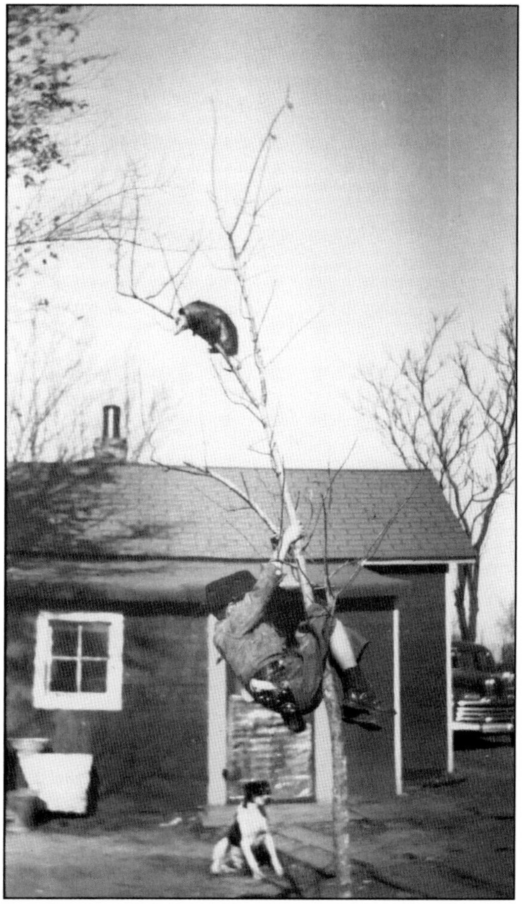

In 1952, with Spike the dog looking on, five-year-old Dave Alkire, six-shooter in tow, trees a possum. This encounter marked the beginning of a long and complicated relationship between Dave and trees, culminating in 2002 when he fell from a deer stand and was, consequently, unable to act as photographer at his niece's wedding. (Courtesy of Barbara Herrell.)

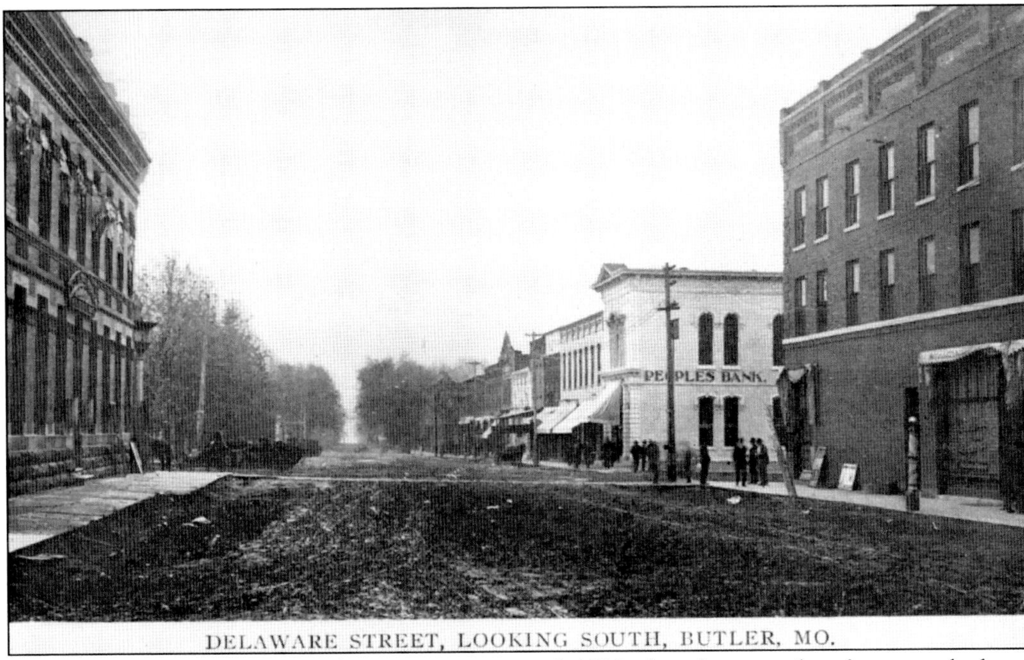

Standing on the square's northwest corner around 1909, the photographer faces south down Delaware Street. At this time, the streets around the courthouse were still a muddy mess, with only the flimsy boardwalk stretched between street corners to protect pedestrians from the slush. In 1910, the brick paving for which Butler is known today was installed for $1.79 per square yard; it was funded by those who owned street-front property. However, while this solved one problem, it created another; while the new paving made the streets safer for human traffic, it made them hard on the horses. The image below from the 1920s illustrates yet another solution. The bricks were covered with a thick layer of sand, preventing slippage but also obscuring the improvements. (Both, courtesy of the Bates County Historical Society and the Eddie Herrman Collection.)

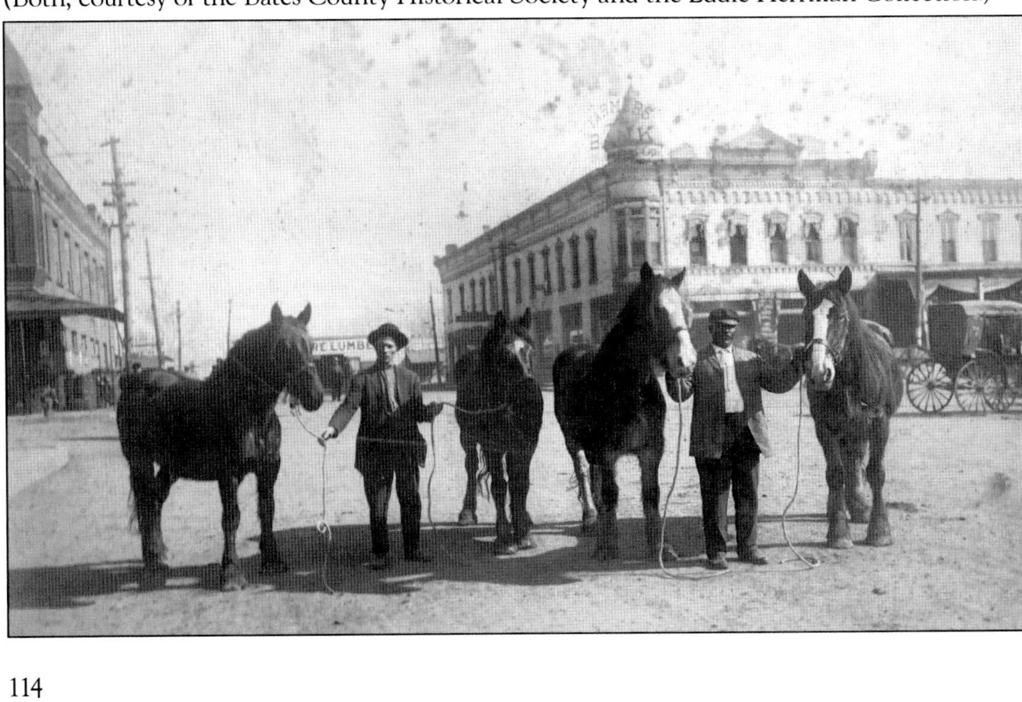

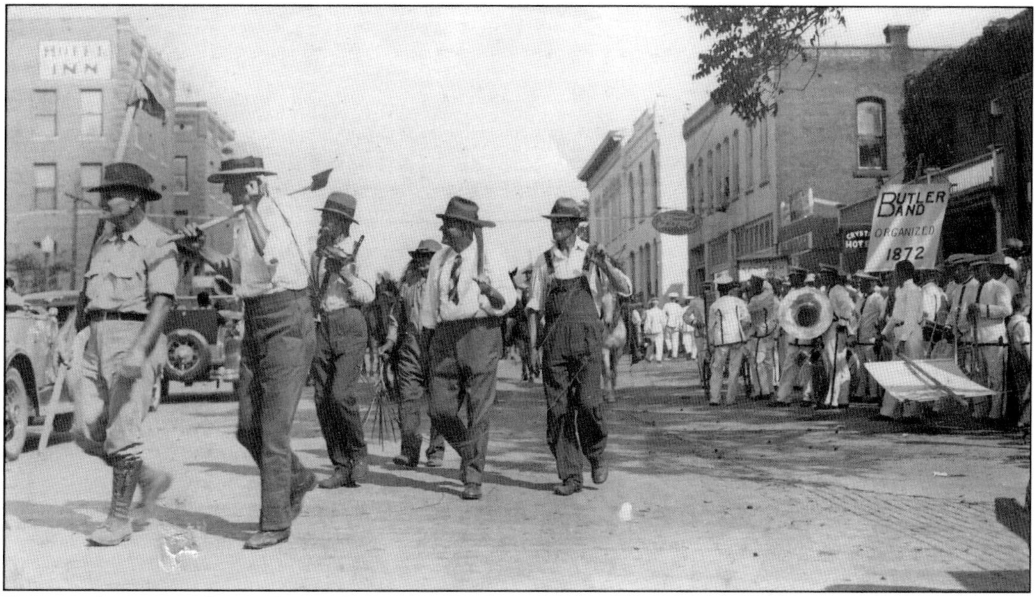

Fraternal societies have always been well represented in Butler. In 1900, the town was home to, among others, Masons, Oddfellows, Knights of Pythias, United Workmen, the Royal Tribe of Joseph, the Knights and Ladies of Security, and (seen here marching in a 1931 parade, hatchets in hand) Woodmen of the World. (Courtesy of the Bates County Historical Society and the Eddie Herrman Collection.)

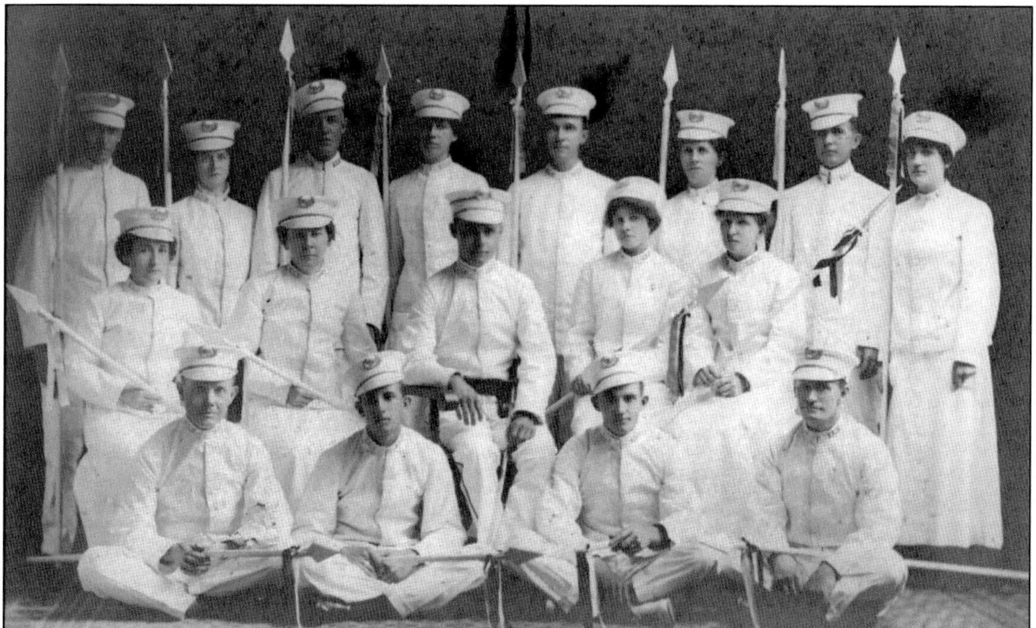

The Knights and Ladies of Security, a mutual aid society, was founded in Topeka, Kansas, in February 1892. The Butler lodge formed soon after. Unlike many of its gender-specific counterparts, the Knights and Ladies accepted both male and female members. Among other activities, the society fielded competition drill teams, like the one pictured here. (Courtesy of the Bates County Historical Society and the Eddie Herrman Collection.)

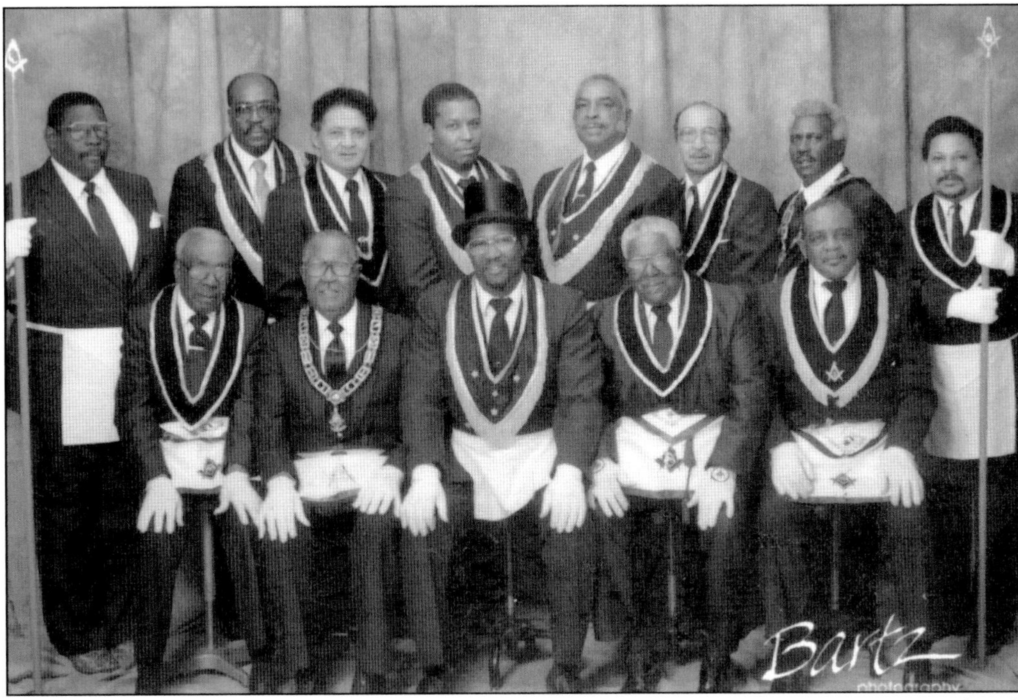

Briscoe Lodge of the Seventh Masonic District of the Most Worshipful Prince meets in the old Douglass School, which they purchased for the purpose in 1956. It is named for its founder, Rev. George Briscoe, minister at Mt. Zion Methodist in the 1870s. (Courtesy of Mildred and Walter Wright; photograph by Bartz Photography.)

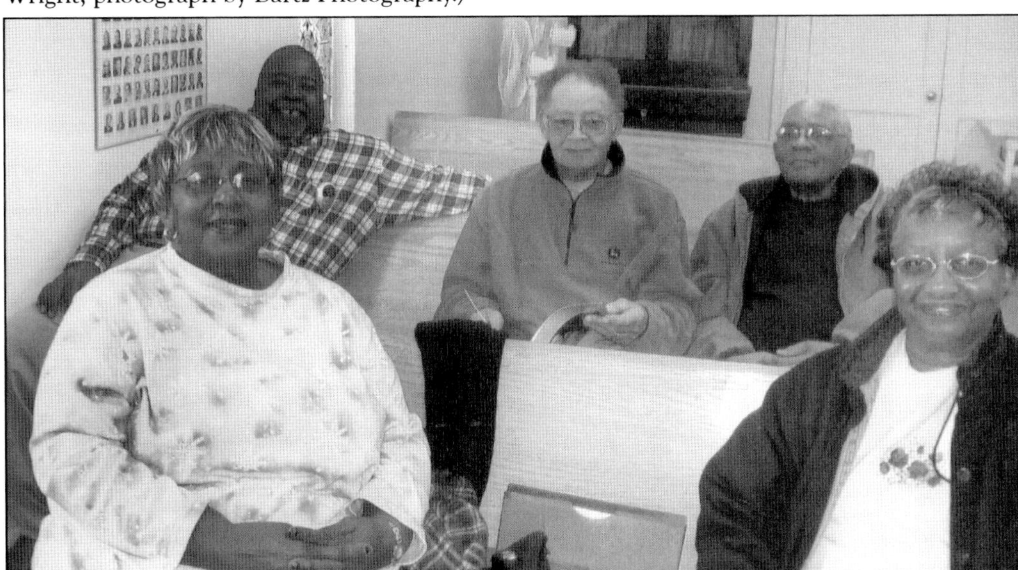

Gathered for a meeting of the Amen Society are, from left to right, (first row) Mildred Wright and Patricia Jacobs; (second row) Rev. Larry Coleman, Troy Burton, and Walter Wright. The society, inspired by the late Elenora Burton, was founded in 1999 by the congregation of Brooks Chapel. The chapel was named after Reverend W.B. Brooks, who, in 1871, purchased an old feed store, moved it across town, and turned it into a church. (Courtesy of Mildred and Walter Wright.)

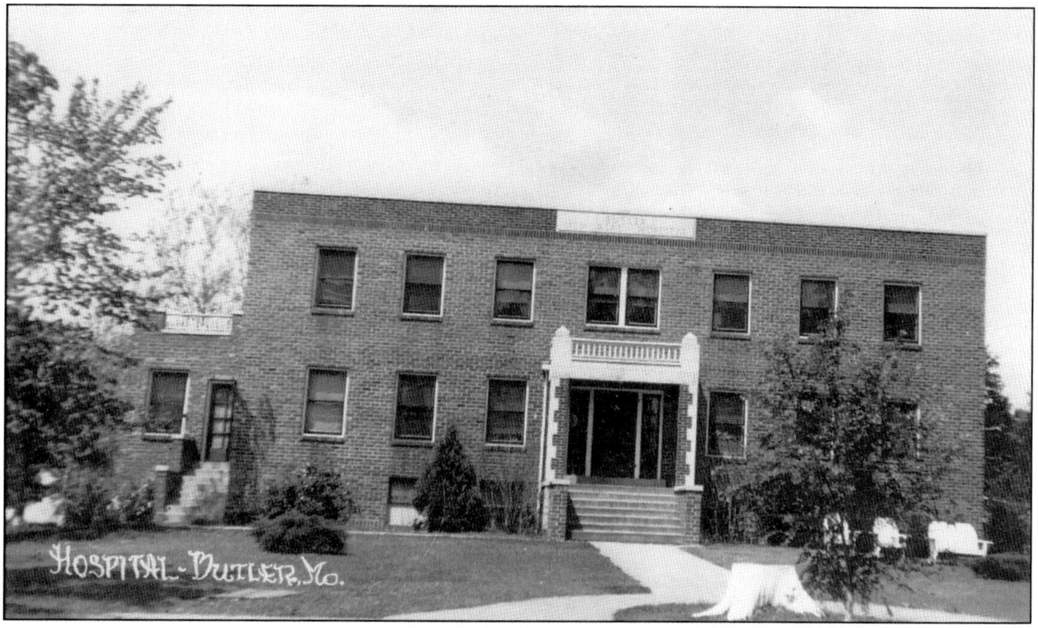

Butler's first hospital facility was set up in 1926 on the second floor of a house on Havanah Street that was owned by Julia Drydon Gaines. It was run by Mrs. S.C. Stayton of Archie, Missouri. Six years later, this was succeeded by a more formal establishment at the intersection of Maple and College Streets. The Butler Memorial Hospital (above), built by Mrs. Stayton in partnership with the chamber of commerce, was officially opened on June 25, 1932. The hospital came under municipal ownership in 1943, but it soon became necessary to consider other alternatives. A proposal was made and approved in 1957 to fund a new hospital on Nursery Street to be called the Bates County Memorial Hospital. The new 50-bed facility (below) opened on September 16, 1960. (Both, courtesy of the Bates County Historical Society and the Eddie Herrman Collection.)

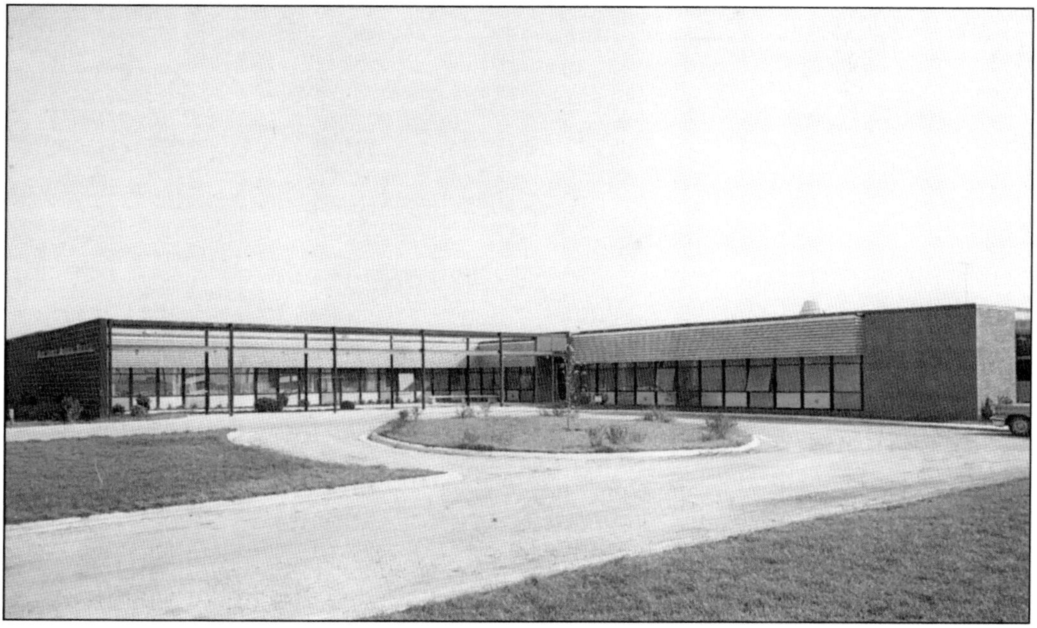

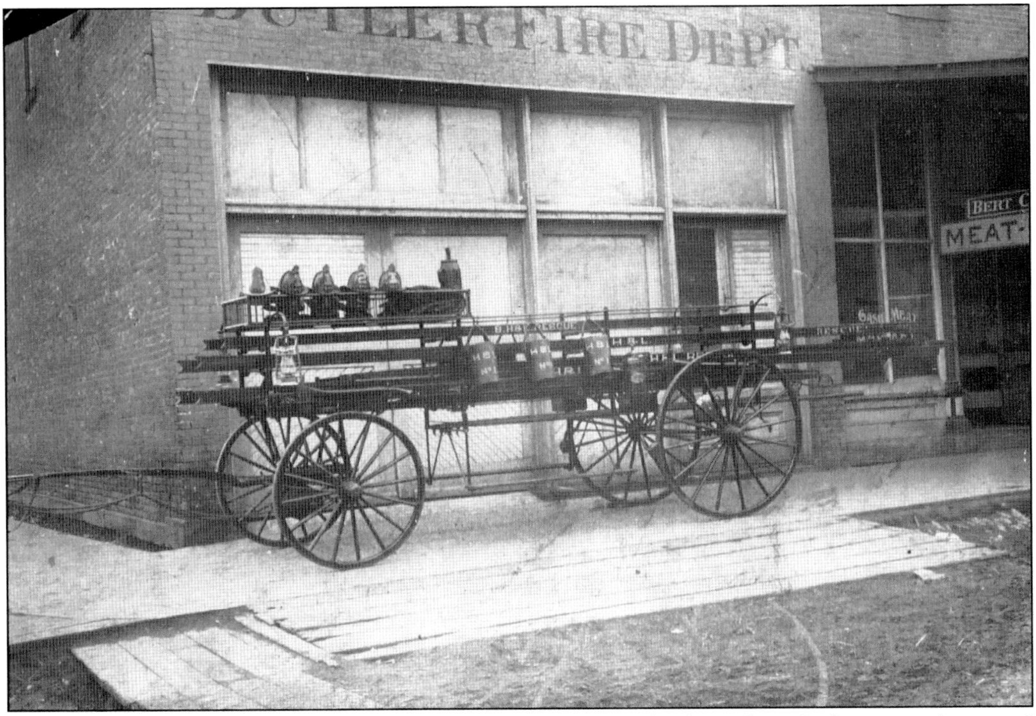

At the turn of the 20th century, the Butler Fire Department had purchased a hose cart (pictured above) and hook and ladder equipment at a yearly cost of $500. They had also participated with honors in several state fire tournaments and were ranked among the fastest and best brigades in Missouri. (Courtesy of the Bates County Historical Society and the Eddie Herrman Collection.)

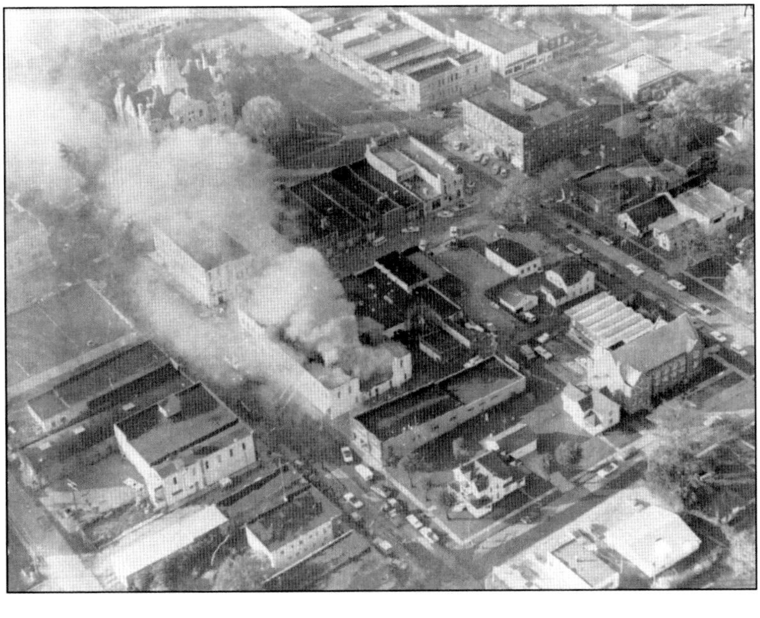

On October 28, 1973, the third major fire in 18 months broke out just to the north of the Butler square, caused by the explosion of a gas heater. The blaze, which destroyed six businesses and did $500,000 in damage, occupied the Butler, Appleton City, Adrian, and Rich Hill Fire Departments for nearly five hours. (Courtesy of the Bates County Historical Society and the Eddie Herrman Collection.)

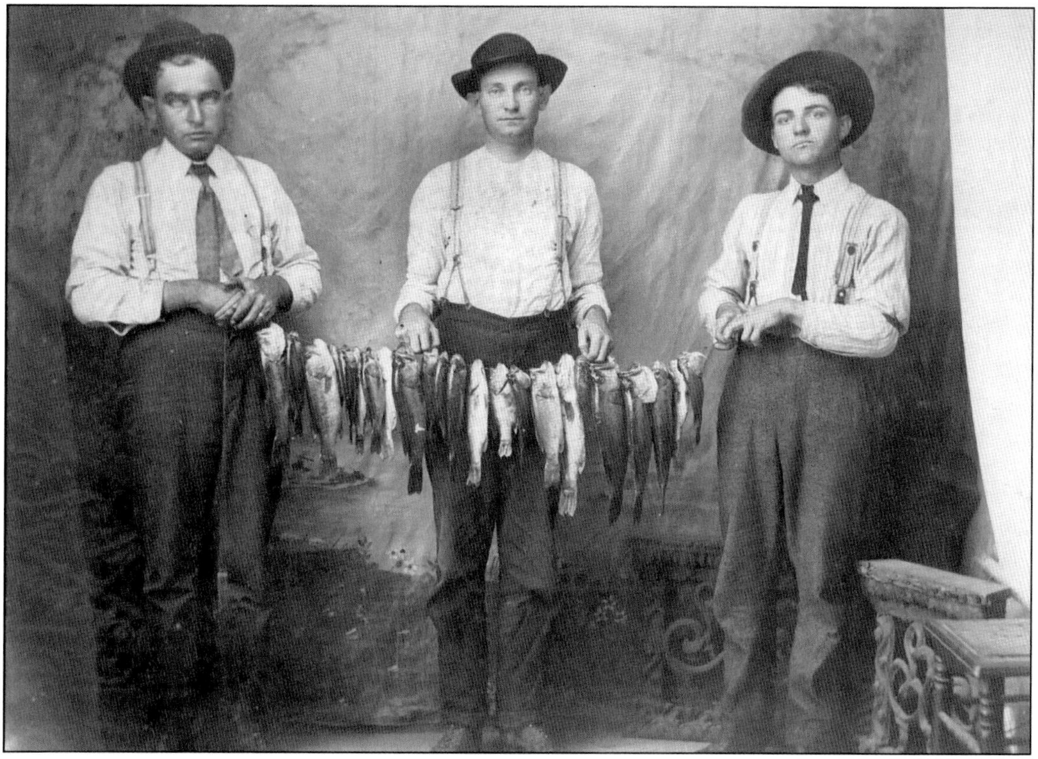

Some folks go to church on Sunday, and some go fishing. Photographed from left to right, F.L. Bennett, a young Mr. Hupp, and Fred Shielder chose the latter course on September 10, 1905. Afterward, they proudly displayed their catch, fresh from Welton Lake. (Courtesy of the Bates County Historical Society.)

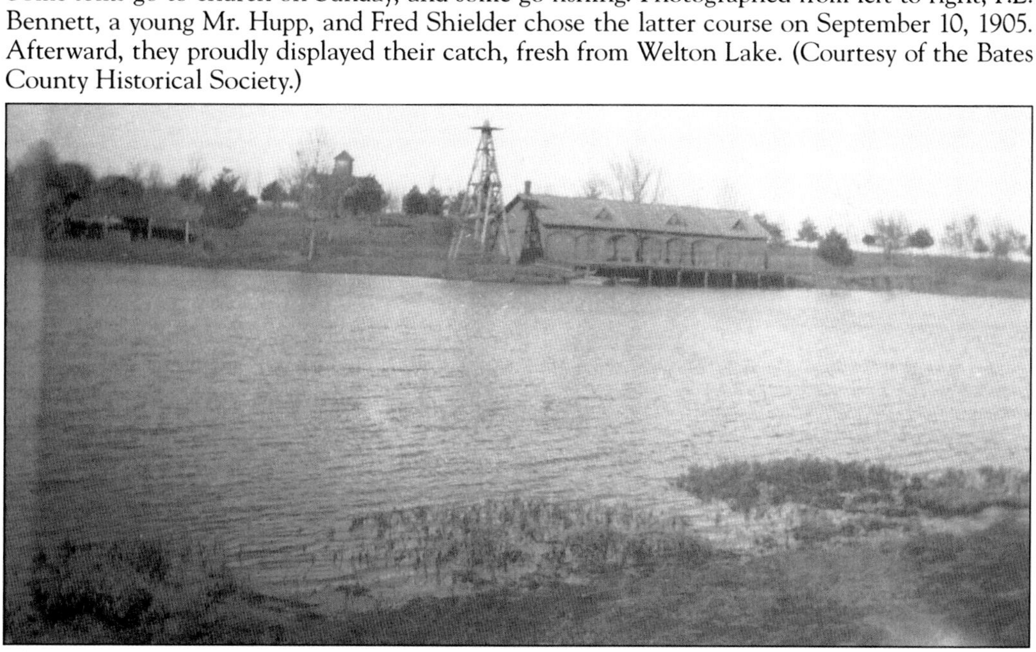

The dancing pavilion at Welton Lake, a man-made lake outside of town, was once a recreational hot spot for the people of Butler, although the lake itself has long since been dry. Built in 1896, the spot's attractions included swimming, boating, bowling, and a picnic area. (Courtesy of the Bates County Historical Society.)

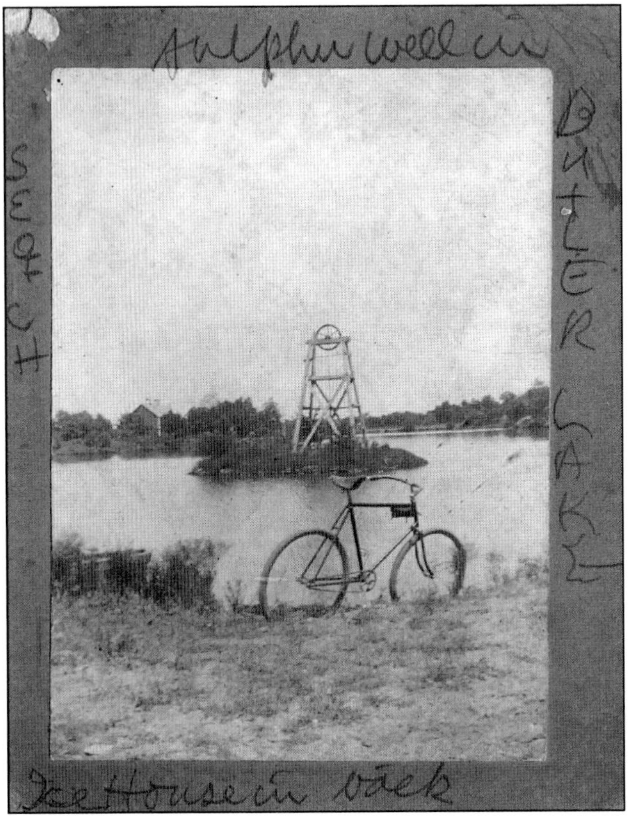

According to Eddie Herrman, Welton Lake was known for its medicinal properties as well as for the recreational opportunities it offered. It was considered something of a health spa, and visitors would come from miles around to sample, among other things, the mineral water from this well. (Courtesy of the Bates County Historical Society.)

Once the ice on the surface of Welton Lake had reached a thickness of six inches, it was harvested and stored in barns like this one, packed under sawdust to prevent it from melting. The slide protruding from the left side of the barn provided the mechanism whereby the harvesters slid the blocks of ice from the surface of the lake into their insulated nest. (Courtesy of the Bates County Historical Society.)

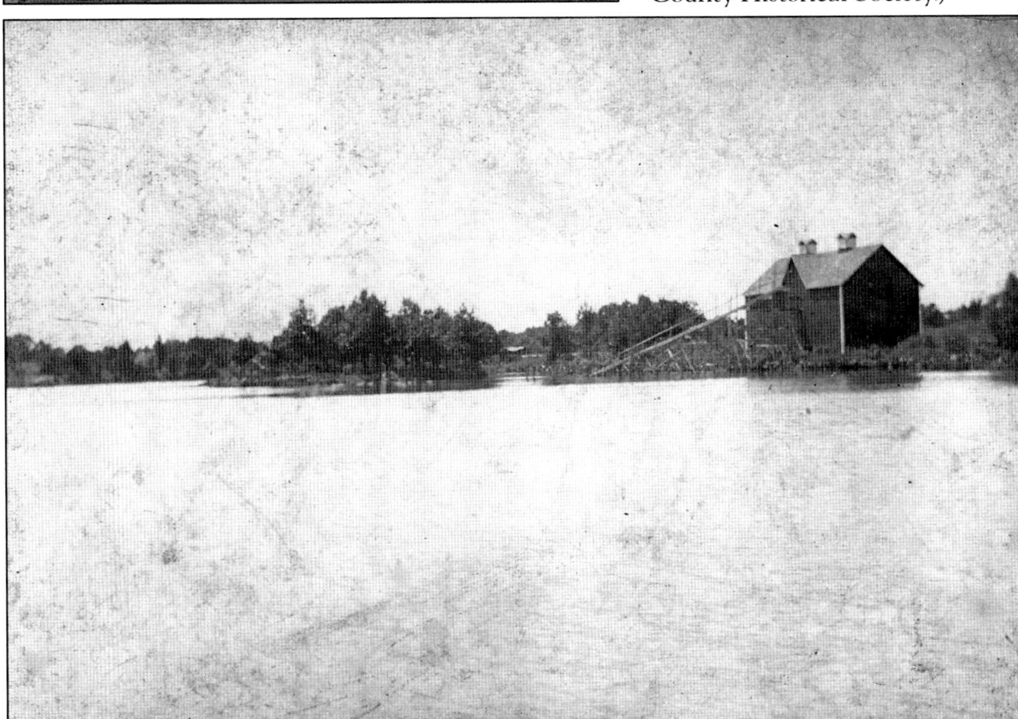

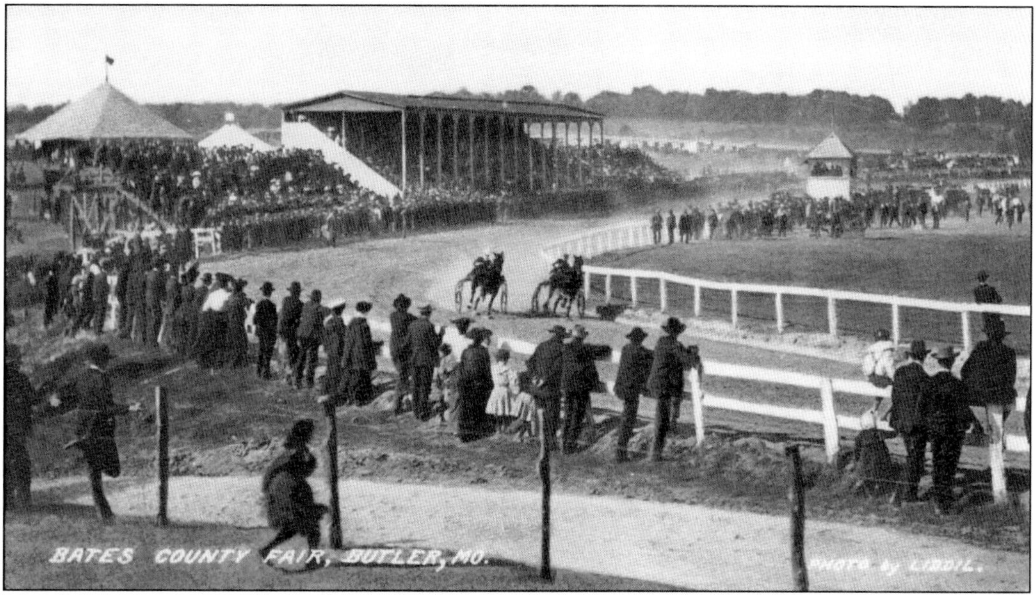

Bates County's original fairgrounds, depicted in this R.L. Liddil postcard, once hosted a range of bustling activities, from produce and livestock exhibitions to horse races. It is now a much quieter place. In the 1880s, the County Fair Association decided to reinvent itself as the Oak Hill Cemetery Association, and the fairgrounds became burial grounds. (Courtesy of the Bates County Historical Society.)

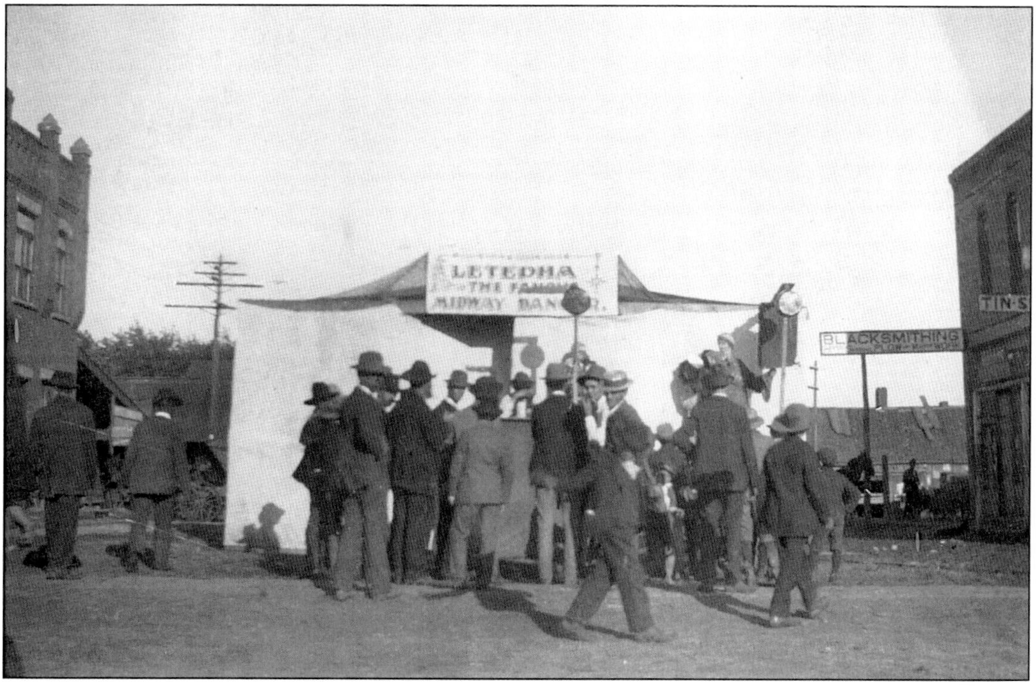

Street fairs and other community celebrations served both to entertain the townspeople and advertise town businesses. Here, Butler men gather at one such event in 1906 outside the tent of Letedha, the Famous Midway Dancer. Strangely, Butler women are nowhere to be seen. (Courtesy of the Bates County Historical Society.)

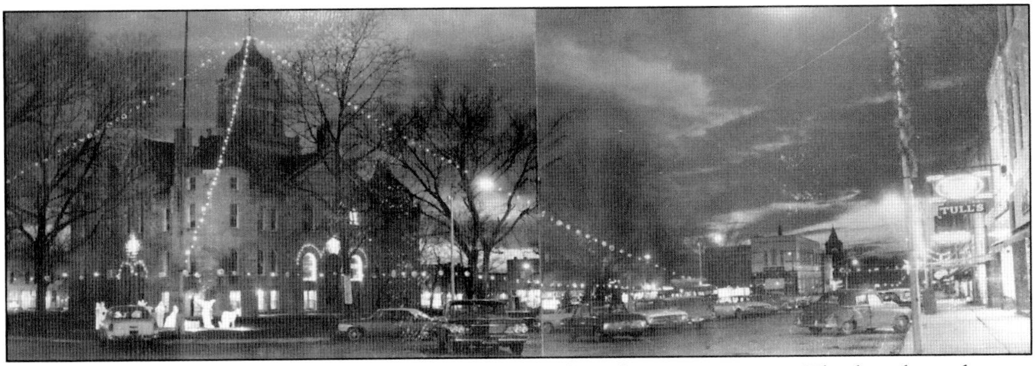

The Butler square becomes a different place during the Christmas season. The bandstand turns into a snow-covered shelter at the North Pole, and Santa comes to town. The Christmas parade rounds the square, featuring floats submitted by churches, businesses, and social clubs. At night, stars come out, lights go on, and all becomes beautiful. (Courtesy of the Bates County Historical Society and the Eddie Herrman Collection.)

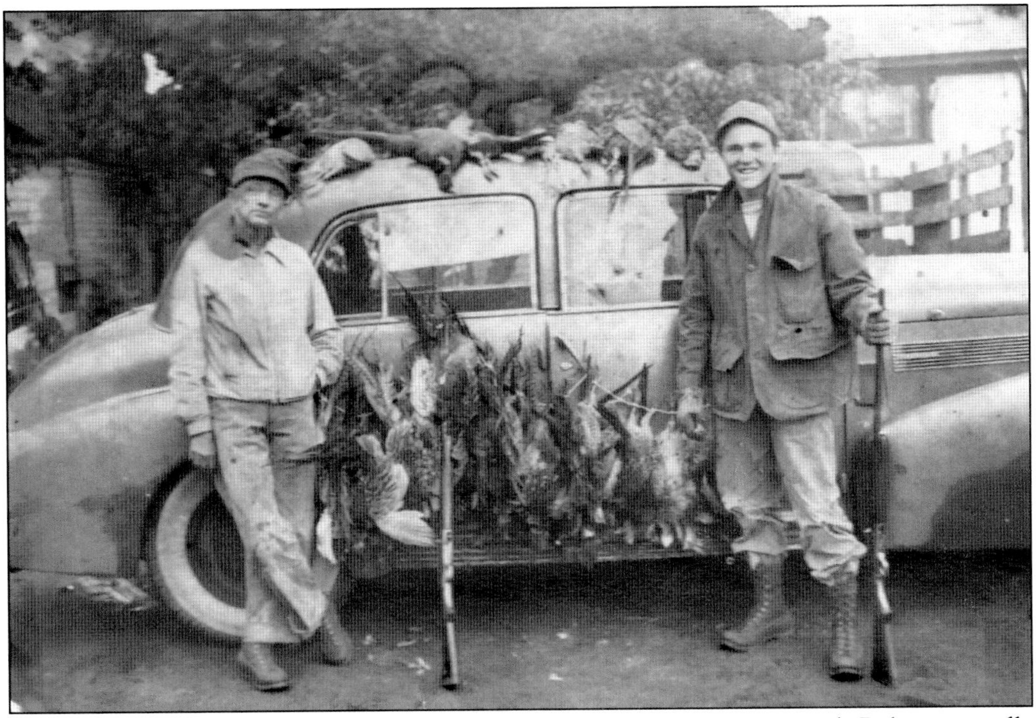

Charles Fisk Sr. and son Joe, just back from a pheasant shoot in Salem, South Dakota, proudly exhibit their spoils. Bates County has always been a community of hunters, from Marshall Lee Wolfe, avid big-game hunter in the 1800s, to Dr. Curtis Long today, whose waiting room was once famous for its taxidermic display of prize kills. (Courtesy of the Bates County Historical Society and the Eddie Herrman Collection.)

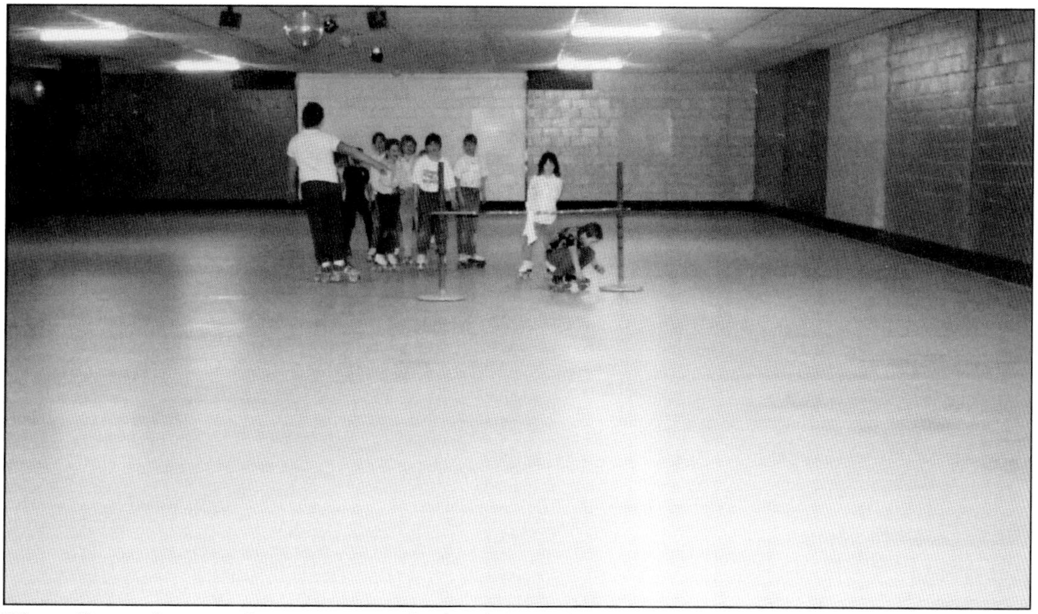

The roller rink was a favorite venue for birthday celebrations. Here, friends of Tammy Herrell do the limbo in honor of her ninth birthday in 1988. Tammy's favorite thing about going roller-skating was the disco ball that reflected spinning light around the darkened rink—even though it usually made her so dizzy, she would promptly fall down. (Courtesy of Barbara Herrell.)

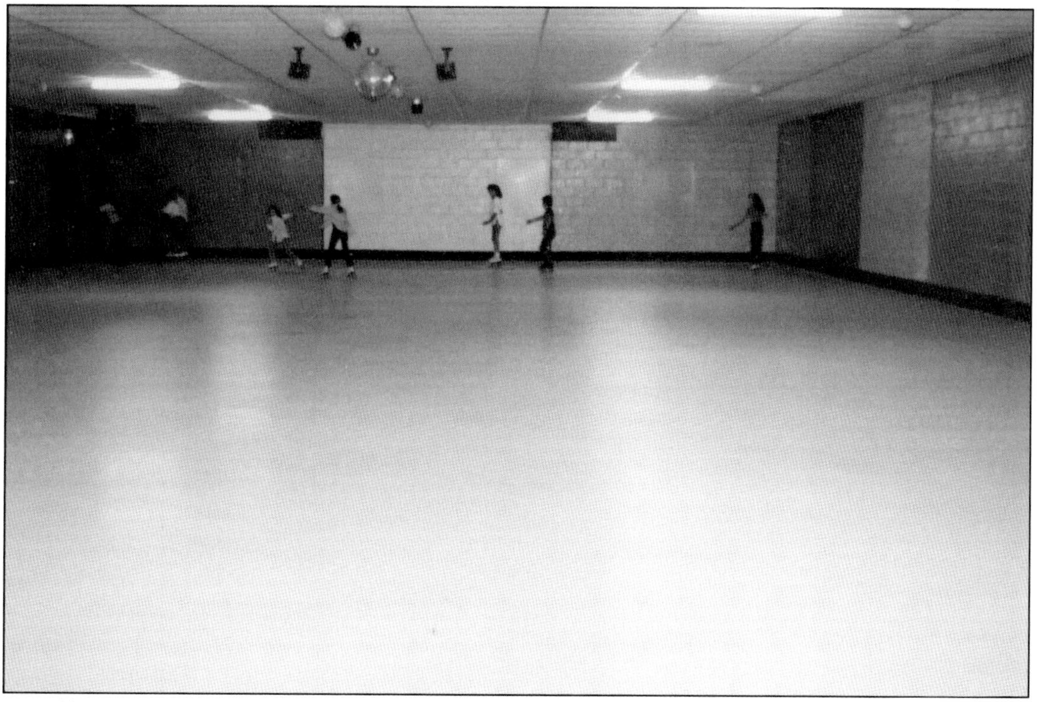

Lowell Logan and his father did the original electrical wiring for the Butler Roller Rink when it opened in 1950. After work was finished, Lowell recalls running to get his skates from their truck, sweeping the loose nails and other debris from the floor, and taking a lap or two to claim the honor of being the first to use the new rink. (Courtesy of Barbara Herrell.)

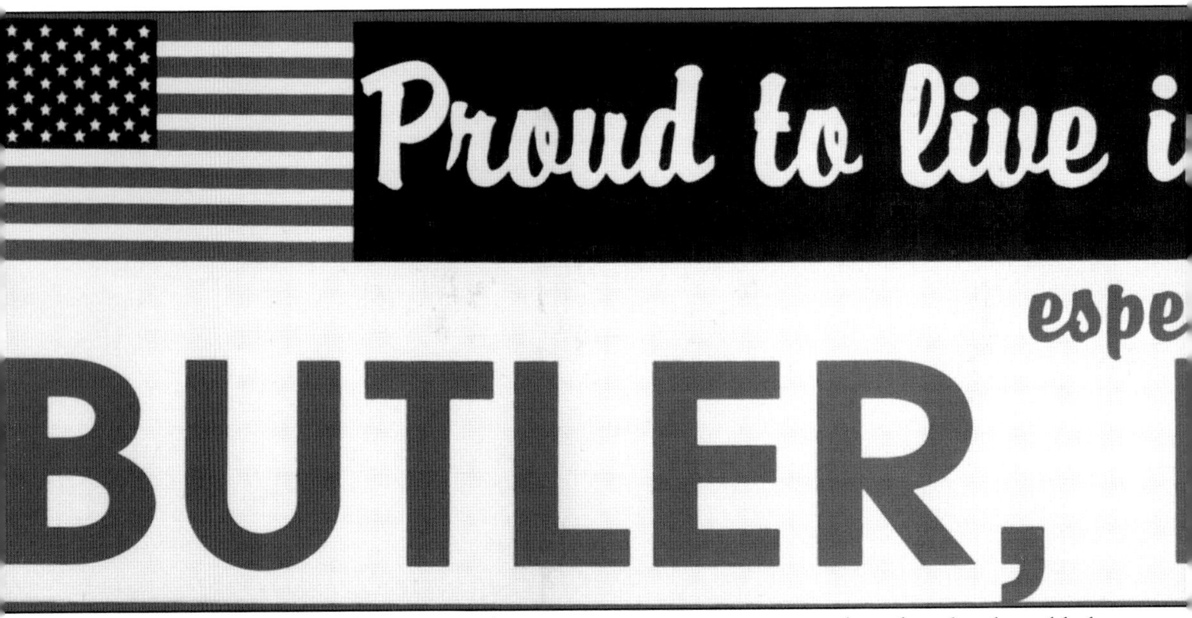

Between April and October 2000, eight automatic weapons were purchased under the table by several part-time Butler police deputies. An article in the *Kansas City Star* took up the story in November 2001, and the gauntlet was thrown. In the article, Butler became Mayberry, populated by a host of Andy Taylors, a number of Barney Fifes, and one "amateur SWAT team," a danger to

itself and to others. In the face of outside ridicule, the townspeople fired back with true small-town flair, and this bumper sticker was the result. What's so bad about Mayberry, after all? (Courtesy of the Bates County Historical Society and the Eddie Herrman Collection.)

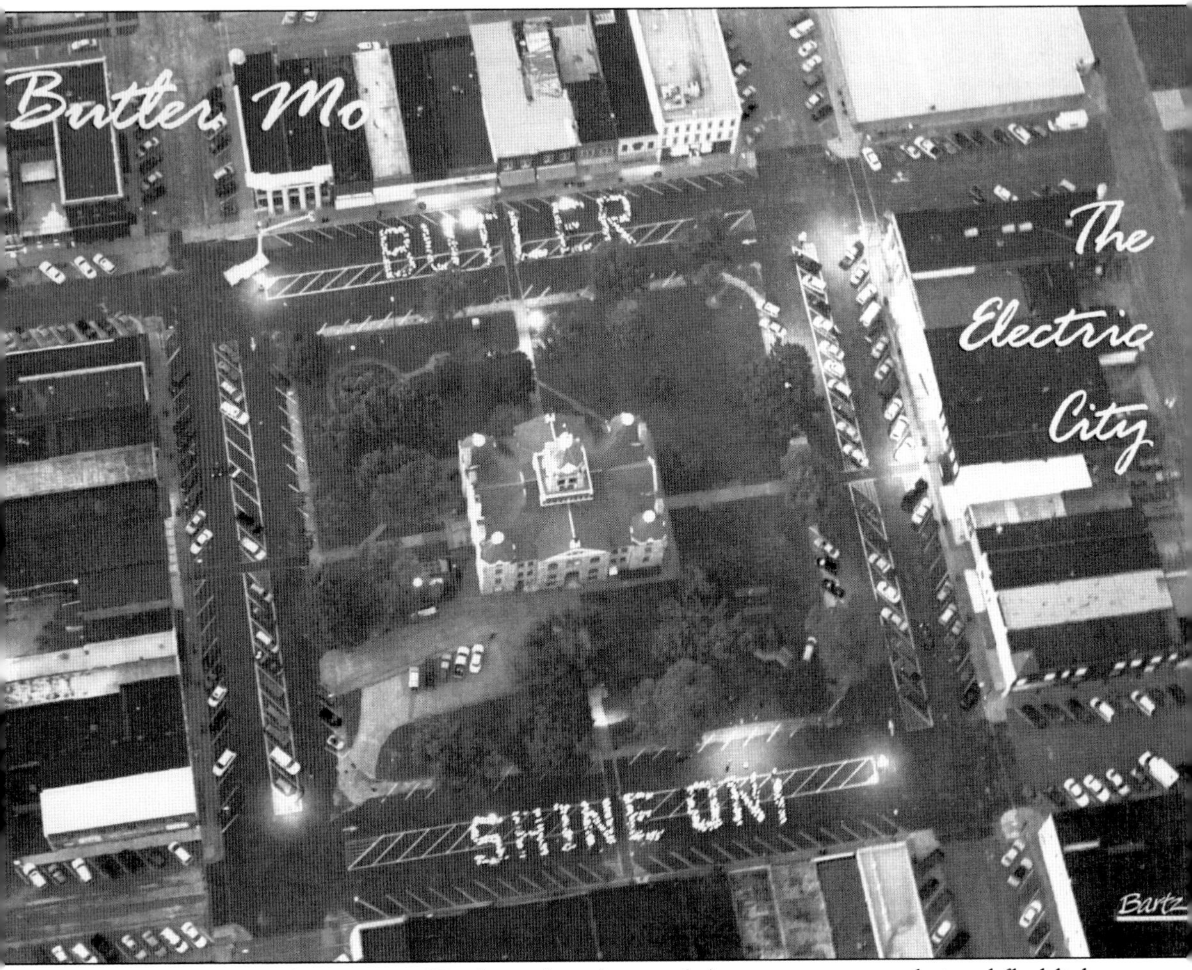

On July 19, 2010, the citizens of Butler gathered around the town square and aimed flashlights into the sky to spell out the message "Butler—Shine On!" Alan Mundey, who organized the letter *H*, recalls a situation both chaotic ("like herding cats") and enjoyable, calling it "small-town fun at its finest." (Courtesy of Bartz Photography.)

About the Organization

The Bates County Historical Society & Museum was established in 1961. History has always played a significant role in the lives of Bates County citizens. There is a common pride in the stories of the past. Children are told of early settlers and the hardships they endured. The Civil War in Bates County was brutal. Neighbor truly fought neighbor, and the final act of unimaginable grief came in 1863 when Union Military Order No. 11 forced every man, woman, and child to evacuate the county while everything was burned to the ground. The war's end brought an era of reconstruction and reconciliation that saw Bates County prosper and flourish. Rich coal deposits brought mining operations to the area, and the railroads soon followed. Agriculture in the rich region brought years of abundant harvests, and farming became the cornerstone of the economy. Today, the Bates County Museum proudly keeps these stories alive so that future generations will fully grasp an understanding of the past. The society's mission is to "preserve our history and sustain our heritage."

—Peggy Buhr
Bates County Museum

Bibliography

Atkeson, William Oscar. *History of Bates County, Missouri.* Topeka, KS: Historical Publishing Company, 1918.

Butler Chamber of Commerce. *Butler, Mo.: My Kind of Town.* Butler, MO: self-published, 1979.

Connelley, William Elsey. *Quantrill and the Border Wars.* New York: Konecky & Konecky, 1909.

Maxey, H.O. and S.L. Tathwell, eds. *The Old Settlers' History of Bates County, Missouri: From Its First Settlement to the First Day of January, 1900.* Amsterdam, MO: Tathwell & Maxey, 1897.